# Damaged Identities, Narrative Repair

# Damaged Identities, Narrative Repair

HILDE LINDEMANN NELSON

CORNELL UNIVERSITY PRESS

ITHACA AND LONDON

First published 2001 by Cornell University Press
First printing, Cornell Paperbacks, 2001

Printed in the United States of America

Library of Congress Cataloging-in-Publication-Data

Nelson, Hilde Lindemann.
    Damaged identities, narrative repair / Hilde Lindemann Nelson.
        p.   cm.
    Includes bibliographical references (p.   ) and index.
    ISBN 978-0-8014-8740-8 (pbk. : alk. paper)
        1. Ethics.   2. Identity (Psychology)—Social aspects.   3. Marginality, Social—
    Psychological aspects.   4. Narration (Rhetoric)—Psychological aspects.   I. Title.
    BJ45.N45 2001
    155.9'2—dc21                                                          00-011733

Cornell University Press strives to use environmentally responsible suppliers and materials to the fullest extent possible in the publishing of its books. Such materials include vegetable-based, low-VOC inks and acid-free papers that are recycled, totally chlorine-free, or partly composed of nonwood fibers. Books that bear the logo of the FSC (Forest Stewardship Council) use paper taken from forests that have been inspected and certified as meeting the highest standards for environmental and social responsibility. For further information, visit our website at www.cornellpress.cornell.edu.


Paperback printing   10   9   8   7   6   5   4   3   2

**Für Elise**

I have tried to remove weight, sometimes from people, sometimes from heavenly bodies, sometimes from cities; above all I have tried to remove weight from the structure of stories.

Italo Calvino, *Six Memos for the Next Millennium*

# Contents

# Preface

How freely we can exercise our moral agency is contingent on a number of things. Most broadly, it depends on the form of life we inhabit: the niche we occupy in our particular society; the practices and institutions within the society that set the possibilities for the courses of action that are open to us; the material, cultural, and imaginative resources at our disposal; the constraints arising from the moral flaws within our roles and relationships; the shared moral understandings that render our actions intelligible to those around us. More specifically, the extent to which our moral agency is free or constrained is determined by our own—and others'—conception of who we are.

In this work I argue that personal identity, understood as a complicated interaction of one's own sense of self and others' understanding of who one is, functions as a lever that expands or contracts one's ability to exercise moral agency. The way in which others identify us establishes what they will permit us to do; if they identify us as morally defective, they will perhaps humor us or hospitalize us, or else treat us with suspicion, contempt, or hostility. This restricts our freedom to act. How we identify ourselves establishes our own view of what we can do; if our self-conception marks us as morally defective, we will mistrust our own capabilities and so treat ourselves with suspicion or contempt, or exempt ourselves from full responsibility for our actions. This too restricts our moral agency.

Identities mark certain people as candidates for certain treatments, and within abusive group relations these treatments are seldom benign.

The connection between identity and agency poses a serious problem when the members of a particular social group are compelled by the forces circulating in an abusive power system to bear the morally degrading identities required by that system. These mandatory identities set up expectations about how group members are to behave, what they can know, to whom they are answerable, and what others may demand of them. Here we may speak of *damaged* identities. A person's identity is damaged when a powerful social group views the members of her own, less powerful group as unworthy of full moral respect, and in consequence unjustly prevents her from occupying valuable social roles or entering into desirable relationships that are themselves constitutive of identity. We may call this harm *deprivation of opportunity*. Further, a person's identity is damaged when she endorses, as part of her self-concept, a dominant group's dismissive or exploitative understanding of her group, and loses or fails to acquire a sense of herself as worthy of full moral respect. We may call this harm *infiltrated consciousness*. Either injury to the identity constricts the person's ability to exercise her moral agency.

The problem of these twin injuries to an identity cries out for a solution. I attempt to contribute to that solution by developing an analytical and practical tool—the counterstory—that can repair the damage done to the identity. I argue that because identities are narratively constituted and narratively damaged, they can be narratively repaired. The morally pernicious stories that construct the identity according to the requirements of an abusive power system can be at least partially dislodged and replaced by identity-constituting counterstories that portray group members as fully developed moral agents.

Counterstories are designed to resist the evil of diminished moral agency in two ways. First, by uprooting the harmful stories that constitute the subgroup members' identity from the perspective of an abusive, dominant group, counterstories aim to alter the dominant group's perception of the subgroup. If the dominant group acknowledges that the counterstory is identity-constituting for the subgroup, it may come to see the group members as worthy of moral respect. It might then be less likely to deprive subgroup members of the goods and opportunities that are on offer in the society, and this would allow the members of the subgroup to exercise their moral agency more freely.

Second, by uprooting the harmful identity-constituting stories that have shaped a person's own sense of who she is, counterstories aim to alter the person's self-perception. If she replaces the harmful stories with a counterstory, she may come to see herself as worthy of moral respect. She might in that case be less willing to accept others' degrading representations of her, and this too would loosen the constraints on her moral agency.

Counterstories, then, are tools designed to repair the damage inflicted on identities by abusive power systems. They are purposive acts of moral definition, developed on one's own behalf or on behalf of others. They set out to resist, to varying degrees, the stories that identify certain groups of people as targets for ill treatment. Their aim is to reidentify such people as competent members of the moral community and in doing so to enable their moral agency. They may, however, fall short of their aim. As not all counterstories are well designed to repair identities, I begin by offering criteria for assessing whether *any* particular story is credible as a contribution to an identity; then I consider criteria for distinguishing counterstories that are morally desirable from counterstories that misfire.

The essay in which I began to develop the concept of the counterstory, "Resistance and Insubordination," was published in *Hypatia* 10, no. 2 (spring 1995). Some of the material in Chapter 3 appears in "Stories of My Old Age," in *Mother Time: Women, Aging, and Ethics,* edited by Margaret Urban Walker and published in 1999 by Rowman and Littlefield. I thank *Hypatia* and Rowman and Littlefield for permission to reprint this material.

If identities are collaborative ventures requiring a number of people to bring them into being, so are books. This one has benefited enormously from the kind efforts of a great many friends and colleagues. The Philosophy Department at the University of Tennessee, where it was written, was extraordinarily generous in its financial, intellectual, and logistical support. Particular thanks are due to Kathy Bohstedt who, as department head, smoothed my path in countless ways with good humor, ingenuity, and enthusiasm. She, Richard Aquila, Jim Bennet, Shelly Cohen, Glenn Graber, Phil Hamlin, Jonathan Kaplan, John Nolt, and Betsy Postow were more than good to me, and I am deeply grateful to them all.

The participants at a working conference on women and aging, hosted by the Ethics Center of the University of South Florida on 20–22 February 1998, provided helpful comments and criticism: I thank Sandra Lee Bartky, Joan C. Callahan, Peggy DesAutels, Robin N. Fiore, Frida Kerner Furman, Martha Holstein, Diana Tietjens Meyers, James Lindemann Nelson, Sara Ruddick, Anita Silvers, Joan C. Tronto, and especially Margaret Urban Walker, who organized the conference.

Conversations with John Hardwig have taught me a lot about the use of narrative in ethics; he and Mary English have aided and abetted the writing of this book in countless ways. Allen Dunn generously imparted his broad and deep knowledge of literary theory and, with Mary Papke, egged me on. Martha Montello coined the phrase "narrative repair" and let me borrow it like the good friend she is. Jeff Blustein, Jonathan Dancy, David DeGrazia, and Naomi Scheman offered useful suggestions that helped me over various difficulties, as did Maggie Little, whose affectionate attentiveness and shrewd philosophical acumen have greatly improved the first three chapters. John Greco and Christopher Gowans read the entire manuscript and pressed me most helpfully on a number of points. My children, Elise, Ellen, and Paul Robinson, and Eric, Laura, and Melissa Nelson, supplied loving confidence in my work and many useful conversations about it; Elise and Ellen in particular read various drafts and gave me good advice.

I was fortunate enough to have not one but two superb editors at Cornell University Press. Alison Shonkwiler acquired the project and line edited drafts of the first two chapters; when she left the press she turned me over to Catherine Rice, who has been unstinting in encouragement, practical help, and sound editorial judgment. I am also much indebted to Cornell's anonymous reviewers and to the production staff, under whose auspices the manuscript became an attractive and readable book.

My deepest thanks, however, are owed to the three philosophers who have been most directly responsible for teaching me my trade. I have been learning from Margaret Urban Walker since 1986 when I heard her give a paper that opened what was for me an entirely new way of thinking about morality. Since then, she has generously shared drafts of her work with me, extended substantial help in revising my own, presented a straight face when I've asked her naïve philosophical questions, lent me her apartment on any number of occasions, gotten fond of my family, repeatedly demonstrated her capacity for mixing wine and wit until the small hours—in short, she has been a dear and good friend. She has patiently and carefully read draft after draft of this book, showing me the importance of looking at actual practices of recognition and response and helping me to avoid a diet of one-sided examples. She is a superb philosopher, an exacting mentor, and a lovely human being.

I have been fortunate in my friendships. Like Margaret, Sara Ruddick has been a blessing in my life. She has been extraordinarily hospitable, welcoming and refining my ideas, collaborating with me on a number of projects, and taking a loving interest in my career and my various extracurricular doings. She too has read every word of this book. As a concept editor there is no one to touch her—she has a talent amounting to genius for delivering hard-headed criticism in an ego-affirming manner, and the book is considerably the better for it. Her wisdom is matched only by her generosity of spirit, and I am grateful for both.

Finally, my deepest thanks are owed to my husband, James Lindemann Nelson, who has been a steady source of love and philosophical savvy for many years. He is my first, last, and most faithful reader; a patient and gentle critic; a nurturer; a scam artist; and my best friend. He has brought books and articles to my attention, allowed me to talk at him about damaged identities for hours on end, helped me over the hard places, and saved me from a number of egregious errors. Let it be said of him as was said of the woman in the Bible—she did what she could. And then some.

HILDE LINDEMANN NELSON

*East Lansing, Michigan*

**Damaged Identities, Narrative Repair**

# 1 Narrative Repair: Reclaiming Moral Agency

Multiplication is vexation,
Division is as bad;
The rule of three doth puzzle me,
And practice drives me mad.
        —Elizabethan manuscript, 1570

In the small city of Cranford somewhere in the Midwest there was a 225-bed hospital. Virginia Martin did her floor training there when she was a nursing student at Eton College, and when she graduated in 1989 she found full-time work on the orthopedic service almost immediately. She was thirty then, kindly and plump, married since nineteen. She'd have liked to go to medical school and was certainly bright enough to get the degree, but since her husband's law school loans still had to be repaid and their two children needed her, nursing seemed the next best thing. She was good at it. She liked it.

Virginia Martin's hospital had four different kinds of nurses. Many of them were young or middle-aged baccalaureate nurses like herself, trained in the work of a particular unit and qualified to rise to the rank of head nurse. The older nurses tended to be diploma nurses with years of practical experience. Then there were RNs with associate degrees, many of whom were part-timers. And finally there were RNs with master's degrees, who served as the hospital's nurse-educators and directed the chemotherapy and nuclear medicine units. Since only 6 percent of nurses in the United States are men, perhaps it's not surprising that, at the time when these events unfolded, all the nurses at Cranford Community Hospital were women.

Like all hospitals, Cranford Community had its frictions. The diploma nurses were galled when they trained a baccalaureate nurse to the work of the unit, only to see her promoted to be their head nurse. As a cost-cutting move, the hospital administrators had hired more unlicensed personnel to do bedside tasks that none of the nurses considered them qualified to do. And physicians at Cranford continued to see their job as "managing the numbers"—getting white cell counts down to normal levels, measuring blood gases, monitoring electrolyte imbalances—while leaving the nurses to do what the chief of medicine was once overheard to call the "touchy-feely stuff" of providing patients and their families with human sympathy.

Every year in the first week of May the nurses at Cranford Community Hospital and Eton College sponsored a Nurse Recognition Day, involving speakers, student events, media attention, and a sit-down dinner for four hundred of the city's RNs to honor the recipient of that year's Distinguished Service Award. Virginia Martin volunteered to serve on the steering committee, which met twice a month throughout the year. She wasn't sure why she'd taken it on. If you needed a Recognition Day, it must be because you knew you weren't recognized, and why would you want to draw attention to that? Doctors don't bother with recognition days, she thought. She found, however, that she really enjoyed getting to know the fourteen other members of the committee. They quickly coalesced into their own little community.

And a diverse community it was. Nursing was about the only thing the committee members had in common. One of them was a fundamentalist Christian, some were atheists, two were observant Jews. Political stances ranged from left-leaning (like herself), to apathetic, to those who favored big business. Three sexual orientations were represented: lesbian, bi, and straight. Most committee members had full-time careers; three were "refrigerator nurses" who saw their jobs mainly in terms of supplemental income. Some, like herself, were comfortably maternal, some feisty and funny, still others quietly elegant, or timid, or driven.

As the committee sifted through the nominations and planned the events, the conversation moved naturally to the qualities that make someone an admirable nurse and to the future of the profession. But the talk also drifted to the ethical problems the nurses encountered in the course of their work. Linda Adams, a public health nurse, had visited a new mother and baby in a tumble-down farmhouse and suspected the baby's failure to thrive was caused by the mother's inability to cope—it was just a feeling she'd had when she was there. Sally Martinson, the emergency room nurse, had started an intravenous drip on a patient without orders because the physician seemed slow and unsure of herself. Chris Johnson, the director of the chemotherapy unit, remarked that she never knew how much she should tell her patients about side effects, since she believed in honesty but not in "truth-dumping." And so on.

At the fourth meeting of the Nurse Recognition Day Committee, Pilar Sanchez arrived with a tale of a sixteen-year-old patient who had been in and out of the hospital many times over the last few years with a form of leukemia that's usually curable in kids of his age. Jake was unlucky, though. His oncologist thought he had defeated the cancer but it came back, and now even a last-ditch bone marrow transplant had failed. Jake's mother insisted that he not be told that he's dying, and the physicians, saying they had to respect her wishes, forbade the staff to discuss Jake's prognosis with him. Pilar Sanchez, who had been taking care of Jake every time he was hospitalized, was very troubled by this. She was convinced that he could handle the truth, and she felt as if she'd lied to him every time she smiled encouragingly when he told her about his plans for the future. She tactfully tried to broach the subject with Jake's oncologist, but he was abrupt, telling her that she was emotionally overinvolved and professionally out of line.

Everybody on the committee was interested and indignant, and everybody had something to say. In Sally Martinson's opinion, this was yet another case of physicians' treating nurses like not-very-bright children. Chris Johnson declared that the reason doctors didn't listen to you is that they didn't take you seriously, and the reason they didn't take you seriously is that you were only doing women's work. Linda Adams bitterly agreed. They do the science. We just do the touchy-feely stuff. Pilar Sanchez added that the oncologist might just as well have said right out that she was an excitable Hispanic. Virginia Martin didn't think they needed to drag gender or ethnicity into this—it was just a doctor-nurse thing. It happened all the time. Only last week, one of the orthopedic surgeons on her unit had put her off when she asked him for a medical consult for a patient with high blood pressure. She hated that. She was the one who would have to cope if the patient stroked out.

And so the committee settled down to a full-bodied grouse.

Then the eldest member, Patricia Kent, a crisply tailored professor of nursing at Eton College, suggested that instead of merely complaining about the friction at the hospital, the committee might take some time at each meeting to figure out how to challenge the "technical" vs. "touchy-feely" division of labor between doctors and nurses. A picture of nursing seemed to be holding the physicians captive—the nurse as Earth Mother with the Bedpan, you might call it. The Earth Mother, of course, was a character in an old story that badly needed to be updated. What better story could be told about the nurses' professional identity that would allow the physicians to see them more clearly? If the nurses could challenge the story about Mothers that the physicians seemed to be telling themselves and substitute one that invited more respectful treatment, maybe it would be easier for them to do their jobs properly.

Nancy Schmidt, one of the older diploma nurses, thought all this business of nursing as a profession had been taken too far, and that if nurses wanted to be professionals, they should become doctors. Virginia Martin secretly agreed with her, but aloud she merely pointed out that there didn't seem to be any one story they could all tell about their professional identity. There were too many differences among them.

Perhaps, Patricia Kent suggested, they could at least agree that the "touchy-feely" story was a damaging one, because it got in the way of their work. And she traced the history of that story, reminding the others of its connections to nineteenth-century military models of nursing, where male officers gave the orders and female nurses served and obeyed them. If the committee members were to resist the "touchy-feely" identity, she argued, they would have to challenge the stories that fed it, including those that identified women as subservient to men, as emotional rather than rational, as mothers rather than scientists. Those were the stories the physicians seemed to endorse. To get them to stop, the nurses would have to counter the destructive stories with better ones of their own.

Virginia Martin drove home feeling a little flat, like a tire without quite enough air. She'd managed to stay clear of the frictions at the hospital by being nice to everybody and keeping her mouth shut, but she'd hoped that this strategy wouldn't be necessary in her newly acquired circle of friends. While she was all for equality with men, she was no feminist. The thought of quoting Gloria Steinem to the orthopods on her unit made her blink. *There* was an image for you. Why were the committee members making such a fuss over what was, after all, just a case of docs being docs? A savvy nurse soon learned how to work around these petty obstructions.

Still, as the weeks went by and many committee members continued to want to use some of the meeting time to think about who they were and whether the physicians would let them be it, Virginia Martin and Nancy Schmidt reluctantly went along. The anecdotes about encounters with physicians displayed a disturbing pattern. For example, there was the story of a dehydrated and disoriented elderly patient with no previous history of dementia who, after being restrained in the emergency room, managed to free her right arm, pull out her IV tubes and Foley catheter, and tangle herself in the bedding, all the while wailing loudly. Sally Martinson helped her to sit in a chair while she remade the bed, gave her juice and water to drink, calmed her by stroking her forehead, roused her hourly all night for fluids, toileting, and neurological checks, and by morning found her oriented and talking of going home. The patient was discharged that afternoon. A week later, the night-shift supervisor formally reprimanded Sally for not following the physician's orders concerning restraints, IVs, and Haldol. Apparently the physician had gone straight to the supervisor to complain. Virginia Martin could identify with this story. She too had been the target of complaints from physicians who didn't bother to talk to her first. And somehow that brought to mind her husband's law firm, where the senior partner had recently made it clear—to her husband, not to her—that he expected her to give a dinner party for an important client.

Over time, Virginia Martin's perception of the hospital underwent a significant shift. In the beginning this was largely due to her respect for Patricia Kent. She had a great deal of affection for her witty and magisterial former professor, and an equally high opinion of her intelligence. And Sally Martinson, who was no fool either, took almost as radical a view as Patricia Kent. Virginia Martin's trust in these women allowed her to try on their perspective.

The stories ultimately contributed just as much to her change of heart as the people who told them, however. They spoke to her own experiences, but because they were the other people's stories, the stories of people she was fond of, they aroused feelings of indignation that her own experiences had never seemed to merit. And since they were *her* stories as well, the patterns they displayed of contempt for women had to be acknowledged as a pattern in her own life. That acknowledgment made it possible for her to agree that the doctors' story about nurses, as the others were piecing it together, needed to be resisted. She saw that, despite their differences, she and the others could construct a better story—one that identified nurses more accurately and respectfully as skilled professionals with serious responsibilities.

Bit by bit, the nurses connected one fragment of their story to another, offering ethical interpretations of the various anecdotes and telling fresh ones that, in the light of these interpretations, now seemed relevant. Some were stories of admirable nursing practice. Patricia Kent, for instance, told the others of the time when Virginia Martin, while a nursing student, had arranged for a dying patient to take a little walk outside the hospital in the spring rain and gotten thoroughly soaked while keeping him company. Others were stories of why the nurses had been attracted to nursing in the first place. As the narrative work went on, the committee members came to a clearer, shared understanding of who they were on the job.

They realized that this shared understanding was only a first step. They knew they'd have to start telling their improved story *within* the hospital if their work conditions were ever to change. Moreover, the physicians would not only have to hear that story but accept it and alter their behavior accordingly. And that would take a lot of doing. The day they succeeded would indeed be a Nurse Recognition Day.[1]

## Counterstories

The cluster of histories, anecdotes, and other narrative fragments the nurses began weaving together is a *counterstory*—a story that resists an oppressive identity and attempts to replace it with one that commands respect (Nelson 1995). By 'identity' I mean the interaction of a person's self-conception with how others conceive her: identities are the understandings we have of ourselves and others. In piecing together the fragments of various narratives that have constructed their oppressive identity and challenging the unjust assumptions that lie hidden in those narrative fragments, the nurses have begun to develop a counterstory that identifies them more accurately and fairly.

The counterstory positions itself against a number of *master narratives*: the stories found lying about in our culture that serve as summaries of socially shared understandings. Master narratives are often archetypal, consisting of stock plots and readily recognizable character types, and we use them not only to make sense of our experience (Nisbett and Ross 1980) but also to justify what we do (MacIntyre 1984). As the repositories of common norms, master narratives exercise a certain authority over our moral imaginations and play a role in informing our moral intuitions. Our culture's foundation myths—the Passion of

1. Jeannine Ross Boyer, RN, supplied the texture for this story. The anecdote told by Pilar Sanchez is adapted from a case study presented by Wayne Vaught at the annual meeting of the Society for Health and Human Values, Baltimore, Md., November 1997. Sally Martinson's story is taken from the *American Journal of Nursing* 89, no. 11 (1989): 1466–67.

Christ, for example, or Washington Crossing the Delaware—are master narratives. So are the best-known fairy tales, landmark court cases, canonical works of great literature, movie classics. Although master narratives need not be oppressive, those that figure into the physicians' understanding of who nurses are supposed to be seem to be sexist, classist, and possibly ethnocentric. It is master narratives of this kind that counterstories resist.

Many counterstories are told in two steps. The first is to identify the fragments of master narratives that have gone into the construction of an oppressive identity, noting how these fragments misrepresent persons—here, nurses—and situations. The second is to retell the story about the person or the group to which the person belongs in such a way as to make visible the morally relevant details that the master narratives suppressed. If the retelling is successful, the group members will stand revealed as respectworthy moral agents. Since a powerful group's misperception of an oppressed group results in disrespectful treatment that can impede group members in carrying out their responsibilities, the counterstory also opens up the possibility that group members can enjoy greater freedom to do what they ought—Virginia Martin and her colleagues may now be able to care for their patients properly.

In what follows, I argue that through their capacity for narrative repair of identities damaged by oppression, counterstories can provide a significant form of resistance to the evil of diminished moral agency. First, by interacting in a number of different ways with master narratives that identify the members of a particular social group as candidates for oppression, counterstories aim to alter the *oppressors'* perception of the group. If the dominant group, moved by the counterstory, sees subordinates as developed moral agents, it may be less inclined to deprive them of the opportunity to enjoy valuable roles, relationships, and goods. This allows members of the oppressed group to exercise their agency more freely.

Second, counterstories aim to alter, when necessary, an oppressed person's perception of *herself*. Oppression often infiltrates a person's consciousness, so that she comes to operate, from her own point of view, as her oppressors want her to, rating herself as they rate her. By helping a person with an infiltrated consciousness to change her self-understanding, counterstories permit her to put greater trust in her own moral worth. If the counterstory moves her to see herself as a competent moral agent, she may be less willing to accept others' oppressive valuations of her, and this too allows her to exercise her agency more freely.

This book is a work of philosophy, but not a philosophy restricted to conceptual analysis in the classical sense. My claims about counterstories are motivated by a combination of purely conceptual points and an attention to broad, general features of human life—features that in themselves are not recondite, although their implications for resisting some of the effects of oppression have not been well understood. Although I won't attempt to identify all the social and material conditions under which counterstories can actually repair a damaged identity, focusing instead on the features that make a counterstory morally desirable, I will rough out the epistemic context that is required for counterstories to be effective. The project I have undertaken, then, is to develop the concept of the counterstory and to offer criteria for assessing stories of this kind.

Counterstories are created much like any story whose aim is to make moral sense of something: their creators choose particulars from the array of experience and look at them in the light of important moral concepts, which in turn show up the relevance of other particulars, which suggest the relevance of other moral concepts, and so on, until the particulars and their moral interpretations have been set into an equilibrium that points to a specific understanding of the state of affairs.[2] Counterstories are the subset of stories developed in this manner that constitute a revised understanding of a person or social group. They are stories that define people morally, and are developed for the express purpose of resisting and undermining an oppressive master narrative. They ordinarily proceed by filling in details that the master narrative has ignored or underplayed. Through augmentation and correction, the master narrative is morally reoriented, thus allowing the counterstory teller to dissent from the interpretation and conclusion it invites. Counterstories take up an oppressive but shared moral understanding and attempt to shift it, rejecting its assumption that people with a particular group identity are to be subordinated to others or denied access to personal and social goods. They are, then, narrative acts of insubordination.

The task of this chapter is to introduce the concept of the counterstory, to explain the kind of moral work that this philosophical tool can do, and to show how a counterstory, by reidentifying a person, can

2. The method is similar to one that has been famously described by John Rawls (1971). Rawlsian reflective equilibrium, however, balances intuitive moral judgments about particular cases against a moral theory, not nonmoral descriptions against moral concepts.

loosen the constraints on her moral agency. Along the way, I begin to collect some of the working parts needed to develop the concept. Counterstories, typically told within the moral space of a *community of choice*, are *stories* of *self-definition*, developed in response to the twin harms of *deprivation of opportunity* and *infiltrated consciousness*. Through their function of *narrative repair* they resist the evil of diminished moral agency. After discussing each of these ideas at some length, I'll begin the central argument by securing the connection between identity and agency that is crucially presupposed by a counterstory.

## Found Communities and Communities of Choice

Marilyn Friedman (1992) has drawn a useful distinction between two sorts of communities. The communities into which we are born and reared—families, neighborhoods, nations—have been accorded special significance by communitarians such as Alasdair MacIntyre and Michael Sandel, who see them as constitutive of self-identity and the source of binding moral norms. But as Friedman points out, these "found" communities have tended to exclude and suppress nongroup members while exploiting and oppressing certain members within the group; women, she observes, have often been on the receiving end of both sorts of treatment. While Friedman grants that found communities play a role in constituting "the unreflective, 'given' identity that the self discovers when *first* beginning to reflect on itself" (Friedman 1992, 92), she notes that on reaching adulthood, women can form radically different communities, those based on voluntary association. She invokes both friendship and urban relationships (her examples are trade unions, political action groups, and support groups) as communities of choice. These, she argues, "foster not so much the *constitution* of subjects but their *re*constitution. We seek out communities of choice as contexts in which to *relocate* and *renegotiate* the various constituents of our identities" (95). This relocation and renegotiation is not always benign, of course. As the Ku Klux Klan reminds us, communities of choice can endorse all kinds of evil that aren't countenanced by a found community.

The distinction between found and chosen communities isn't a hard and fast one, as the associations we elect voluntarily are typically nestled within the larger communities we inherit at birth or through forcible displacement. Some found communities can be exited at will while others can't, or can't easily. A neighborhood into which one chooses to move isn't as "found" as the neighborhood in which one has lived all one's life; the long-term, intimate relationships one enters into aren't as "found" as are one's affinities to parents, siblings, and other blood kin. The boundaries may be blurred, but there is nevertheless a difference between the two sorts of communities that has important implications for the viability of a counterstory: a found community operates on a given set of shared moral understandings, while a chosen community can operate on quite another. I'll argue, in Chapter 5, that the alternative evaluative standards of a chosen community are what make it possible to legitimate the person who develops a counterstory.

Both kinds of communities are present in the story about Virginia Martin. Cranford Community Hospital is arguably a found community. While it's true that the nurses chose their profession, most did not choose the setting in which they practice it. Virginia Martin, for example, is restricted because of her husband's job to the city of Cranford, which has only the one hospital. If she wants to be a floor nurse—and she does—then the hospital is her community. Like some other found communities, this one is "exploitative and oppressive toward many of [its] own members, particularly women." Like some other found communities, this one "*complicate*[s] as well as *constitute*[s] identity" (Friedman 1992, 91, 93).

The steering committee, by contrast, is clearly a community of choice. Its members are all volunteers. Virginia Martin, like the other committee members, gravitated toward the committee out of her "own needs, desires, interests, values, and attractions, *rather than* . . . from what is socially assigned, ascribed, expected, or demanded" (Friedman 1992, 94). Virginia Martin thinks of the committee members as friends, not just colleagues. And as we have seen, it is in this community, rather than in the hospital where many of the members happen to work, that the nurses have found a context in which to "relocate and renegotiate" the various constituents of its members' identities.

Either kind of community could function as a moral space (Walker 1993) in which people subject what they do to ethical examination and reflection, but in our story, Virginia Martin and her friends used the community of choice for this purpose. We saw them undertaking such an examination as they worried about the baby in the farmhouse, the emergency room physician who seemed unsure, the chemotherapy patients who wanted to know the truth. And because nursing practice says something significant about the nurses' identities, the moral space created by the chosen community was also a space for reflecting on who the nurses are and want to be.

When a person engages in ethical reflection within the moral space of a chosen community, the others who inhabit that space perform a number of useful functions that fit roughly under the heading of what Cheshire Calhoun has called "emotional work"—the work of managing another's feelings. Calhoun argues that the work of "soothing tempers, boosting confidence, fueling pride, preventing frictions, and mending ego wounds" (Calhoun 1992, 118) is critical to the transformation of moral belief systems. "Because what we feel is tied to how we interpret situations," she writes, "helping others get the right moral perspective cannot be detached from working to correct their emotional attitudes" (120). The members of the chosen community thus help the deliberator to manage her emotions about what she has done or what has been done to her, and they tell stories that help her to correct inappropriate feelings arising from misinterpretation of other people's intentions. They supply further information that is relevant to the deliberations, or fresh perspectives on the morally troubling situation. They serve as a check on the deliberator's self-understanding by providing new interpretations of her interactions with others—"was the ER physician really slow, or were you feeling especially impatient that day?"—and offering their own intuitions as sounding boards against which to test her conclusions. And because the knowledge of what she ought to do now or how she should feel about what has already happened is not already there, fully formed, inside the deliberator's consciousness, the others within her moral space lend a hand in shaping her deliberations. They help her to know her own thoughts.

## Stories

What makes a counterstory a *story*? Does just any depiction of a logically related, chronological sequence of events count? How are the elements of a story connected to one another? Where do a story's meanings come from? I want here to draw attention to the features of stories that are important for my purposes: they are *depictive*, being representations of human experience; they are *selective* in what they depict; they are *interpretive*, offering a particular way of construing the acts, events, and personae that are represented; and they are *connective*, creating relationships among their own elements and to other stories.[3] Once we have rehearsed a story's characteristics, it will be easier to see how stories figure into the construction of an identity. Throughout this work, I'll use the terms "story" and "narrative" interchangeably.

First, a story is *depictive*. It is a representation of some actual or imaginary set of events, brought about or suffered by actors, that takes place over time. The raw material for any story is the stuff of actual people's lives—the things they do and experience, what they believe, their interactions with other people and the rest of the world.[4] Stories depict these events and experiences by describing them in words or other symbolic systems that are capable of representing a temporal sequence. Not all symbolic systems can depict successive moments in time; photographs, for example, usually represent only one such moment. Narrative representations, by contrast, must depict time passing.

Depictions of logically related events, actors, and places can be arranged into a simple chronological succession, but this is not yet a story. It is simply a *chronicle*. A chronicle represents events as occurring in a strict temporal sequence, but the events of a story can deviate from this sequence. Stories can contain flashbacks or flash-forwards, or rapid switches between the two. An event can be separated by an interval from the narrative present ("Last year I went to India") or it can be presented as occurring at some unspecified time. A story can linger over an event so that its representation takes up more time than did the event itself, or time can be compressed or skipped. An event that occurs only once can be presented a number of times, or a whole series of similar events can be presented simultaneously (Bal 1985, 49–79). In a story, then, time's arrow can fly in a number of directions.

Second, stories are *selective* in what they depict. Chronicles too are somewhat selective—a chronicle of the kings of England doesn't contain depictions of, say, domestic life in a contemporary Inuit village—but they are indiscriminate about which events in the lives of the kings they might include. Unlike a chronicle, which simply tells you that this happened, and then this, and then this, the elements of a story must be chosen in such a way as to represent a "process of happening,

---

3. My thanks to Elise Robinson for these four rubrics.
4. Even a fantasy begins with the stuff of actual people's lives: the depiction of a planet that is lit by two green suns draws on the actual experiences of "green" and "sun."

which is thought to possess a discernible beginning, middle, and end" (White 1973, 5). The chronicle becomes a story when its elements are restricted to inaugural, transitional, or terminating motifs. "Chronicles are, strictly speaking, open-ended. In principle they have no *inaugurations;* they simply 'begin' when the chronicler starts recording events. And they have no culminations or resolutions; they can go on indefinitely. Stories, however, have a discernible form (even when that form is an image of a state of chaos) which marks off the events contained in them from the other events that might appear in a comprehensive chronicle of the years covered in their unfoldings" (6).

Third, stories are *interpretive.* They don't just select the actors, events, and places that go into their creation—they characterize these elements. One means of characterizing the actors in a story is by showing what they do, and when characters are depicted as doing certain things repeatedly, we conclude that they have particular preoccupations or habits. *Round* characters are complex and undergo change; *flat* characters are stable stereotypes (Bal 1985, 79–80). The protagonist may, depending on how the story is plotted, be an active and successful hero, an unsuccessful victim (tragic hero), or a patient who suffers events rather than bringing them about (think of the character Dude, the protagonist of the Cohen brothers' film *The Big Liebowski*). Places are characterized in terms of the events that occur in them, or through descriptions that create an atmosphere inviting a particular emotional response.

The elements of a story can also be interpreted through a character who perceives and reacts to them—through what the character sees, hears, or touches. In a story (but not a chronicle), the depictions of time, events, actors, and places are always presented from within a point of perception—from a particular angle or way of seeing that offers a specific interpretation of what's going on. Mieke Bal's term for the relation between the elements that are presented and the perspective through which they are presented is *focalization* (Bal 1985, 100), and the person from whose point of view the story is told is the focalizer. Sometimes the story in its entirety is seen from a particular focalizer's point of view, but different people can also play the role of focalizer at different points in the story. In one scene we might see a setting or character from one character's angle of vision, while in the next the focalizer might be someone outside the action, such as the narrator.

A story offers an interpretation of its characters and events not only through its focalizers and what it shows people doing, but through its plot and the genre to which that plot belongs. A story's plot invites the receiver of the story (the reader, spectator, listener) to draw a conclusion about what happened: he really loved her but didn't know how to show it; the wrath of Achilles was the cause of the trouble; it was sad when the great ship went down. The *mode* of emplotment, or genre, invites the receiver of the story to interpret the depiction of events as farcical, as tragic, as an instance of chaos in a meaningless universe, and so on. The mode of emplotment thus relates a given story to other stories that offer the same kind of explanation of people's place in the cosmic (or local) order of things, of whether reconciliation among people is possible, of whether what happened was inevitable or just a matter of bad luck.

In the mode of emplotment's ability to relate one story to another we can see a fourth feature of stories: they are *connective*. They draw connections not only among themselves but also within themselves. As we just saw, setting can be related to event or character, and action is often related to character as well: the courtier's kiss shows him to be a traitor; the stifled laugh displays the worker's contempt for a colleague. By depicting events as causally (and not just temporally) linked; by the use of symbolism, which allows the depiction of a person or thing to stand for something greater than itself; by patterns and motifs that connect one set of events to another; and by connections between setting and event (such as a declaration of love on a moonlit balcony), the story's capacity for connection allows us to make sense of what has been represented.

Stories create meanings through the relationships of their internal elements, but also through their relationships to one another. While a story's mode of emplotment connects it to other stories generically, stories also draw explicit connections to particular stories (Bal 1985, 7). A contemporary story, for example, can contain a reference to a "Judas" or a "Scrooge" and so establish a narrative connection to the Passion of Christ or Dickens's *Christmas Carol*. This narrative connection, established through allusive nods to other stories, also sets up interconnections among various elements *within* the story. Character types and the stock plots that are associated with these characters can be lifted from stories that are familiar cultural staples and be reworked as variations on old themes. Or fragments of one story might be spliced to those from another story and so shed light on both. As we'll see later on, the connective feature of stories is absolutely central to the narrative construction of identities.

The depictive, selective, interpretive, and connective features of a story all work together to give the story its overall meaning. Indeed, it's in a story's ability to mean and to convey meaning that it differs most notably from a chronicle. A chronicle is just one damned thing after another, whereas a story embodies an understanding. Through its selective, interpretive, and connective representation of human experience over time, it makes a certain sort of sense of some part of what it is to be human. A personal identity likewise embodies an understanding. Through one's own and others' selective, interpretive, and connective representations of the characteristics, acts, experiences, roles, relationships, and commitments that contribute importantly to one's life over time, an identity makes a certain sort of sense of who one is. It does so because it is essentially narrative in nature.

## Self-Definition

Counterstories are stories of self-definition. In general, stories of self-definition can be grouped roughly into three categories: nonmoral self-definition, weak moral self-definition, and strong moral self-definition. They might be stories that define (or redefine) a group to which an individual belongs and from which the individual takes some significant part of her identity, or they might be stories that define (or redefine) the individual directly.

A story of group nonmoral self-definition merely identifies the group as one thing rather than another—the board of directors of a theater company, for example, might recount the history of past performances as a way of identifying the theater primarily with comic revivals instead of contemporary drama. Similarly, a story of individual nonmoral self-definition might identify the person as a good cook. A story of weak moral self-definition constructs a group or an individual as morally competent. A corporation tells such a story when it advertises itself as socially and environmentally responsible, and a teenager does the same when she recounts instances of good judgment to persuade her parents that she can be trusted with the car keys.

The concept of strong moral self-definition requires a more extensive explanation. In Margaret Urban Walker's terms, strong moral self-definition is a kind of moral competence. It is "the ability of morally developed persons to install and observe precedents for themselves which are both distinctive of them and binding upon them morally" (Walker

1987, 173). Walker has argued that, contrary to universalist moral theories, which assume that all relevant considerations regarding what any moral agent is required, permitted, or forbidden to do in a situation are exactly the same for any other agent similarly placed, there are identity-constitutive features of a moral agent's life that can give content to the particular ways in which this particular agent may or must act. On Walker's view, *this* agent might have commitments or priorities that differ from those of another agent in a similar situation. She might not need to do what the similarly situated agent does; she might aim to be a different kind of person from the one the similarly situated agent tries to be.

In deliberating about what she ought to do, the agent reviews her personal history, weighs the particulars of her past in terms of more general moral values, and discerns or constructs a course of action that expresses a commitment to those particulars. The person either ratifies her history—"I've always believed in telling the truth, but not in truth-dumping"—and remains on her present course, or repudiates it and charts a new course: "I've always been too quick to blame the mother when a baby doesn't thrive. I'll try not to do that this time." Either way, she creates a moral track record that commits her to certain values for the future. The review of her history is a backward-looking story that explains to her who she has been. The commitment to a future course of action is a forward-looking story that shows her where she wants to go. Strong moral self-definition thus allows certain individuating features of the person's life to matter in ways that aren't universally generalizable but remain specific to the person and so contribute to her identity.

We may contrast purposeful strong moral self-definition, whereby the agent deliberately sets out to define herself in terms of the values, experiences, and commitments she takes to be identity-constituting, with inadvertent strong moral self-definition, whereby the agent non-purposefully and perhaps even unconsciously makes of herself a particular sort of person. Consider Virginia Martin's young friend Megan O'Brien, a nurse-practitioner at a not-for-profit family planning clinic. A year or so ago, shortly after she began her practice, a sixteen-year-old high school dropout asked Megan O'Brien for birth control. On being presented with a number of options, the girl thought a long-acting contraceptive would be best, so Megan O'Brien gave her Norplant, inserting six flexible strips under the skin on the girl's upper arm. The implants, designed to release the hormone progestin slowly, protect the recipient against pregnancy for five years. Nine months later, however, the girl returned to ask that the Norplant be removed, because she was experiencing breakthrough bleeding and her boyfriend didn't like the feel of the strips under the skin. Megan O'Brien hesitated. As she started to think about it, she concluded that her patient was too young to appreciate fully what a disaster for her a pregnancy at this point would be. Moreover, she didn't trust the girl to remember to take a daily birth control pill. So she refused to remove the implants.[5]

This is a moment of strong moral self-definition, but it's inadvertent. Megan O'Brien might purposefully have mined her past for the commitments and experiences that have made her who she now is, and used these particulars not only to guide her care of the young patient but to set a precedent for the care of future patients. That she didn't do this, however, doesn't mean that she is not now defining herself morally. In acting as she does, she has begun to fashion herself into a nurse who controls and manipulates underage patients. If she controls and manipulates often enough, she becomes a controlling person.

When she originally inserted the contraceptive, something important about her action was indeterminate. Was she acting as her young client's agent? Was she implementing her own views about adolescent sexuality, or attempting to stand in for the girl's parents? None of this was clear, either to herself or to anyone else. The girl thought it was clear, however. She had agreed to accept Norplant on the understanding that she was in charge of her own body. But now, by refusing to remove the implants, Megan O'Brien retroactively changes what it was that her patient originally consented to. Her present refusal makes visible what could not be seen earlier—that not only for the immediate moment but for the past nine months the contraception has been coercive. Christine Korsgaard echoes this idea of strong but retrospective moral self-definition when she writes,

> You cannot, just by making a resolution, acquire a virtue or recover from a vice. Or better still, we will say that you can, because you are free, but then we must say that only what happens in the future establishes whether you have really made the resolution or not. I do not

5. For ethical analyses of health care providers' refusal to remove Norplant, see Macklin 1996.

mean that only the future will produce the evidence: I mean that only
what you do in the future will enable us to correctly attribute a resolu-
tion to you. There is a kind of backwards determination in the construction of one's character. (Korsgaard 1989, 45)

The backward determination of a morally opaque action that is nevertheless identity-constituting is more complicated in a case of purposeful strong moral self-definition, because there the agent, *intending*
that the action should say something about who she is, issues herself a
promissory note which she must later make good. How well she succeeds in this depends in part on her later choices, but these may be constrained by events over which she has little control. She cannot know
until her life-story plays itself out whether the commitment she made
could actually be adhered to in the way she anticipated. Something
might turn up or have been overlooked that sends her story off in an un-
expected direction, so that, in the event, there is cause for regret.

A story of strong moral self-definition is always told *from here*, but
like any sort of moral choice, its assessment is necessarily *from there*
(Williams 1981a, 35). Whether a person has succeeded in defining herself by charting a present course of action depends on how well she
stays on course, and that depends not only on her own resolve but on
whether subsequent events knock or nudge her in a different direction.
Living up to one's resolutions requires luck as well as persistence. Because one can't foresee how one's life will go, from here it is somewhat
indeterminate; from there, it might mean something morally that can't
now be seen.

## Two Kinds of Counterstories

Unlike an act of backward determination, which defines a past that
has been, until now, morally opaque, counterstories redefine a past
that has been, until now, characterized incorrectly. They take a story
that has (for the moment at least) been determined, undo it, and reconfigure it with a new significance. If individuals or groups can *identify*
themselves through stories of nonmoral self-definition, weak moral
self-definition, or strong moral self-definition, though, they can *repair*
their identities only through the last two kinds. Counterstories such as
the ones the nurses told in the moral space of the steering committee
are stories of strong moral self-definition, told both for the individuals

and the group. Each person uses the story to repudiate an incorrect understanding of who she is, and replaces this with a more accurate self-understanding. Reidentifying herself in this way commits her to a future course of action that expresses who, morally, she takes herself to be.

Other counterstories do their repair work more minimally, resisting master narratives' morally degrading depictions of an oppressed group by representing the group members as morally upright human beings. These are stories of weak moral self-definition. Harper Lee's *To Kill a Mockingbird* is such a counterstory, bidding readers to resist the master narratives that identify black men as sexual predators of Southern white women. While the counterstory concerns a particular black male character, there is no one existing person who is reidentified by it. Instead, the story can be set to the moral task of shifting racist understandings of black men in general. If it succeeds, then individual black men whose identities have been damaged by those same master narratives can also be seen as morally trustworthy.

Individual and group counterstories can shade off into one another. Just as a counterstory could be developed by an individual to define herself morally, so a counterstory that reidentifies an individual can be generalized to revise a moral understanding about the group to which the individual belongs. Counterstories move in this way between individuals and groups because oppressive identities are imposed on individuals precisely because of their membership in a despised group.

No counterstory can be nonmorally self-defining, though it may identify the individual or group in nonmoral terms. For example, I might tell a story to establish that, despite what others may think, I am bad at managing money and have no head for business. If I am a Jew and am purposefully resisting the stereotypes that depict Jews as avaricious usurers, my story is a counterstory even though it doesn't employ moral terms, because it repudiates a pernicious master narrative. Groups too can tell self-defining counterstories that, on their face, say nothing about their moral character but instead identify them in nonmoral terms. The nonmoral terms take on a moral valence when the stories are used to repair the group identity.

Counterstories can be created *by* or *for* the person whose identity needs repair. In the moral space within a corporation (perhaps by the water cooler) I can construct a story with my coworkers that lets me reidentify a gay colleague, who has been isolated and passed over for

promotion on account of his sexual orientation, as a talented and trustworthy person. If my gay colleague takes up my counterstory, it has
corrective powers not only for me and my coworkers but also for him.
We now see him as someone to be respected and treat him accordingly,
and he too, perhaps, sees himself in a new light. The reason that counterstories can be told to reidentify someone other than the teller, as I'll
explain in Chapter 3, is that identity is a function not only of how a
person perceives himself but also of how others perceive him. Counterstories told to repair someone else's identity obviously aren't self-
defining, but they can identify the other person in terms that acknowledge the person's moral competence. They are, in other words, stories
of weak moral definition. In certain instances of prolonged and deep intimacy it may also be possible for one person to define another in
strong moral terms (J. Nelson 1999), but I shall not explore that possibility here.

## Narrative Repair

The immediate purpose of a counterstory is to repair identities that
have been damaged by oppression. Identities—as I'll argue in Chapter
3—are complex narrative constructions consisting of a fluid interaction
of the many stories and fragments of stories surrounding the things that
seem most important, from one's own point of view and the point of
view of others, about a person over time. Because identities are constructed from both points of view, there are, broadly speaking, two
ways in which they can be damaged. First, a person's identity is damaged when powerful institutions or individuals, seeing people like her
as morally sub- or abnormal, unjustly prevent her and her kind from occupying roles or entering into relationships that are identity-constituting. If a woman is denied custody of her child solely on the grounds that
she is lesbian, her relationship with her child is attenuated; this impairs
her ability to hold on to her identity as a mother. If a company's offices
are accessible only by means of stairs and this prevents a person in a
wheelchair from taking a lucrative job there, the person's potential relationship with the company never gets off the ground; this slightly
erodes his identity as an economically self-sufficient person. Japanese
Americans interned during World War II were forcibly confined because
of their supposed threat to the country; their identities as U.S. citizens
were taken away from them. And in the story of the Nurse Recognition

Day committee, the physicians' "touchy-feely" characterization of nurses makes it difficult for them to fulfill their nursing roles; this is an injury to their professional identities. Harm to an oppressed person's identity that takes this form may be called *deprivation of opportunity*. The kind of counterstory that is required to repair deprivation of opportunity is one that will change others' perception of the person. The judge, the employer, the government,[6] the physicians must either *endorse* counterstories told by those suffering the deprivation or *develop* counterstories on the sufferers' behalf.

Although oppression always damages people's identities by depriving them of opportunity, it frequently also has a second kind of destructive impact. A person's identity is twice damaged by oppression when she internalizes as a self-understanding the hateful or dismissive views that other people have of her. The lesbian mother, the wheelchair-bound worker, the Japanese American might all come to see themselves in the terms reserved by the oppressive institutions of their society for people like them. They then lose, or fail to acquire, self-respect. If John Rawls is right in identifying self-respect as a primary good (Rawls 1971, 178), then its absence is perhaps even more significant a harm than the deprivation of an identity-constituting role or relationship. This second sort of damage to an oppressed person's identity can be called *infiltrated consciousness*.

Notice that, like deprivation of opportunity, infiltrated consciousness admits of degrees. In the story of the Nurse Recognition Day committee, Virginia Martin had partially internalized the physicians' opinion of nurses. She had unreflectively believed that physicians did the real work in the hospital and that the nurses' work was not merely different but somehow second best. She would have gone to medical school rather than nursing school if she could; she dismissed the physicians' lack of respect toward nurses as simply a matter of docs being docs. But she also took pride in her work and enjoyed doing it. To the extent that the physicians' characterization of who nurses are had invaded her own sense of herself, her identity has been damaged. The kind of counterstory that is required to repair an infiltrated consciousness is one that will change the person's self-perception. The person must either tell a counterstory for herself or endorse one that is told on her behalf.

---

6. I take it that collectives and not just individuals are capable of moral agency. For arguments in defense of the idea that collectives can be persons, see Rovane 1998.

## Identity and Agency

So far, I have been collecting some of the working parts that contribute to the concept of the counterstory: community of choice, story,
self-definition, deprivation of opportunity, infiltrated consciousness,
narrative repair. Now I want to secure the connection between identity
and agency. My claim, if you recall, is that counterstories allow oppressed people to refuse the identities imposed on them by their oppressors and to reidentify themselves in more respectworthy terms. I
further claim that this reidentification permits oppressed people to exercise their moral agency more freely. These claims are plausible only if
identity and agency are closely connected. With the help of two important papers by Paul Benson (1990, 1994), I argue that the connection between the two is an internal one, since not only do my actions disclose
who I am, but who I am taken—or take myself—to be directly affects
how freely I may act.

Identity is a question of how *others* understand what I am doing, as
well as how *I* understand what I am doing. If other people perceive my
actions to be those of a morally trustworthy person, then they will permit me to act freely. In addition, though, I must see *myself* as a morally
trustworthy person if I am to act freely. Both others' recognition that I
am a morally responsible person and my own sense of myself as a
morally responsible person, then, are required for the free exercise of
moral agency.

Following Benson, I argue that agency is freer or less free to the extent
that two conditions obtain. The first, control over one's actions, ranges
over both one's ability to act willfully and the ability to regulate one's
will reflectively. The second, normative competence, involves three capacities: (1) the ability to understand moral norms, act in accordance
with them, and reveal who one is, morally speaking, through what one
does; (2) the ability of others to recognize by one's actions that one is a
morally responsible person; and (3) the ability of the agent to see herself
as a morally responsible person. If others' conception of who I am keeps
them from seeing my actions as those of a morally responsible person,
they will treat me as a moral incompetent. This is the problem of deprivation of opportunity. If my own conception of who I am keeps me
from trusting my own moral judgments, I will treat *myself* as a moral
incompetent. This is the problem of infiltrated consciousness.

I'll make my argument in two steps. First, I'll make the case that how
others identify me has a direct bearing on how freely I can exercise my

agency. Second, I'll demonstrate that how I see myself also determines how freely I can act.

## How Others Identify Me: Deprivation of Opportunity

Modern and contemporary philosophers often talk of moral agency as if it were merely a capacity one has, involving competencies that we possess in our own right. Many prominent contemporary theories, including Gerald Dworkin's (1970, 1988), Harry Frankfurt's (1971), Wright Neely's (1974), Gary Watson's (1975), and Daniel Dennett's (1984), have characterized free agency as consisting in the competency to govern one's conduct willfully and the capacity to regulate one's will reflectively—neither of which is represented as having anything at all to do with one's relationships to other people. In his classic "Freedom of the Will and the Concept of a Person," for example, Harry Frankfurt writes,

> The unwilling addict identifies himself, . . . through the formation of a second-order volition, with one rather than with the other of his conflicting first-order desires. He makes one of them more truly his own and, in so doing, he withdraws himself from the other. It is in virtue of this identification and withdrawal . . . that the unwilling addict may meaningfully make the analytically puzzling statements that the force moving him to take the drug is a force other than his own, and that it is not of his own free will but rather against his will that this force moves him to take it. (Frankfurt 1971, 13)

Similarly, Wright Neely contends:

> A man is freer not only to the extent that he does as he pleases and to the extent that his pleasing as he does follows from a coherent life plan, but also to the extent that this life plan and the character which goes with it have been forged by him through time with due attention to the satisfactions which he may be missing as a result of lacking certain desires, with due consideration of those of his character traits which lead to painful consequences, and with due sensitivity to other types of lives which may serve as ideals for him to follow. (Neely 1974, 54)

Although Susan Wolf does not restrict her account to the content-neutral capacities of governing one's conduct and regulating one's first-order desires, her theory of agency is just as individualistic as the others. She argues that free agents must have a metaethical commitment to some degree of objectivism, as this grounds "the ability to do the right thing for the right reasons" and "the ability to act in accordance with, and on the basis of, the True and the Good" that are, on her view, necessary for moral agency (Wolf 1990, 71). Here again, though, there is no acknowledgment that the agent acts in conjunction with other agents, much less that this fact might have a bearing on the conditions for free agency.

It's my contention, however, that freedom of agency requires not only certain capacities, competencies, and intentions that lie within the individual, but also recognition on the part of others of *who one is*, morally speaking. To see how this works, let's return to the story of the young leukemia patient who was not told that he was dying. Because the physician identified Pilar Sanchez as a fond (in the sense of foolish) care giver, her considered moral judgment that Jake be told of his prognosis didn't get registered as a *moral* judgment at all. It got registered as emotional overinvolvement—assisted, perhaps, by ethnic stereotypes about excitable Hispanics. The physician's inability to identify Pilar Sanchez as a morally developed agent forecloses the possibility of any discussion with him, let alone a case consult, and this deprives her of the opportunity to care for Jake as well as she thinks she should.

In "Feminist Second Thoughts about Free Agency," a paper that develops the point about recognition, Paul Benson contends that most theories of free agency have misdescribed cases of diminished freedom in which the agent is, say, a young child or someone who has been diagnosed with a serious mental illness. In cases of this kind, the theories hold, the agents have no "power to control their conduct through deliberate choices which express what they 'really' want to do" (Benson 1990, 52). So, for example, Frankfurt classifies young children as "wantons," incapable of adopting second-order desires that control which first-order desires they are willing to act on (Frankfurt 1971). The insistence on a control condition as sufficient for free agency, Benson suggests, is a mistake that could only be made by a philosopher who has never been the primary care giver of a young child. Who else would think that a five-year-old boy who has been warned not to tease his baby sister but does it anyway must be out of control, incapable of stopping what he is doing? That the control condition is inadequate is, to harken back to the title of the essay, Benson's "first feminist thought" about free agency.

The five-year-old may be perfectly capable of leaving his sister alone, says Benson. What he has not yet developed, however, is the capacity for "normative self-disclosure"—the ability to reveal through his actions who he is as a person (Benson 1990, 53). To revert to the language I was using earlier, the little boy's teasing does not count as an instance of inadvertent strong moral self-definition. Unlike Megan O'Brien's refusal to remove her patient's contraceptive device, which disclosed a controlling and manipulative streak in her character, the boy's behavior doesn't tell us anything much about who he is. Since the capacity for normative self-disclosure is, for Benson, a crucial component of normative competence, and the boy hasn't fully attained normative competence, his agency isn't free even though he *can* control his behavior.

On Benson's view, then, agency is free to the extent that two conditions are present. One is the control condition, and the other is normative competence, which involves the ability to express one's identity through what one does. As Benson puts it,

> Powers of control are only one part of a much broader, and hopefully more adequate, conception of free agency. On this new conception, free agency requires *normative competence*, an array of abilities to be aware of applicable normative standards, to appreciate those standards, and to bring them competently to bear in one's evaluations of open courses of action. . . . At the heart of free agency is the power of our actions to reveal who we are, both to ourselves and to others, in the context of potential normative assessments of what we do. Our level of awareness and understanding of the standards expressed in those assessments is as crucial to our freedom as our ability to control what we do. (Benson 1990, 55)

In keying free agency to the power of our actions to reveal who we are, Benson points to something that P. F. Strawson has famously described in "Freedom and Resentment." In that essay, Strawson contrasts our ordinary attitudes of interpersonal engagement, such as "gratitude, resentment, forgiveness, love, and hurt feelings" (Strawson 1962, 62), which we display toward people whose actions reveal them to be participants in the moral community, with attitudes that preclude such engagement, because the persons' deeds show them to be morally sub- or abnormal. "Participant reactive attitudes," says Strawson, "are essentially natural human reactions to the good or ill will or indifference of others towards us, as displayed in *their* attitudes and actions." They are attitudes we take toward people who by their attitudes and actions have shown themselves to be among "the normal and the mature" (Strawson 1962, 67).

Objective attitudes, by contrast, are those we exhibit toward people whose actions disclose them to be psychologically abnormal or morally undeveloped (note that these are Benson's two cases of unfree agency). "To adopt the objective attitude to another human being," as Strawson memorably puts it, "is to see him, perhaps, as an object of social policy; as a subject for what, in a wide range of sense, might be called treatment; as something certainly to be taken account, perhaps precautionary account, of; to be managed or handled or cured or trained" (Strawson 1962, 66). Which attitude we take toward someone depends on whether we think they are morally responsible or morally defective, and we decide this by interpreting, in accordance with some set of evaluative standards, what their actions say about who they are. How we register what someone is doing thus determines whether we will allow them to exercise their agency freely, on the one hand, or constrain them by disciplining them, refusing them a driver's license, denying them custody of their children, or confining them to a locked psychiatric ward, on the other.

But, as Benson goes on to point out (this is his "second thought"), whether we will be seen as the sorts of people who can be held morally responsible for what we are doing has as much to do with the norms of those who assess us as with our ability to understand those norms (58). Not all of us who fail to qualify as fully free agents do so because we don't appreciate the evaluative standards that others use to take our measure. We may know those standards very well but reject them, and so court persistent misreading. Here Benson is thinking, for instance, of a woman in a sexist society. She may be perfectly aware of how others will perceive her "unladylike" behavior, but not accept mainstream standards of how a lady should behave. It's possible that those in the mainstream will then judge from her actions that she is not morally trustworthy—she obviously doesn't know the rules. As Benson points out, agents who are at the margins of society are particularly open to having their actions evaluated as evidence of sub- or abnormality, precisely because they don't conform to the standards adopted by those in the mainstream.

If Benson is right—and I think he is—then normative competence isn't just a matter of capacities and capabilities that reside within the agent. As capacities and capabilities are always relative to an environment, the ability to exercise them successfully depends in part on the others who inhabit that environment. Normative competence is therefore genuinely interpersonal: the capacity for normative self-disclosure embraces not only the agent's ability to appreciate the moral construction that others will place on her actions but also the recognition by those others that her actions are those of a morally developed person. The role that other people's recognition of one's identity plays in Benson's account of free agency explains, in a way that most contemporary theories can't, what went wrong between Pilar Sanchez and the dismissive oncologist. According to the standard theories, Pilar Sanchez is a free agent. She is able to govern her behavior by means of her will and is also capable of regulating the content of her will. So the control condition is met. Yet there are good reasons to think that her moral agency is less than fully free, and that is because one component of the normative competence condition is not met. She is aware of and appreciates applicable normative standards and can bring them to bear in her assessments of her options, but she can't make her actions reveal who she is, because others have imposed an oppressive identity on her.

The oncologist has perceived Pilar Sanchez's involvement with her young dying patient as saying something morally discreditable about her. He sees her as a defective agent, and therefore in no position to hold him accountable. By his standards, which are the mainstream standards in the hospital, she is someone to be managed or handled (if not cured or trained). The problem is not, however, that Pilar Sanchez is morally underdeveloped. Rather, it's that there is something wrong with the norms in the mainstream. These norms produce the oncologist's objective attitude toward her, and it's that which keeps her from being fully free.

If the constrictions on her agency are to be loosened, the oncologist must be persuaded to identify Pilar Sanchez differently. If he comes to perceive her as a colleague rather than an emotional Latina, he is more likely to include her in the moral deliberations regarding Jake's care. The damage the oncologist has inflicted on her identity is that of deprivation of opportunity. The counterstory that's required to reidentify her, then, is a story about her moral trustworthiness that *he* is willing to endorse. The difficulty, of course, lies in getting the oncologist to listen to such a story.

So far, it looks as if the degree to which agency is free depends on how well two conditions are met. One is the control condition, which ranges over both one's ability to act willfully and the ability to regulate one's will reflectively, and the other is normative competence, conceived as (1) the ability to understand moral norms, act in accordance with them, and reveal who one is, morally speaking, through what one does; (2) the ability of others to recognize by one's actions that one is a morally responsible person. Alternatively, the normative competence condition may be thought of as a refinement of the control condition: control over one's actions requires that others not put obstacles in one's path. Seeing that self-disclosure is a matter of what others perceive, as well as what a person expresses, helps us to explain why repairing the damage to a person's identity allows her to exercise her agency more freely, at least when the damage in question is that of deprivation of opportunity.

## HOW I IDENTIFY ME: INFILTRATED CONSCIOUSNESS

When we consider the *other* sort of damage that oppression inflicts on people's identities, however, it quickly becomes apparent that our understanding of the normative competence condition needs to be expanded. In a second paper, "Free Agency and Self-Worth," Benson considers the problem of what I have been calling infiltrated consciousness, arguing that in addition to whatever other capacities are necessary, "free agents must have a certain sense of their own worthiness to act" (Benson 1994, 650). In other words, not only do others have to identify the agent as morally trustworthy—she has to identify herself as trustworthy as well.

Benson begins by looking at an instance, not of oppression, but of personal domination.[7] In the 1944 film *Gaslight*, the character played by Ingrid Bergman is the wife of an evil man, played by Charles Boyer. The Boyer character, who has murdered the Bergman character's aunt, marries the Bergman character so that he can steal the valuable jewels the aunt hid before she died. Bergman, of course, is unaware of his nefarious intent and believes he truly loves her. To keep her from finding out what he is doing, Boyer tries to confuse and disorient her, making her believe that she can't remember things she has recently done, that she loses things, that she has hallucinations. Through plausible suggestions he isolates her from people, reducing her to bewildered helplessness. By these means he dramatically diminishes her freedom as an agent.

---

7. Oppression consists in systematic institutional processes that prevent certain groups of people from developing and exercising their capacities or gaining access to material goods (Young 1990, 38, 40). Personal domination consists in one person's preventing another from determining her own actions.

She can act intentionally even though she believes she is going mad, and her will doesn't seem to be plagued by unregulated motives. As most free agency theorists understand it, then, the control condition is met. Likewise, her normative competence, as we understand it so far, seems to have survived intact. She can wield moral norms and reveal herself through her actions, and others identify her as the sort of person toward whom one appropriately takes the reactive attitude. But she is still not free. Why? Benson's answer is that "she has lost her former sense of her own status as a worthy agent. She has ceased to trust herself to govern her conduct competently" (Benson 1994, 657). If he's right, then we have to refine the normative competence condition. We must now conceive of normative competence as: (1) the ability to understand moral norms, act in accordance with them, and reveal who one is, morally speaking, through what one does; (2) the ability of others to recognize by one's actions that one is a morally responsible person; and (3) the ability of the agent to see herself as a morally responsible person.

Benson thinks that a historical theory of free agency, such as John Christman's (1991), could explain Bergman's lack of freedom by showing that the process by which she came to her present beliefs couldn't bear her scrutiny. If she knew what Boyer had done to manipulate her, "she would surely resist the beliefs and desires that resulted from it" (Benson 1994, 656). So Benson moves to a case of oppression, which he views as blocking this response. He imagines a feminist remake of *Gaslight*, also set in the 1880s, in which the husband is a kindly soul who takes his wife's interests to heart, but, because he is a physician and the medical science of his day pathologizes women, he regards the wife's active imagination and strong passions as symptomatic of a serious psychological illness. The wife trusts her husband's diagnosis and comes to believe that she is mentally ill. In this case, Benson argues, "the woman would not be likely to resist the process by which her beliefs and desires were altered in the wake of her diagnosis, if she were to attend reflectively to that process. For she arrives at her sense of incompetence and estrangement from her conduct on the basis of reasons that are accepted by a scientific establishment which is socially validated and which she trusts" (657).

Here the loss of free agency extends beyond the institutional impediments that others place in the agent's way. Whereas the social mechanisms that sustain oppression thwarted Pilar Sanchez's ability to register a moral judgment regarding her young patient, the mechanisms reach even further in Benson's case of medical gaslighting, infiltrating the agent's consciousness and destroying her sense of who she is. Oppression takes the place of Boyer's machinations to bring it about that the medically gaslighted wife should lose, to a significant degree, confidence in her worthiness to be the author of her own conduct. Like Bergman in the original film, her view of herself has been altered so that she no longer regards herself as competent to answer for her actions in light of normative demands that she herself thinks other people might reasonably apply to her (Benson 1994, 660).

While Benson's explanation of why someone with an infiltrated consciousness is not a free agent strikes me as largely correct, I believe that he has misdescribed what happens when one is gaslighted by deceit, as opposed to being gaslighted by oppression. Benson accepts Christman's view that an agent's regulative power over her will is free just in case "the agent's will was acquired through a process that could be sustained under reflection" (Benson 1994, 654). Under reflection, the agent concludes that her beliefs about her will have been formed in the right way: they have been properly connected to reality and are therefore warranted. Because Bergman's belief that she ought not to trust her judgment was formed by Boyer's systematic deception, rather than by any actual psychological impairment, it is not warranted, and so, Christman would say, she is not free.

Benson endorses this account of how deception takes away an agent's freedom and follows it up by a psychological claim: when an agent whose beliefs about her unworthiness to act aren't warranted, she can repair the damage and free her will simply by reflecting on the process by which her beliefs were formed. That's why Benson thinks that if Bergman were aware of Boyer's manipulation, she would "surely resist the beliefs and desires that resulted from it." This is an argument about transparency. Benson claims that if Boyer's chicanery could be made transparent, Bergman would drop her beliefs that her judgments are worthless: what was done by deceit can be undone by unmasking the deceiver. The unstated inference is that because the medically gaslighted wife has no way to see through the medical ideology of her day, she cannot, like Bergman, free herself.

But Benson ought not to suppose that the Bergman character would "surely" resist the belief in her own unworthiness if only she knew the belief wasn't warranted. He attaches too much importance to the consequence of being shown the hidden mechanism. Knowing that there is no rational warrant for the belief that she is morally untrustworthy doesn't guarantee that the agent can rid herself of the belief. Her ability to resist depends on *her ability to trust her own judgments*, and in both of the gaslighting cases, that is precisely what has been so badly broken down.

In the original case, Bergman might discard the belief in her own untrustworthiness if she knew of Boyer's deception and if he had only been playing with her mind for a few days or weeks, because that is too short a time to do a thoroughgoing job of corrupting someone's sense of self-worth. Self-worth is resilient and survives repeated blows. As long as Bergman retains enough of it to believe that her mental processes are reliable, she may be able to assess the evidence pointing to her husband's machinations and draw her own conclusions, and that will be enough to restore her to her premarital level of confidence in her agency.

If, however, Boyer is given sufficient time to destroy Bergman's sense of self-worth altogether, and if her loving trust in him causes her to accept his verdict regarding her mental state as definitive, then Bergman will not be able to rely on her judgments, no matter how much evidence presents itself regarding her husband's deception. Her beliefs will be evidence-resistant, precisely because she no longer trusts herself to exercise her moral agency competently. She is then in no better an epistemic position than the medically gaslighted wife who, having lived all her life in a society that discounts women's judgments, and having now been authoritatively diagnosed as seriously ill, no longer regards herself as mentally competent. For the doctor's wife too, the ability to resist the belief that she is crazy depends less on *whether* she is shown the hidden mechanism that drives the diagnosis than on *when*. If the evidence that the science is wrong comes too late and she no longer has any faith in her ability to judge it for herself, the evidence will not free her.

The relevant difference between the two gaslighting cases, then, is not (as Benson supposes) that there is something the wife could find out that would free her agency in the first case but not in the second. Rather, the difference is that, in the first case, the wife's sense of self-worth hasn't yet been completely corrupted. If it were, what she knew or didn't know about the warrant for her beliefs could make no positive difference to her, because her ability to know anything would be precisely what she no longer trusted. Indeed, the knowledge that her beliefs are without rational warrant could well serve to make her feel even more crazy.

There are other relevant differences, too, and these have to do with both the extent to which the women's beliefs have been manipulated and the means used to manipulate them. The woman who has been medically gaslighted has been extensively manipulated. Because hers is a case of oppression, she has perhaps never seen herself as a fully competent moral agent. Those in authority are likely always to have treated her as if she were morally deficient, and this means the normative competence condition was never fully met. The social constriction on her agency would then have been compounded by the medical judgment that she is hysterical, which corrupts what little sense of self-worth she might once have had. She, having internalized both the prevailing judgment about women and the judgment of medical science, is thereby thrice bound: once by patriarchy, again by doctors, and finally by herself. As she has never exercised her agency very freely, talk of narrative *repair* seems inappropriate. What the medically gaslighted woman needs are stories that let her *acquire* ordinary levels of free agency for the first time. She needs counterstories that her husband and his colleagues will endorse and counterstories that she can endorse. Only when her identity is more fully formed—in terms of how others see her and how she sees herself—can the normative competence condition be satisfied. The resources available to her for telling either kind of story lie in her communities, especially her communities of choice.

The Bergman character's problem lies more in the *means* by which her beliefs are manipulated. Once, it appears, she enjoyed normal levels of free agency: before she was married, both conditions for freedom were met reasonably well. That being the case, we can say that her beliefs have not been extensively manipulated. Nevertheless, if Boyer had been given a long enough time, he might have been able to corrupt her will even more thoroughly than did the husband of the medically gaslighted woman because the means Boyer employed were Bergman's own love and trust in him. He used the special vulnerability that is attendant on intimacy to bend her to his will, taking advantage of the confidence she placed in him, not only to implant the suggestion that she was going mad, but also to isolate her from anyone who might reassure her as to her sanity.

Had he been completely successful in this program of personal deception, he might well have stripped her of all the resources that would allow her to take back her normal epistemic position. Bereft of everything except her intimacy with him and no longer able to trust herself, she would have had to rely entirely on his judgments rather than her own. There would be no communities to which she could turn for help, for her world would now contain only herself and her husband. In that world there would be no one to free her, for she could no longer convincingly tell a counterstory on her own behalf and her husband would be the last person to tell it for her.[8]

Sustained and systematic deception by an intimate, then, is potentially even more destructive to a person's sense of her own worthiness to act than is oppression. In either case, however, the difficulty for someone who identifies *herself* as unworthy of answering for her own conduct is that she can't reidentify herself as morally accountable simply by coming to the rational conclusion that her feelings of worthlessness aren't warranted, or by having others point this out to her. Because she doesn't trust her own judgment, it will be hard for her to hear, much less create, a counterstory that reidentifies her as a worthy person. She can always come up with another story that explains why she *ought* to be treated badly. She can always remind herself, as Virginia Martin did, that docs will be docs.

How, then, can a counterstory serve to repair an infiltrated consciousness? The short answer is that sometimes it can't. As in the case of deprivation of opportunity, where there can be a great deal of difficulty in getting the persons who are misperceiving someone to endorse a counterstory that identifies the person as morally competent, so, in the case of infiltrated consciousness, the necessary story of weak or strong moral self-definition may be impossible for the oppressed person to develop. Since, however, consciousnesses can be infiltrated to greater or lesser degrees, the agent whose trust in herself is not yet completely corrupted might be able, under the right conditions, to tell the story she needs in order to free herself.

Virginia Martin, for example, has a comparatively mild case of infiltrated consciousness. When the Nurse Recognition Day committee meetings first began, she shared the mainstream view in the hospital that a nurse is a kind of second-rate doctor who doesn't deserve a great deal of professional courtesy. When she encountered evidence that this view was unwarranted, she was generally able to resolve the cognitive dissonance this set up in her by dismissing the evidence as unimportant or telling a story about it that made it fit better with her other beliefs.

8. In the film, Boyer makes the mistake of permitting his wife to go out with him on a sightseeing expedition. Her beauty and mystery attract the attention of a handsome police investigator, played by Joseph Cotten, who ultimately comes to Bergman's rescue. So her world never does consist of just herself and her husband.

She resisted the idea that she and her colleagues needed to reidentify themselves and was equally suspicious of the move to link this reidentification to any kind of feminist framework.

Because the committee meetings provided a moral space in which to reflect—in the company of other nurses whose opinions she respected—on who she was, and because these others had a very different view of nurses from the one that infiltrated her consciousness, a cognitive dissonance arose that she couldn't simply dismiss. She tried to laugh it off, caricaturing the project of strong moral self-definition as a Gloria-Steinem-meets-orthopedic-surgeon absurdity. Ultimately, however, her affection for, and trust in, her former professor and the new friends of her chosen community made it possible for her to take for her own the counterstory the others were telling about themselves.

As Benson's two papers suggest, identity and agency are both interpersonal notions. Who I am, morally speaking, is in some measure a matter of who others say I am, and this has a direct bearing on how freely I am able to exercise my moral agency. Moreover, how others perceive me also influences how I perceive myself, and that too has a direct bearing on my freedom to act.

## Questions Raised by Counterstories

Counterstories, I have argued, permit people whose identities have been damaged by oppression to see themselves, and to be recognized by others, as morally trustworthy persons. But it is important to note precisely what role recognition plays here. By itself, recognition does not stop persons from being oppressed, as oppression is the product of a dialectic between people's understanding of themselves and of one another, on the one hand, and the material conditions of an oppressive community of place, on the other. The nurses' counterstory cannot—is not designed to—end oppression. It is instead a tool for reidentifying the nurses as respectworthy professionals, and so freeing their agency.

The story of the nurses raises a number of philosophical and ethical questions. First, what is it about the story that allows the nurses to refigure their own role? This is a question about *identity*. Second, what is the connection between the stories they have been hearing in their community of place and what is morally owed them? This is a question about *oppression*. Third, how should the nurses respond? This is a question about *resistance*. In the chapters to come, I take up each of these questions, using the concept of the counterstory to trace the connections among them.

Before doing so, however, I wish to situate my project with respect to other recent philosophical work. The growing body of literature within moral philosophy that has argued for the importance of narratives to the moral life has not paid much attention to oppressive identities and the possibility of narrative resistance. In the next chapter, then, I survey the work that has been done and examine some of the difficulties that arise as a consequence of this neglect.

# 2  Narrative Approaches to Ethics

> Don't take it as a matter of course, but as a remarkable
> fact, that pictures and fictitious narratives give us pleas-
> ure, occupy our minds.
> ("Don't take it as a matter of course" means: find it
> surprising, as you do some things which disturb you.)
> —Ludwig Wittgenstein, *Philosophical Investigations*

To say that counterstories are capable of reidentifying people whose
identities have been damaged by oppression is to claim that narratives
do moral work. Over the last two decades a number of literary critics,
psychologists, sociologists, religious studies scholars, bioethicists, and
moral philosophers have defended the idea that narratives figure importantly in the moral life, producing a small but illuminating body of literature that is commonly called "narrative ethics." Because narrative
ethicists have put a wide array of stories to a wide variety of moral uses,
there is no single theory that the term "narrative ethics" picks out. In
general, however, narrative ethics accords a central role to stories, not
merely employing them as illustrations, examples, or ways of testing
our intuitions regarding moral theories or principles, but regarding
them as necessary means to some moral end. Narrativists have
claimed, among other things, that stories of one kind or another are required: (1) to teach us our duties, (2) to guide morally good action, (3) to
motivate morally good action, (4) to justify action on moral grounds, (5)
to cultivate our moral sensibilities, (6) to enhance our moral perception, (7) to make actions or persons morally intelligible, and (8) to reinvent ourselves as better persons.[1] Often, though not always, narrativists have distanced themselves from Enlightenment views of
morality that work with universalizable principles deduced from ab-

---

1. For (1) see MacIntyre 1984; Nussbaum 1990; Murray 1997. For (2) see MacIntyre
1984; Nussbaum 1990; Rorty 1990. For (3) see Nussbaum 1990; Hunter 1991. For (4)
see MacIntyre 1984. For (5) see Nussbaum 1990; Rorty 1989; Charon 1997; Hawkins
1997. For (6) see Nussbaum 1990; Hunter 1991; DePaul 1993; Rorty 1989. For (7) see
MacIntyre 1990; Taylor 1989; Frank 1995; Brody 1987. For (8) see Frank 1995; Rorty
1989.

stract moral theories, opting instead for a virtue ethics or various forms of moral particularism.

Although there are important differences among narrative ethicists, regarding not only what kind of moral work specific stories do but also what narrative implies about the nature of morality in general, anyone adopting a narrative approach to ethics must answer, at a minimum, four key questions. First, what is done with the story? This is a question about the *narrative act*. Second, with what kind of story is it done? This is a question about *genre*. Third, who does something with the story? This is a question about the *narrative agent*. And fourth, why is this done? This is a question about *moral purpose*. In this chapter, I'll use the light shed by the concept of the counterstory to assess how the four moral philosophers who have most influenced the turn to narratives—Martha Nussbaum, Richard Rorty, Alasdair MacIntyre, and Charles Taylor—have answered these questions. Although there is much of value for narrative ethics in all four approaches, each philosopher's work poses problems, for which, I'll conclude, the counterstory offers solutions.

## Nussbaum: Perception

Martha Nussbaum is perhaps best known for her exploration of the role of artistically sophisticated fiction in developing moral perception. Like Henry James, Nussbaum believes that the terms of a good novel can sharpen the reader's moral vision because they are not the shopworn terms of ordinary ethical discourse—"the standing moral terms," as James calls them, indicating both their habitual character and their inertia. Rejecting the shopworn, the novelist uses "the immense array of terms, perceptional and expressional, that . . . simply looked over the heads of the standing terms—or perhaps rather, like alert winged creatures, perched on those diminished summits and aspired to a clearer air" (James, preface to *The Golden Bowl*, quoted in Nussbaum 1990, 149). Nussbaum contends that by reading "alert winged" novels, one can make of oneself a person "on whom nothing is lost" (James, *Princess Cassimissima*, quoted in Nussbaum 1990, 148). One does this by allowing the author of the work to direct one's attention to the rich and subtle particulars of the narrative—the moral, intellectual, emotional, and social nuances. When the author has set these out with skill and imagination, overlooking no meaningful detail, the attentive reader can see what is morally at issue. Having refined her perception, she can then respond to actual others in her own life not merely adequately but excellently: she becomes "finely aware and richly responsible" (Nussbaum 1990, 148).

In *Love's Knowledge,* Nussbaum argues that moral philosophy requires the study of selected works of literary fiction in order to pursue its own tasks in a complete way (Nussbaum 1990, 23–24). Without literary works, she contends, we can have no fully adequate statement of the conception of ethics that centers on the question, How should a human being live? This conception, famously articulated by Aristotle, leaves much to the moral inquirer's judgment, as it rests on a fine responsiveness to the concrete rather than relying exclusively on general rules. How well the inquirer judges, however, depends on how clearly she sees. Cultivating perception is thus crucially important for the Aristotelian enterprise, and fiction—especially novels, Nussbaum believes—can help cultivate that perception.

Works of fiction that look over the heads of the standing terms play a role in one kind of Aristotelian ethics at two levels. First, they help assure that we get a rich and inclusive conception of the question of how to live and the dialectical process through which the question must be pursued. Second, they display, in their forms and structures, certain features that are also the features of an Aristotelian ethics: a plurality and incommensurability of values, the priority of the particular over the general, an acknowledgment of the cognitive role of the emotions, and an insistence on human vulnerability and the fragility of goodness (Nussbaum 1990, 25, 36–44). Through these features, fiction makes possible the sustained exploration of particular lives, sharpening the reader's perception and teaching her the fine-grained attention that is necessary for good moral judgment. And as Nussbaum makes clear in *The Fragility of Goodness* and elsewhere, these features can also be used to criticize the axiology, methodology, and epistemology of standard deontological and consequentialist moral theories.

Well-chosen novels, Nussbaum argues, extend our experience beyond our own particular parish boundaries. In addition to broadening our horizons, however, they also give us experiences that are "deeper, sharper, and more precise than much of what takes place in life" (Nussbaum 1990, 48). In most of our experience of life we allow a rough, sketchy understanding of some state of affairs to stand proxy for this depth and precision, but novels don't let us get away with that. They convey, in a way that texts written in a traditional philosophical style seldom do, the mystery, conflict, and risk of human deliberation about how to live well. Because such deliberation lies at the heart of Nussbaum's view of the moral life, she believes we need "—either side by side with a philosophical 'outline' or inside it—texts which display to us the complexity, the indeterminacy, the sheer *difficulty* of moral choice" (141). If we ourselves are to attain the moral virtuosity that consists in choosing exactly the right response to another, we need to see these choices modeled by particular characters in particular settings, in the kind of detail that lets us appreciate how easy it is to miss something crucial, how hard it is to get it right.

In response to Hilary Putnam's 1983 criticism that Nussbaum's morality of perception is dangerously insular, lacking the "general rule-guided toughness" (Nussbaum 1990, 198) that is required for the liberal political project of righting large-scale social injustice, Nussbaum contends that public deliberations in a democratic state can also benefit from the sort of clear-eyed perception that is cultivated and sustained by the literary imagination. Stressing the cognitive role of the imagination and the emotions in bringing us into contact with the complexity not only of our own lives but also of the lives of people who are situated very differently from us, Nussbaum argues in *Poetic Justice* that literary works develop our feelings of compassion, enabling us "to imagine what it is like to live the life of another person who might, given changes in circumstance, be oneself or one of one's loved ones" (Nussbaum 1995, 5). She suggests that "the ability to imagine the concrete ways in which people different from oneself grapple with disadvantage" (xvi) can have great public and practical value, given the vast amounts of racism, homophobia, ethnic animosity, sexism, and contempt for the poor that run rampant in the world.

Using the example of development economics, Nussbaum contends that social science needs to take account of more than population statistics and cost-benefit analyses predicated on utilitarian rational-choice models; it also requires a sense of how people within a population live their lives, what they feel and imagine. Because the right sorts of novels embody and generate the "ability to see one thing as another, to see one thing in another" (Nussbaum 1995, 36), they subvert crude social scientific thought and foster the perceptive understanding that good social science requires. Novels "present persistent forms of human need and desire realized in specific social situations. These situations frequently, indeed usually, differ a good deal from the reader's own. Novels, recognizing this, in general construct and speak to an implicit reader who shares with the character certain hopes, fears, and general human concerns, and who for that reason is able to form bonds of identification and sympathy with them, but who is also situated elsewhere and needs to be informed about the concrete situation of the characters" (7).

And finally, Nussbaum argues that narrative understanding is of value in the law. If judges and juries are to do their work well, she thinks, they must learn a flexible, context-specific way of judging whose neutrality is linked with rich historical concreteness—a rationality whose norms are supplied by the literary imagination (Nussbaum 1995, 80–82). If we follow a novel, Nussbaum writes, "with eager attention, succumbing to its invitations and being moved by its people, then we are, in the process, making judgments—about the industrial revolution, about utilitarianism, about divorce law, about the education of children— . . . we are, in effect, being constituted by the novel as judges of a certain sort" (83). The judge is to examine the realities that lie before her with imaginative concreteness and the emotional responses that are proper to the person of detached sympathy. She will notice especially vividly the disadvantages faced by the least well off, having been trained to such attention by reading novels that invite her to identify with people whose liberty has been severely constricted by social prejudice. "A literary imagining of the importance of various liberty and equality interests for citizens offers valuable guidance in cases dealing with those interests" (118). In our political dealings as well as in our more personal interchanges, Nussbaum claims, certain novels serve as important sources of deliberative enrichment.

The *narrative act* that interests Nussbaum, then, is that of reading "with eager attention." The *genre* of story that is to be read is the novel, understood as a work of fine literary art. The *narrative agent* is the reader. The *moral purpose* is that of refining the inquirer's moral perception, which in turn permits the agent to respond excellently, above the common run, not only to those with whom she stands in a relationship of intimacy, but to people from whom she is separated by the barriers of race, class, culture, or economic standing. One problem raised by this set of answers to the questions posed by a narrative approach to ethics is, as I'll argue in a moment, that of choosing the right books in the genre. A second problem has to do with the social privilege that must be enjoyed by any narrative agent using Nussbaum's approach.

And a final problem is whether the perceptivity learned by reading books in this genre translates readily into moral excellence in any case.

## Problems with the Stories We Read

Any approach to ethics that centers on the stories we read raises the question of *what* to read. Which novels ought the inquirer to adopt as moral guides? Obviously, not just any story in the genre will do. If certain novels are capable of refining our perception, others, perhaps, are capable of blunting it. Nussbaum nods to this problem when she talks of the power of "certain carefully selected works of narrative literature" to enhance our perception (Nussbaum 1998, 346). Implicit in this locution is the idea that carelessly selected works of narrative literature could diminish us—or at least, fail to improve us.

Michael DePaul offers an insightful analysis of the difficulty of choosing the right kind of literature in *Balance and Refinement*. There, he imagines a naïve young man named Billy who, taking seriously the task of moral inquiry, wishes to improve his epistemic position. So, following Rawls (and DePaul), Billy puts his moral beliefs into reflective equilibrium. He balances his considered moral judgments against the moral theories he's adopted, and widens the equilibrium by setting all those beliefs into balance against his background beliefs. Billy's beliefs are now coherent and therefore rational. But, as DePaul argues, "balance" isn't enough. Like any coherence method of moral inquiry, reflective equilibrium is open to the no-contact-with-reality objection. That is to say, Billy's beliefs might all cohere with one another but have nothing to do with how things actually are. For his beliefs to be grounded in reality, they have to be formed in the right way, properly connected to the phenomenological character of Billy's experiences.

If Billy is thus to secure *warrant* for his beliefs, as well as coherence, DePaul argues, he needs to broaden the limited range of his experiences so that his beliefs are likely to be true (DePaul 1993, 74). He's had plenty of reasoning experiences, but he's short on what DePaul calls formative experiences—experiences that influence one's perceptions so that one sees situations in a different way (146–47). Billy needs to seek out activities that might be formative for him, such as exposure to "literature, film, art, and so on" (150), and so become more adept at perceiving what's morally at issue in a given set of circumstances. This is the "refinement" part of DePaul's method.

In particular, Billy wishes to acquire warranted beliefs about how he should treat some future soulmate. His moral and political opinions incline him to egalitarian, liberal views regarding women, but he wants to ground those views in a firmer foundation. So he begins by reading John Stuart Mill's *On the Subjection of Women* and discovers that he is quite sympathetic to the arguments he finds there. They cohere with his other beliefs. But, because he's sexually inexperienced, he recognizes that he's in a poor position to be making judgments about what sorts of relationships are appropriate between men and women. He would like to broaden his experiential base so that it contains more formative experiences. "At this point," DePaul tells us,

> Billy makes a serious blunder. He correctly decides that more philosophical argument will not significantly improve the epistemological status of his moral judgments, but makes a very poor choice about how to broaden his imaginative experience—he picks up a romantic novel on his way out of the supermarket. As a result of reading this novel, which Billy really enjoys, he starts to form the opinion that what a woman really wants is to be "swept away" by a "real man," that women need to be dominated by men, both emotionally and sexually, and that rough treatment, bordering on rape, is often appropriate and even desirable. (DePaul 1993, 163)

Realizing that he can't overcome his naïveté by reading just one novel, Billy continues to broaden his experience, reading more novels and short stories, watching more plays and movies. But because he has so little to go on, that first bodice-ripper becomes the standard against which these further experiences are measured. The only literary and cinematic episodes that ring true to him are those that endorse the "treat 'em rough" school of thought he first encountered at the supermarket. And then, DePaul argues, we can imagine that the same holds for his personal life—the relationships with women that he finds the most satisfying are the ones that conform to his favorite depictions of sweet savage love. "The end result of the whole affair," DePaul remarks sadly, "is that Billy's moral judgments regarding appropriate relations between men and women are thoroughly fouled up" (164).

Billy may be naïve about women, but that's not all that ails him. He also pretty clearly lacks narrative competence, and this might be what's gotten him into his present predicament. Narrative competence may be defined, first, as the ability to *choose* good literature, and second, as the ability to *read* good literature with care, skill, and critical judgment. It's the capacity for selecting works of fiction that are worth one's time and attention, and then reading these works shrewdly, with an awareness of the literary techniques the author employs and a sense of how the text relates to other literary texts. Narrative competence involves knowing the standards for what makes a work of literary art good or great and either using those standards to evaluate what one reads or calling the standards into question.

Note, however, that the relevant standards are primarily *aesthetic* ones—the ones we use for judging literature as a work of art. But if Billy is trying to refine his *moral* perception, why should those be the right standards? Mightn't it be more important for him to learn how to choose books that can improve his moral position, even if they are of poor literary quality, and then learn how to read these books in ways that make him a morally better person? If choosing and reading books for these purposes involve standards other than aesthetic ones, then Billy's attaining *narrative* competence won't solve his problem.

There seems no good reason to think that people who have attained high levels of narrative competence are also necessarily skillful at choosing books that allow them to enhance rather than corrupt their moral perception, or that they are necessarily capable of reading such books in ways that make them morally better. While Nussbaum appreciates the importance, for improving one's moral position, of approaching great literature in the right spirit (Nussbaum 1998, 343), she doesn't seem to appreciate that the reader must then, in addition to having cultivated higher than average levels of *narrative* competence, also have attained a high degree of *normative* competence.

It might be argued that narrative competence comprises normative competence. This could be the case if a work of fine literature cannot truly be beautiful unless it also contains what is morally highest and best. Such was Friedrich von Schiller's contention in "Naïve and Sentimental Poetry," where he claims that the common task of both the naïve and the sentimental poet is to "give human nature its full expression," either by displaying prelapsarian mankind in harmony with itself and nature, or by showing man striving to "make a whole of himself" (Schiller 1966, 155). Indeed, Schiller concludes his famous essay by arguing that because the naïve represents unstudied, innocent experience while the sentimental represents reflective reason, the ideal of a perfect humanity requires a commingling of both temperaments for its completion. If it is the business of the poet to represent this ideal, then it would seem that reading the best poetry well requires a great deal of moral as well as literary discernment.

Whether good literature must be morally edifying as well as aesthetically pleasing is an ancient and much debated question. Nussbaum, however, never addresses it, even though it seems to lie right at the heart of her method. She seems merely to suppose that the narrative competence required for reading "certain carefully selected works of narrative literature" is sufficient to achieve her moral purpose. But if I am right about the difference between the ability to read good literature and the ability to read literature in a way that makes you good, it turns out that the narrative competence presupposed by Nussbaum's approach is at best insufficient to the task of improving one's moral perception.

Who has access to narratives in the genre? Not very many people, really. Even among those for whom the enjoyment of sophisticated literary fiction is a live possibility, quite a few have never cultivated a taste for it, and for most people, the material conditions, institutions, trainings, and experiences that would allow serious fiction to enter their lives are simply not available. *The Golden Bowl*, to name a favorite of Nussbaum's, or Beckett's *Molloy* trilogy, to name another, can daunt even well-educated readers. Such books are likely to appeal only to persons of a certain social standing, and then only if they have been shown how to read works of this kind.

That the enjoyment of fine novels, good plays, and the right kind of film aren't genuine possibilities for most people mightn't matter very much to Nussbaum, considering the very specialized purposes to which she wants this enjoyment to be put. She might argue that if the reader of Henry James or Beckett is likely to be a member of a privileged social class, so too is the inquirer who reads Nussbaum to learn of the need to employ great literature to the end of moral excellence. And she would be right. For such people it might indeed be the case that enriching, morally formative experience can be acquired vicariously through exposure to these refined and refining narratives, but they will be successful only if they somehow hit upon the right criteria for choosing literature that lends itself to that end, read it in the right spirit, and already engage in the moral practices that are the preconditions for the cultivation of the kinds of moral virtuosity that interests Nussbaum. No doubt there is a considerable body of literature that is both aesthetically good and capable of producing the formative experiences that refine one's moral perception, which is why I don't rule out the possibility that the sort of person who reads *Poetic Justice* might profit in the way Nussbaum suggests from reading *Hard Times*. Such a person, however, will already be highly competent both normatively *and* narratively. Billy, alas, is neither of these things. For him, the door to this approach is shut and bolted.

There is a deeper problem. Even if the inquirer could combine a high degree of narrative competence with a high degree of moral competence, it is not at all clear that she can as readily use her newfound powers of perception to "read" and respond to actual others as Nussbaum supposes. For one thing, even the most artfully drawn, complex, and fully realized fictional character does not much resemble, either in her subjectivity or in the range of her experiences, any actual, flesh-and-blood person. The novelist selects only certain incidents and actions as a means of bringing a character to life. The well-trained reader can fill in other details for herself, note tensions between what is said and what is left unsaid, and use the caesurae and silences in the novel to resist the novelist's interpretation of events, but even the most carefully attentive reader cannot in these ways collaborate with the author to make of a fictional character anything approaching a living human being.

Moreover, we can see and know things about characters in a novel or play that we can't possibly hope to know about ordinary people, as the author or playwright carefully directs our attention toward desires, emotions, and thoughts that ordinarily remain hidden from view. As Jesse Kalin puts it, "Novels tend to provide a kind of information about their characters that is not available for people, but it is just this information that makes judgment and sensitive response so possible in those cases" (Kalin 1992, 145–46). The mistake here is to suppose that the skills one learns in becoming a reader on whom nothing is lost are the same as the skills needed for being a perceptive moral agent—on whom much must *of necessity* be lost. Even trompe-l'oeil art doesn't imitate life as faithfully as that. Making sense of a work of art requires a certain kind of interpretive ability, but it is far from clear that it is the same kind that is required for making sense of a person. René Magritte put the point nicely: "Ceci n'est pas une pipe." The image painted on the canvas is only a painted representation. You can't fill it with tobacco and you can't smoke it either.

Nor is it so very evident that the highly refined perception of particu-

lars learned by reading novels could equip the inquirer to respond excellently to evils whose eradication requires concerted political action.
Nussbaum assumes that the moral skills cultivated for the project of
interpersonal responsiveness are equally applicable to the project of
making society more just, but if the narrative agent emulates Nussbaum's concentrated focus on the psychologies of a novel's characters,
she is likely to lose sight of the *societal* failings and *institutional* flaws
that are the stuff of political critique. While Nussbaum has plausibly
defended the need for clear-eyed perception if social ills are to be addressed, that defense doesn't eliminate the tension between the generalizable precepts that would seem to be required for any tenable political theory, on the one hand, and the insistence on the particular that
characterizes a personalist perspective, on the other. Because of Nussbaum's emphasis on the specific and the concrete, the personal and the
perceptual, it would seem rational for the narrative agent who reads for
the moral purposes she recommends "to choose local perspectives over
global ones, private, personal solutions over institutional ones, and
charity over welfare" (Dunn 1999, 21). It isn't obvious that such choices
can do much to eradicate social ills.

## Rorty: Solidarity and Self-Invention

Rorty too is interested in the effect on us of the stories we read. Like
Nussbaum, he sees in this narrative act the potential for attaining a certain kind of moral virtuosity that is the product of a carefully cultivated
practical discernment. In *Contingency, Irony, and Solidarity*, Rorty
sets himself a double task: finding ways to make our institutions and
social practices less cruel, and finding ways to invent oneself on one's
own terms, rather than accepting someone else's description of oneself.
Doing either task well, he believes, requires stories. The demands for
human solidarity and self-creation are equally valid, Rorty insists, but
they are incommensurable: we cannot hold private perfection and justice in a single vision. "The vocabulary of self-creation is necessarily
private, unshared, unsuited to argument. The vocabulary of justice is
necessarily public and shared, a medium for argumentative exchange"
(Rorty 1989, xiv).

Rejecting the "illusions" of the metaphysician, who pins his faith on
the existence of "true" selves or deep facts about human nature that are
beyond the reach of time and chance, Rorty urges us instead to be "iro-

nists" who "substitute a tissue of contingent relations, a web which stretches backward and forward through past and future time, for a formal, unified, present, self-containing substance, something capable of being seen steadily and whole" (41). As historicists and nominalists, ironists don't believe that the truth about themselves or anything else is "out there." The world is out there, but descriptions of the world are not, and it's descriptions that are truth-bearing. Descriptions are elements of human languages and languages are human creations.

Rorty acknowledges that the world contains the states of affairs that allow us to decide among competing descriptions—descriptions that are sentences in some particular language game. But, he points out, it doesn't follow that the world can tell us how to choose among language games. "When the notion of 'description of the world' is moved from the level of criterion-governed sentences within language games to language games as wholes, games which we do not choose between by reference to criteria, the idea that the world decides which descriptions are true can no longer be given a clear sense" (Rorty 1989, 5). Language games aren't given up because people discover that they are not world-guided, Rorty contends. They are given up because linguistic communities gradually lose the habit of using certain words and gradually acquire new concepts. In this sense, Rorty remarks, the Romantics were right to say that truth is made rather than found. Rorty believes it would pay us to drop certain expressions like "intrinsic nature," since these have caused more trouble than they are worth. We ought instead to redescribe things in new ways until we have created a pattern of linguistic behavior that allows us to look for "new forms of nonlinguistic behavior, for example, the adoption of new scientific equipment or new social institutions." The method of redescription "does not pretend to have a better candidate for doing the same old things which we did when we spoke in the old way. Rather, it suggests that we might want to stop doing those things and do something else" (9).

By describing themselves in their own terms, Rorty declares, ironists re-create themselves. They see "self-knowledge as self-creation. The process of coming to know oneself, confronting one's contingency, tracking one's causes home, is identical with the process of inventing a new language—that is, of thinking up some new metaphors" (Rorty 1989, 27). Ironists who are liberals, however—on Judith Shklar's definition of liberals as a people for whom "cruelty is the worst thing they do"—must on Rorty's view confine their project of self-creation to the private sphere, where they can't hurt or humiliate other people. In the public sphere, their task is to foster institutions and customs that diminish cruelty and promote freedom, since those goals are just as important as the goal of self-creation. "The compromise advocated in this book," declares Rorty, "amounts to saying: *Privatize* the Nietzschean-Sartrean-Foucauldian attempt at authenticity and purity, in order to prevent yourself from slipping into a political attitude which will lead you to think that there is some social goal more important than avoiding cruelty" (65).

The private project of self-invention, since it is a project of redescription, involves looking for a better vocabulary than the one that is ready to hand. Rorty calls the set of words we use to justify our actions, beliefs, and lives our "final" vocabulary—final in the sense that if the worth of these words is challenged, their user has no further words that could be used to validate them. It's this final vocabulary that the ironist wishes to replace—not because she thinks a new final vocabulary will be closer to reality than the one she currently employs, but because she worries that the final vocabulary she has inherited might belong to the wrong language game, and so have turned her into the wrong kind of human being (Rorty 1989, 73–75). The ironist's "description of what she is doing when she looks for a better final vocabulary than the one she is currently using is dominated by metaphors of making rather than finding, of diversification and novelty rather than convergence to the antecedently present. She thinks of final vocabularies as poetic achievements rather than as fruits of diligent inquiry according to antecedently formulated criteria" (77).

Literary works that enlarge the ironist's vocabulary show her new possibilities for self-creation. These may be works of fiction or "dialectical" writing in the style of Hegel, Nietzsche, Heidegger, and Derrida, since both sorts of works attempt to play off vocabularies against one another, to produce gestalt switches by making smooth, rapid transitions from one terminology to another. Rorty calls all such writing "literary criticism," and, because it's the final vocabularies and the beliefs that are characteristic of their users that interest him, rather than the texts per se, he does not attempt to draw any distinction between the authors and the characters in their own books. "We do not bother to distinguish Swift from *saeva indignatio*, Hegel from Geist, Nietzsche from Zarathustra, Marcel Proust from Marcel the narrator, or Trilling from The Liberal Imagination. We do not care whether these writers managed to live up to their own self-images. What we want to know is whether to adopt those images—to re-create ourselves, in whole or in part, in these people's image" (Rorty 1989, 79–80).

By redescribing their pasts and their present situations in terms of the new final vocabularies that literary critics have created, and then comparing the results with alternative redescriptions that use the vocabularies of alternative critics, Rorty claims, ironists hope to make the best selves for themselves that they possibly can (Rorty 1989, 80). The ironist who, to take one of Rorty's examples, reads *Remembrance of Things Past* can look to Proust/Marcel as a moral adviser who will help her to do what he did—to free himself from other people's descriptions of him (80–81). Or she can try on Nietzsche's final vocabulary, or that of any other literary critic who gives her a language that is better than the one she's using.

The project of personal self-invention thus revolves around two narrative acts. The first is to *read* sophisticated literature, and the second is to use that literature as a guide to *retelling* one's own story. While the ironist uses a narrative means of resisting other peoples' descriptions of her, her story is not a counterstory. Judging from Rorty's examples, she does not tell it to repair an identity that has been damaged by oppression. For Rorty the counterstory is a poetic rather than a political achievement, and requires the moral advice of people who are specially adept at thinking up new metaphors. Not just anyone can tell this kind of story. What's required, first, is that one adopt an ironist stance toward the world; second, that one be well trained in reading "dialectical" writing; and third, that one use this writing to make of oneself a poet whose artistic achievement is a new self.

Books that are needed for Rorty's second project—the public project of solidarity—are of two kinds. The first sort (for example, *Uncle Tom's Cabin, Les Miserables,* or *The Well of Loneliness*), Rorty claims, helps us to see how our social practices have made us cruel. The second sort (Rorty's examples are *1984* and *Lolita*) warns us of the tendencies to cruelty inherent in the project of self-invention. "Such books show how our attempts at autonomy, our private obsessions with the achievement of a certain sort of perfection, may make us oblivious to the pain and humiliation we are causing" (Rorty 1989, 141). These books aim at working out either a new *public* final vocabulary or a new *private* final vocabulary and so, although they are very few in number when compared to books whose purposes are presently stateable within a familiar final vocabulary, Rorty says, they are also "the most important ones—those which make the greatest differences in the long run" (143). Cruelty, not self-creation, is their topic.

Given his insistence on historical contingency and his skepticism regarding metaphysical claims about human nature, Rorty can't, of course, provide any noncircular way for the liberal to defend his belief that cruelty is the worst thing we do. He can't, for example, appeal to a standard of human solidarity that stands beyond history and institutions, since his views commit him to the position that what counts as being a decent human being is a matter of transient consensus about what attitudes are normal and what practices are just. But he declares that "a belief can still regulate action, can still be thought worth dying for, among people who are quite aware that this belief is caused by nothing deeper than contingent historical circumstance" (Rorty 1989, 189). Instead of the metaphysician's certainties, Rorty offers us the picture of a society in which the notion of something standing beyond history has become unintelligible, but in which a sense of human solidarity remains intact. In such a society, solidarity would not be thought of "as recognition of a core self, the human essence, in all human beings. Rather, it is thought of as the ability to see more and more traditional differences (of tribe, religion, race, customs, and the like) as unimportant when compared with similarities with respect to pain and humiliation—the ability to think of people wildly different from ourselves as included in the range of 'us'" (192). On that understanding of solidarity, the detailed descriptions of humiliation and pain that are found in novels offer a hope of moral progress, since they teach us to see the implications of our personal projects and social practices.

For Rorty, then, as for Nussbaum, the *primary narrative act* is that of reading. Part of his project, however, also involves the *secondary act* of revising one's own story. And just as Rorty's method requires two narrative acts, so it employs two *genres*. The first is "literary criticism," understood as novels and other writings that play off vocabularies against one another; the second is autobiography—but autobiography that, in describing a life, also constitutes it. The ironist *narrative agent* is a reader—but one of the narrative purposes to which she puts her reading is that of revising her own story. And the *moral purpose* of her primary narrative activity is to learn new vocabularies that permit the exercise of personal excellence, allowing her to identify herself on her own terms rather than someone else's, on the one hand, and make herself less blind to cruelty, on the other. Rorty's answers to the questions posed by narrative approaches to ethics thus raise many of the same questions that are raised by Nussbaum's approach: Which works in the genre should one choose? How much social privilege is needed to achieve this sort of moral purpose? Can the narrative act of reading actually fulfill the moral purpose in any case? Rorty, however, has the additional problem of explaining how self-invention could be confined purely to the private sphere.

## More Problems with the Stories We Read

Whereas Nussbaum is silent regarding the problem of what stories to select for the purpose of becoming a better person, Rorty has a specific recommendation. He advises us to be guided in our choices by literary critics.

> Our doubts about our own characters or our own culture can be resolved or assuaged only by enlarging our acquaintance. The easiest way of doing that is to read books, and so ironists spend more of their time placing books than in placing real live people. Ironists are afraid that they will get stuck in the vocabulary in which they were brought up if they only know the people in their own neighborhood, so they try to get acquainted with strange people. . . . Ironists read literary critics, and take them as moral advisers, simply because such critics have an exceptionally large range of acquaintance. They are moral advisers not because they have special access to moral truth but because they have been around. (Rorty 1989, 80)

But whether literary critics are competent moral advisers has less to do with where they have been than with how they behaved when they got there. Surely Rorty isn't so green as to uncritically emulate people who have "been around." As medieval morality plays, sentimental comedies of the eighteenth century, and any number of Victorian novels have enthusiastically pointed out, the naïf who falls in with the sophisticate may become a person whose wide-ranging, vicarious acquaintance with all sorts of people teaches him to be dismissive, envious, self-absorbed, or profligate.

Rorty's advice thus embogs us once again in the problem of corruption. To return to DePaul's naïve inquirer, if Rorty were to instruct Billy to take literary critics as his moral advisers, Billy might reasonably wonder what these people know about life that he doesn't. He's probably met literary critics who are just as naïve about their relationships with women as he is—and if he hasn't, I have. The literary critic who is a poetic genius but a contemptible human being does not create her own texts or read other people's with a view to making herself a "better" person. She does not approach these texts in the right spirit, or use them for the purposes Rorty recommends. Why, then, should her tastes guide Billy's choice of literature?

Nor does Rorty fare any better than Nussbaum with the problem of access to the genre. Few people are in a position to cultivate a taste for Proust or Hegel, let alone set Proustian or Hegelian insights to the ironist tasks of self-invention and eschewing cruelty. And, like Nussbaum, Rorty faces the Magritte problem: the difficulty of translating a savvy appreciation of fictional characters into the skills that are necessary for remaking oneself or responding compassionately to others. Like Nussbaum as well, Rorty's focus on the psychologies of a literary character presents difficulties for the liberal who is concerned to eradicate cruelty at the social and institutional level.

Rorty's approach—but not Nussbaum's—poses a final problem. His private project of ironist self-creation seems oddly (given his other views) to assume that "we" are largely independent of the social and political forces of "our" culture and so may reinvent ourselves at will. Consider this passage, where Rorty describes Proust/Marcel's self-invention in *Remembrance of Things Past*:

> Proust . . . did not want to befriend power nor to be in a position to empower others, but simply to free himself from the descriptions of himself offered by the people he had met. He wanted not to be merely the person these other people thought they knew him to be, not to be frozen in the frame of a photograph shot from another person's perspective. . . . His method of freeing himself from those people—of becoming autonomous—was to redescribe people who had described him. He drew sketches of them from lots of different perspectives—and in particular from lots of different positions in time—and thus made clear that none of these people occupied a privileged standpoint. Proust became autonomous by explaining to himself why the others were not authorities, but simply fellow contingencies. (Rorty 1989, 102)

Is it in fact so easy to become autonomous by shaking off the descriptions that other people impose on us? Can Pilar Sanchez, to return to my opening story, really free herself to care properly for the dying Jake by redescribing the oncologist who persists in describing her as an emotionally overinvolved, excitable Hispanic? Can the medically gaslighted woman free herself from physical confinement in an asylum for the mentally ill by explaining to herself why her doctors were not authorities but simply fellow contingencies?

Rorty's insouciance about the ease with which we can slide out from under other people's descriptions of us betrays a disconcerting lack of appreciation of the very real ways in which powerful people's representations of who we are can constrict our freedom of movement. The slave can't just *say* that her owner has no authority over her and expect to walk away. The lesbian who wants custody of her child can't hope to get it by redescribing the judge. The truth of the matter is that self-invention is a real possibility for nobody, and even the more modest project of self-modification fares better if one is insulated from the contingencies of fortune by substantial amounts of power and privilege.

That Rorty has missed such an obvious point is perhaps explained by his unshakable (and unargued-for) faith in the existence of a bright line between the public and private spheres of human life. He seems to believe that the spheres can be kept from influencing one another. That is to say, not only does he seem to take it for granted that public arrangements and practices have no impact on our private poetic achievements, but he also imagines that our private projects, however cruel, will have no effect on our public project of eradicating cruelty. Despite what he seems to think, if he is giving "public" and "private" their ordinary meanings, confining self-invention to the private sphere does not keep the ironist from hurting or humiliating others. The ironist might beat his wife in private, neglect his children in private, betray his friends in private, even if Rorty's method requires him to behave himself in public.

Rorty's position suggests (strangely, for a postmodernist) that individuals are ontologically prior to society; but, as I shall argue in the next chapter, this gets it backwards: persons are largely what they are in response to the languages, institutions, political and economic arrangements, roles, and shared understandings of their society. When all these forces from the public sphere are brought to bear on the ironist, there is less room in the private sphere than Rorty supposes for her to make herself over in new images of selfhood. Makeovers are possible but not simple. Their success depends on a complicated interaction of social forces, of one's position with respect to powerful people and institutions, and of the possibilities that either already exist or can be created for personal and group self-definition. Yet Rorty seems oblivious to these complications.

The questions for narrative ethics that are posed by approaches involving the stories we read, then, are these: (1) What are the criteria for selecting stories that will improve rather than corrupt the narrative agent? (2) Who gets to be a narrative agent, given the amount of social privilege that is required for access to these stories? and (3) Are the skills and vocabularies we learn when we engage in the narrative act the ones we must actually put to use in any quest, whether personal or political, for moral excellence? An additional question, posed by the demand that we reidentify ourselves only in private, is: (4) What are the limits to narrative self-creation?

## MacIntyre: Justification

Alasdair MacIntyre takes a radically different narrative approach to ethics, not only in the narrative act and in the genre used to perform it, but also the moral purpose to which he employs narratives. His claim in *After Virtue* is that morality is at present in a state of grave disorder, consisting of "fragments of a conceptual scheme, parts which now lack those contexts from which their significance derived. We possess indeed simulacra of morality, we continue to use many of the key expressions. But we have—very largely, if not entirely—lost our comprehension, both theoretical and practical, of morality" (MacIntyre 1984, 2). His response to this catastrophe is to call for a return to Aristotelian ethics, as he believes "the Aristotelian tradition can be restated in a way that restores intelligibility and rationality to our moral and social attitudes and commitments" (259).

In particular, MacIntyre draws on the Aristotelian concepts of the "narrative unity of human life and of a practice with goods internal to it" (228). Combining those concepts, he arrives at the idea that human actions are *intelligible* only within some temporally ordered, unified narrative sequence, and that *rationality* is always dependent on a set of specific practices growing out of a community's historical tradition. It is the stories of one's community—ancient Greece, medieval Paris, or eighteenth-century Edinburgh—that develop one's capacity to see things as reasonable, appropriate, valuable, and so on, and that also supply the norms for such seeing.

Because "action itself has a basically historical character" (MacIntyre 1984, 212), MacIntyre believes we can understand our own and other people's actions only by discovering the narratives in which they play a part. He offers us the example of a man standing next to me at the bus stop who suddenly says: "The name of the common wild duck is *Histrionicus histrionicus histrionicus*" (210). On MacIntyre's view, the only way I could possibly render the act of uttering this intelligible is by supplying the narrative. Perhaps the man has mistaken me for someone who yesterday asked him if he happened to know the Latin name for the common wild duck. Or maybe he's just come from a session with his therapist, who wants him to strike up random conversations with strangers as a means of overcoming his shyness. Or possibly he's a spy, and this sentence is his contact code. "In successfully identifying and understanding what someone else is doing," MacIntyre argues, "we always move towards placing a particular episode in the context of a set of narrative histories, histories both of the individuals concerned and of the setting in which they act and suffer" (211).

Through the act of supplying narrative histories we become authors: "man is in his actions and practice, as well as in his fictions, essentially a story-telling animal" (216). But, MacIntyre cautions, "we are never more (and sometimes less) than the co-authors of our own narratives. . . . We enter upon a stage which we did not design and we find ourselves part of an action that was not of our making" (213). For MacIntyre, then, what constrains our storytelling is not, as for Rorty, the act of will by which we relegate our personal redescriptions to the private sphere, but rather the fact of our participation in a narrative that began long before we were born and which contains many other characters.

If, as a condition of the possibility of intelligibility, narrative is an epistemological tool, it is also, as MacIntyre sees it, an ethical tool. MacIntyre insists that "we all live out narratives in our lives" (212). He claims that each human life is a narrative possessing *unity,* although modern life renders this unity socially and philosophically invisible. "To ask 'What is the good for me?' is to ask how best I might live out that unity and bring it to completion. To ask 'What is the good for man?' is to ask what all answers to the former question must have in common" (MacIntyre 1984, 218–19). MacIntyre conceives of any individual life as the story of a quest for the human good. Like the heroes of a medieval quest narrative, he thinks, we not only seek to attain that good but also to understand the nature of that which is sought. The virtues we cultivate along the way enable us to overcome the temptations and dangers we encounter, for such overcoming "will furnish us with increasing self-knowledge and increasing knowledge of the good" (219).

In MacIntyre's view, however, the most important stories are not the ones we enact but the ones we were born into, for these bestow meaning on the stories we enact. "I can only answer the question 'What am I to do?' if I can answer the prior question 'Of what story or stories do I find myself a part?' We enter human society, that is, with one or more imputed characters—roles into which we have been drafted—and we have to learn what they are in order to be able to understand how others respond to us and how our responses to them are apt to be construed" (MacIntyre 1984, 216). The moral inquirer, MacIntyre argues, can never seek the good life or exercise the virtues simply as an individual. "I am someone's son or daughter, someone else's cousin or uncle; I am a citizen of this or that city, a member of this or that guild or profession, I belong to this clan, that tribe, this nation. Hence what is good for me has to be the good for one who inhabits these roles" (220). It's the found communities to which I belong that give me my identity. So if I am to know who I am, I have to know the communities' stories.

MacIntyre accordingly calls for an ethics based on what might be called the "just-so" stories of one's culture: like Rudyard Kipling's stories of how the elephant got his trunk or the camel his hump, the high mythical and historical narratives of our communities explain who we are as a people and how we came to be this particular "we." These foundational narratives (they are, of course, master narratives, although not all master narratives are foundational) serve as the community's source of moral normativity, and on MacIntyre's view we are to invoke them as a means of ethical *justification*. When we have run out of reasons for acting as we do, we appeal to the norms that are internal to the social practices of the community, norms which are in turn justified by the final vocabulary of the community's "just-so" stories. So, to take an obvious example, physicians might look to the history of medicine and the physician's traditional role in society as justification for refusing to participate in physician-assisted suicide. The norms internal to the practice of medicine forbid physicians to kill their patients, and the rightness of these norms is explained by invoking the master narrative of the Hippocratic tradition.

Because the narrative tradition of the community subtly shapes all its members' knowing and valuing, there is no one model of moral reasoning that can be used as a vantage point from which to pass judgment on all the many cultures within which human beings live. Standard Enlightenment accounts of morality, taking themselves to be precisely such a vantage point, are thus dismissed as a philosophical cul-de-sac, a dead hope. And indeed, MacIntyre's historical narrative approach to ethics has obvious advantages over the standard moral theories. A complaint commonly lodged against Kantian ethics, for example, is that any maxim to be universalized in accordance with the Categorical Imperative must be couched at such a high level of abstraction that it can't tell us what we ought to do in a given set of circumstances, but only (sometimes) what we mustn't do. The corresponding complaint against utilitarian ethics is that its prescriptions, when they aren't platitudes, are often counterintuitive or hopelessly vague, since they depend heavily on uncertain predictions and interpersonal comparisons of utility that are difficult to make. On MacIntyre's historical approach, by contrast, one need merely invoke the master narratives of one's tradition to find the rationale for one's actions.

For MacIntyre, then, the *primary narrative act* is that of invoking the historical narratives of the communities of which one is a part. The *secondary act* is to live out in one's life the unified story of one's quest for the good. The *narrative agent*, both enactor and storyteller, is the citizen of a community. The *genres* are the foundational master narrative and, as for Rorty, the autobiography that both describes and constitutes the self. And the *moral purpose* of the primary act is justification; of the secondary act, making moral sense of one's life. The questions MacIntyre's approach raises for narrative ethics are, first, how to keep the stories of a community from unfairly subordinating certain people while at the same time excluding others altogether, and second, whether the story that identifies the narrative agent must take any specific form.

Before discussing these problems, however, I want to examine what Charles Taylor does with MacIntyre's notion of living out in one's life the unified story of a quest for the good. Since he believes that MacIntyre is correct in his claim that this quest constitutes the good life for a human being, his use of narrative also raises the question of the form of the story that identifies the narrative agent.


## Taylor: Self-Understanding

In *Sources of the Self*, Taylor undertakes a history of the concept of personal identity, arguing not only that our notion of selfhood is a peculiarly modern one which is by no means shared by other cultures or other eras, but also that it's a notion that has profoundly shaped our epistemology and philosophy of language—largely without our having noticed. Like MacIntyre, Taylor rejects the standard theories of contemporary moral philosophy, complaining that they have no conceptual place for a vision of the good life as "the object of our love or allegiance" (Taylor 1989, 3) and insisting, again with MacIntyre, that selfhood is inextricably bound up with conceptions of the good. Like MacIntyre, Taylor sees present-day morality as fragmented. No moral framework "is shared by everyone, can be taken for granted as *the* framework tout court, can sink to the phenomenological status of unquestioned fact" (17). Yet not to have a framework, he believes, is to live a life that is spiritually meaningless.

Indeed, not to have a framework is on Taylor's view not to have a self at all. "To know who you are," Taylor argues, "is to be oriented in moral space, a space in which questions arise about what is good or bad, what is worth doing and what not, what has meaning and importance for you and what is trivial and secondary" (Taylor 1989, 28). We are selves, he claims, only insofar as "we seek and find an orientation to the good," and we do that seeking and finding within a framework that both defines the shape of the good and provides a sense of where we stand in relation to this (34, 41–42). The framework thus defines who we are. It provides the background, even if we can't explicate it philosophically, for our moral judgments, intuitions, or responses (21, 26).

Being "rightly placed in relation to the good" (Taylor 1989, 43) is a matter not only of how near or far we are from our vision of the good, but also of whether we are moving toward or away from it. "The issue for us has to be not only where we *are*, but where we're *going*" (47). Since we can't be selves without an orientation to the good, and since our place relative to the good is something that always changes over time, our sense of the good has to be incorporated into our understanding of our lives as an unfolding story. "We grasp our lives in a *narrative*," Taylor declares. "In order to have a sense of who we are, we have to have a notion of how we have become, and of where we are going" (47).

On Taylor's view, making sense of a present action in terms of one's orientation to the good requires a sense of what one has become that can be given only in a story. Similarly, when one endorses an existing direction to one's life or changes one's course, one is projecting a future story. "This sense of my life as having a direction towards what I am not yet is what Alasdair MacIntyre captures in his notion . . . that life is seen as a 'quest'" (Taylor 1989, 48). And for Taylor as for MacIntyre, that quest is what gives meaning to our lives as a *whole*. We don't, Taylor thinks, want to settle for making sense of just this or that time of our lives. We want to integrate the past by taking it up into the future "in a meaningful unity" (51). Taylor can imagine a culture in which a human life might be split—for example, that at the age of forty people go into ecstasy and emerge as a reincarnated ancestor. But in "our world," he insists, "there is something like an a priori unity of a human life through its whole extent" (51). No matter where we are in our lives, we must see ourselves as approaching or receding from the good, taking account of where we once were with respect to it and where we now seem to be going. Because we can't help but do this and so determine the direction of our lives, "we must inescapably understand our lives in narrative form, as a 'quest'" (52).

For Taylor, then, the *narrative act* is that of living out the story of a quest. The *narrative agent* is "inescapably" everyone. The *genre* is, again, self-constituting autobiography. And the *moral purpose* is to make moral sense of who we are. The question that Taylor's approach raises for narrative ethics is one that is raised by MacIntyre's secondary narrative act as well: Must the genre exhibit any one specific form?

## Problems with the Stories We Invoke

Before we consider the problems attendant on the act of living out a story, let's return to the difficulties created by MacIntyre's primary narrative act—namely, that of invoking the foundational master narratives of the community's traditions. The trouble with MacIntyre's claim that we can't know how we ought to lead our lives without appealing to the self-defining histories of our culture is that "our" culture's traditions aren't apt to yield a picture of the good life that could ever be adopted by those who find themselves on the margins of the culture, or those who are subordinated within the culture. MacIntyre seems not to notice how his use of narrative unjustly excludes certain people from the community altogether, while at the same time it problematically includes certain other people by characterizing their lives within the community as unsuccessful or fit only for others' purposes. And what of people within the culture whose positions are liminal? What, for example, of the Capulet in love with the Montague, the mulatto, the transgendered person? How are *they* to understand themselves with respect to the community's traditions?

If the "just-so" stories of my tradition embody the community's norms but take *no* account of me and my kind—think of the New Testament, which depicts Jesus' blessing a heterosexual union but seems nowhere to acknowledge the worth of homosexual relationships—the people in my group can't invoke those stories to justify good and rightful places for ourselves within the community's practices. I and my kind are thus not only excluded from useful participation in social life, we're also deprived of the opportunity to exercise the capacities our community values—and deprived as well, incidentally, of material goods. On the other hand, if the "just-so" stories embody the community's norms but take the wrong sort of account of me and my kind— the tales of Uncle Remus serve as an example here—others can invoke the stories to justify arrogating to themselves the labor, health, dignity, or bodies of the people of my group. Either way, I and those like me have to look elsewhere for moral recourse. There's little or nothing in the master narratives to which we can appeal directly that would permit us access to the goods of the community.

Moreover, if MacIntyre's primary narrative act is fraught with problems of inclusion and exclusion *within* a community's traditions, there are similar problems in his account of how to reconcile the traditions *between* communities. As John Arras has pointed out, "foundational stories not only tell us who we are; they also tell us who we are not" (Arras 1997, 75). As a community, we define ourselves against other communities, positioning ourselves as not-Protestant if we are Catholic, not-Israeli if we are Palestinian. Often, these "not" relationships involve the domination of the one over the other, and usually this Other figures in the community's foundation myths as an objectified element rather than a subject community with myths of its own. So, as Arras points out, "for contemporary Palestinians the relevant story is the history of their oppression at the hands of the Jewish state; conversely, for contemporary Israelis the relevant foundational story is the history of Palestinian aggression and terrorism. The subjects of these historical narratives are thus locked in a perpetual struggle, not only over land, but also over the meaning of their common history" (75).

When cultures clash and traditions are at odds, the exhortation to invoke one's own tradition offers no political or moral relief. If the impasse is to be resolved peacefully, each side will likely have to make an effort to hear and understand the other's story. Often, such efforts fail or never get off the ground. But supposing the parties do somehow manage to hear one another, it's possible that they might come to question their own stories, and they would then need some standard for judging which story is better—or indeed, whether either story is morally adequate. Simply invoking their own tradition to settle the dispute won't help, for that is to use as a yardstick the very thing that one was trying to measure.

MacIntyre's solution to the problem of competing stories is to tell further stories. In *Whose Justice? Which Rationality?* he claims that some new stories do a better job than the old ones of solving the problems that prompted people to call the old stories into question in the first place. When members of a narrative tradition come to see the tradition as ultimately unable to resolve its problems, the tradition experiences an "epistemological crisis" (MacIntyre 1988, 361) for which its resources are no longer adequate. At that point, says MacIntyre, the members may look to outside traditions to show them not only a new set of social roles and new narratives to justify them but also a way out of the crisis. MacIntyre insists that the adoption of new stories constitutes epistemological and moral progress. The new story is *better* than the old at solving the problems set for it—"better" according to the evaluative standards inherent in the old narrative tradition—so we haven't settled for a mere succession of one story after another. In this way, he claims, the historical narrative approach to ethics can remain critical without ultimately abandoning narrative for transcendental principles.

MacIntyre's solution may well be the right one, especially when one considers that the evaluative standards inherent in any tradition are often at odds with one another, such that a new story can appeal to norms that were present but not taken seriously enough in the old ways of understanding the tradition. The difficulty with his analysis, however, is his failure to recognize that disenfranchised or subordinated members of the community were in epistemological crisis *all along*. They cannot rely on the modes of thought and evaluation made available by the tradition, because they are either alienated from those modes or connected to them in morally troublesome ways. This is not to say that they can't at all draw on the resources implicit in the standing narratives. But it does mean they have to approach those narratives with suspicion and distrust, and that they must continually challenge their authority. Once it's acknowledged that the normativity of the "just-so" stories *must* be called into question by some of the community's members all of the time, and by all of the community's members in times of crisis, we have a more complicated picture than the one MacIntyre offers us of how stories perform the work of moral justification.

## Problems with the Stories We Enact

Whereas MacIntyre's primary narrative act raises questions of exclusion and inclusion, his secondary narrative act—that of living out in one's life a unified story of one's quest for the good—is problematic in other ways. First, to say that our lives *are* stories because "action itself has a basically historical character" (MacIntyre 1984, 212) is to misunderstand what a story is. As my overview of the depictive, selective, interpretive, and connective features of stories makes clear, the temporal sequence of spatially located acts, experiences, and relationships that are the stuff of our lives can't by themselves take on the form of any particular story (Bal 1985, 5–7). We have to *make* it a story, and we do this by selecting incidents and themes from the minutiae of our existence and explaining their importance by how we represent them in narrative form. Autobiography, then, isn't life. It's a narrative structure that makes sense of a life.

The second difficulty here is with the supposition that the lives of all persons are best understood as a unified narrative with a linear plotline. The sort of life story that MacIntyre and Taylor take as paradigmatic of persons is arguably nothing more than a moral construction put on one very particular kind of life. It is a way of understanding what is supposed to be significant about the life course of what Iris Marion Young calls "respectable" people (including most philosophers) who have professional or corporate careers (Young 1990, 57–58). The "career self" (Walker 1998, 131–52) whose life trajectory is plotted as a linear progression toward a goal also surfaces in John Rawls's assumption that persons have a "rational life plan." The more or less explicit view of Rawls, MacIntyre, and Taylor is not merely that human beings cannot make sense of themselves outside a narrative in which each meaningful incident counts as progress in positioning oneself properly with respect to some end, but that the meaning of a life consists precisely in planning for, striving after, and attaining that end. The career self presupposed by this view is the protagonist of a *Bildungsroman*, whose chapters record the early training, the "wasted" time, the "recovered" sense of a calling, the self-doubts and failures, the achievements and public recognition, and finally, the "tapering off" into old age.

But this is a stock plot from a particular culture's store of master narratives, not a transcendent fact about persons. While the career self is a dominant ideal among professionals and business executives in postindustrial Western societies, it is only one of very many ways to conceptualize the story of a life. It seems improbable that human persons are selves just in virtue of their ability to sustain a unified narrative, as Taylor and MacIntyre would have it. What of lives, asks Walker, for which a yarn can be spun like Wittgenstein's thread, twisting fiber on fiber so that no one fiber runs through the whole length, but the strength is in the overlapping of many? (Walker 1998, 147). If MacIntyre and Taylor were to object, "But there *is* something common to all these fibers—namely, the plot that unites them in the quest narrative of a whole life"—we might offer them Wittgenstein's reply: "Now you are only playing with words. One might as well say: 'Something runs through the whole thread—namely the continuous overlapping of those fibres'" (Wittgenstein 1958, remark 67).

The third difficulty raised by the insistence on understanding one's life as a unified story of a quest for the good is that this arbitrarily restricts the author of a life-story to only one mode of emplotment. As Hayden White defines it, "Emplotment is the way by which a sequence of events fashioned into a story is gradually revealed to be a story of a particular kind" (White 1973, 7). We can see, for example, in the way the events surrounding Hamlet unfold that his story is a tragedy rather than a comedy. It's the plot structure itself, says White, that tells us what we are to make of it all, what ultimate meaning we are to attach to the story of the Danish prince.

White argues that any given history (whether of a nation-state, a community, or a person) explains a past set of events and processes by representing them in the form of a story with a specific plot (White 1973, 2). But the plot structures of these representations can embody very different perspectives on history in general and on the data that a particular history sets out to explain. When, for example, we look at autobiographical narratives we see that they display radically different conceptions of what "autobiography" should consist of, and radically different conceptions as well of the functions to assign to various events as elements in the story. These differences are given expression through (among other things) the story's mode of emplotment. If a historian provides her narrative with the plot structure of a tragedy—think of Edward Gibbon's *Decline and Fall of the Roman Empire*—he has explained what the story adds up to in one way. If he has structured it as a satire—Lytton Strachey's *Lives of Eminent Victorians* springs to mind—he's offered a different explanation.

Following Northrop Frye's *Anatomy of Criticism,* White identifies at least four distinct archetypal modes of emplotment. In *comedy,* there is an affirmation of the possibility that human beings can be reconciled to one another and to the natural forces at work in the world; the "inalterably opposed elements in the world" are revealed to be ultimately in harmony with each other. In *tragedy,* there are "intimations of states of division among men more terrible than that which incited the tragic agon at the beginning of the drama," and while these divisions are inalterable and eternal, the spectators of the contest come to their own moment of reconciliation, resigned "to the conditions under which they must labor in the world." *Satire* views the hopes, possibilities, and truths of human existence ironically, on the presupposition that it is ultimately impossible either "to live in the world happily or to comprehend it fully"; aware of its own failure to represent reality adequately, it is a "repudiation of all sophisticated conceptualizations of the world." Finally, *romance* "is fundamentally a drama of self-identification symbolized by the hero's transcendence of the world of experience, his victory over it, and his final liberation from it—the sort of drama associated with the Grail legend or the story of the resurrection of Christ in Christian mythology. It is a drama of the triumph of good over evil, of virtue over vice, of light over darkness" (White 1973, 8–10).

There are arguably other modes of emplotment as well: I am thinking, for example, of the "restitution" and "chaos" modes discussed by Arthur Frank (1995). Given this variety, why should MacIntyre and Taylor insist that only a quest narrative offers the correct conception of an autobiography, that only something like the Grail legend assigns proper functions to the various elements of the story? It's hard to see why the vast variety of human lives should all be forced into one particular mold, or what is accomplished by doing this. Lives run wildly different sorts of courses, and while a particular segment of someone's life might best be understood by plotting it one way, a later segment might be better understood by giving it a different sort of plot altogether. There seems no reason to think that everything we want or need to make sense of about ourselves and one another can be subsumed under the quest plot of the search for the good.

The question for narrative ethics posed by approaches involving the stories we invoke, then, is: How do you keep stories from unfairly *edging some people out* or *forcing some people in?* And the question posed by approaches involving the stories we enact is: What's the *form* or *mode* of the stories that identify you?

## Faulty Linkups

Each of the four philosophers thus poses problems for narrative ethics. But note that the problems stem mainly from faulty linkups among the narrative act that is recommended, the narrative agent who is to perform this act, the narrative genre that the agent employs, and the moral purpose that is sought. By 'faulty' I mean that the linkups might function properly on some occasions for certain people, but, like an electric cord with a short in it, they're unreliable and don't work consistently.

Nussbaum's narrative act—that of reading fine literature attentively—raises the problem of what literary works to read. Here the faulty linkup lies between the genre and the narrative agent, who not only might become corrupted if she chooses the wrong work, but can't connect to the work at all unless she's been well trained to read works in the genre, has developed a taste for this sort of literature, and has sufficient money and leisure to enable her to devote her attention to the narrative act. There's also a fault, on Nussbaum's approach, in the linkup between the narrative act itself and the moral purpose, as, at best, the act refines the agent's ability to respond sensitively to *fictional* characters, and this skill carries over only awkwardly from literature to life.

Because Rorty's primary narrative act is the same as Nussbaum's, his approach suffers from the same faults in the linkup between genre and agent, on the one hand, and narrative act and moral purpose, on the other. His recommendation that we take literary critics as guides again raises the problem of corruption; his use of sophisticated literature again presumes a narrative agent who enjoys a fair amount of social privilege. And to the extent that literature is not life, there's no consistently reliable connection between the act itself and the moral purpose. In addition, however, Rorty's secondary narrative act—that of redescribing oneself privately—opens up the problem of how private these redescriptions really are, and whether most people can redescribe themselves with the kind of impunity Rorty seems to suppose. Here the fault is in the link between the narrative agent and the moral purpose, since only some agents are sufficiently insulated from others' descriptions so as to be able to make themselves over in their own terms.

MacIntyre's primary act of invoking the community's "just-so" stories suffers from a fault in the link between the genre and those narrative agents who are either excluded from or subordinated within the community. The approach works properly only for people who can identify unproblematically with some character represented in the foundational narratives, and then only if the character in question occupies a respected niche within the community. MacIntyre's secondary (and Taylor's only) narrative act—that of living out a story—also mis-connects the genre and the narrative agent, since at most, only some agents' lives could best be understood as a single unified narrative with a linear plotline.

My critique does not show that these four moral philosophers are simply mistaken in their claims to represent moral life. Rather, I have argued that they depict only the self-images, the prerogatives of choice, the social positions and relations, the possibilities for both personal and moral agency, of *some* people in a particular culture (see Walker 1997a). People who can't be sophisticated readers of literary texts, whose options for redescribing themselves are severely limited by how other people identify them, who don't comfortably fit into established and well-respected social roles, or whose life histories seem to mean something that can't be captured by a quest narrative can't ultimately achieve the moral purposes adopted by these approaches through the narrative means that the approaches recommend.

Counterstories are one solution to most of these problems. The narrative agent who *constructs*, rather than reads, stories to enhance her own and others' perception of herself requires no particular narrative or normative expertise, nor need she strike up an acquaintance with any literary critics. While novels might be among the imaginative resources she draws on when creating a counterstory, the success of a counterstory doesn't depend on reading the right kind of fiction, so the question of criteria for selecting such fiction needn't arise—although the problem of selecting good counterstories still remains to be dealt with. Similarly, the narrative agent who tells a counterstory need enjoy none of the social privileges that are necessary for the understanding and appreciation of "alert, winged" novels employing new vocabularies. For reasons that will become clear, inventing good counterstories requires only ordinary amounts of narrative and normative competence, and these may be exercised by even minimally educated people, inhabiting forms of life far removed from Rorty's ironist or Nussbaum's student of Beckett or Henry James.

Do counterstories engage directly with the moral purpose for which they are told? I argue that they do. They are not vehicles for learning skills that carry over only somewhat awkwardly from art to life, but are instead useful tools for participating directly in practices of personal, interpersonal, or political responsibility. As for the problem of the limits on narrative self-invention, which Rorty tries to solve by a sharp (and sharply problematic) public/private split, the concept of the counterstory as I have described it is premised on a more nuanced understanding of the interaction between the public and private spheres. In fact, the possibility of the success of counterstories rests precisely on their engagement with master narratives that embody our publicly shared moral understandings; the possibility of their failure on their inability to shift those understandings. While my conception of the counterstory sidesteps Rorty's problematic solution to the problem of setting limits on personal redescription, that there is such a problem seems clear enough. Giving a better account of where these limits lie and how some might be overcome is a task I'll take up shortly.

Counterstories are also a solution to the questions posed by MacIntyre's and Taylor's narrative approaches to ethics. Rather than *invoking* master narratives as a means of moral justification, counterstories *resist* these narratives by attempting to uproot them and replace them with a better alternative. They operate on the supposition that the norms of the community are to be found not only in its foundational narratives, but also in stories that offer other vantage points from which to assess a community's social practices. The teller of a counterstory is bound to draw on the moral concepts found in the master narratives of her tradition, since these played a key role in her moral formation regardless of how problematic her place within that tradition has been, but she isn't restricted to just these concepts. To the extent that her experiences of life and considered judgments make them available, she can also help herself to alternative understandings of lying, heroism, fairness, or propriety, testing her conceptions of these things for adequacy against conceptions offered by people within both her found communities and her communities of choice. The narrative agent who tells counterstories thus commands a wider range of moral resources than are available on MacIntyre's account to persons who are unjustly subordinated or excluded by a community's foundational narratives.

Moreover, since counterstories can employ any of the four archetypal modes of emplotment and probably quite a few other modes besides, and since they are capable of highly localized jobs of narrative repair rather than being required to represent (as Taylor would have it) "a human life through its whole extent," they can reidentify people in ways that don't run afoul of the difficulties arising from the insistence that human lives make sense only within a unified plot structure that unfolds the tale of a quest.

Counterstories thus seem less susceptible to the problem of faulty linkups than do the narrative approaches of Nussbaum, Rorty, MacIntyre, and Taylor. But before I describe what I take to be the more reliable linkup between the narrative act of telling a counterstory and the moral purposes to which this act can be put, I'll have to demonstrate that personal identities are the sorts of entities on which narrative acts can have an effect, and then that the damage inflicted on identities by oppression is amenable to narrative repair. That is the task of the next two chapters.

# 3 The Narrative Construction of Personal Identities

> "Identity?" said Jack, comfortably pouring out more
> coffee. "Is not identity something you are born with?"
> "The identity I am thinking of is something that hov-
> ers between a man and the rest of the world: a mid-point
> between his view of himself and theirs of him—for each,
> of course, affects the other continually. A reciprocal flux-
> ion, sir. There is nothing absolute about this identity of
> mine."
> —Patrick O'Brian, *Master and Commander*

What is it about personal identities that permits them to be refigured by means of counterstories? How, for example, is it possible for the nurses in the story of Virginia Martin to perform narrative acts of purposeful strong moral self-definition—redefinition—that could successfully counter the identities ascribed to them by the physicians at Cranford Community Hospital? In this chapter I'll argue that identities are narratively constructed and that, within limits, narrative constructions can be narratively reshaped.

First, however, let me recapitulate the argument up to this point. I began by defining a counterstory as a narrative that takes up a shared but oppressive understanding of who someone is and sets out to shift it. If the counterstory is successful, it allows the person who is reidentified by it to be seen by herself and by others as someone worthy of moral respect—a good in itself. But because moral respect is necessary for the free exercise of moral agency, the counterstory's function of reidentification also contributes to the person's freedom to act.

I then argued that a counterstory frees up a person's agency because personal identity and agency are intimately connected. Not only do my actions have the potential to disclose who I am, but how I and others understand who I am profoundly affects the range of actions that are open to me. So, for example, if I am not understood to be a surgeon, I may not cut into a living person. Here my freedom to act depends on others' recognition that the identity of a surgeon is properly mine, and that I can therefore be trusted to perform surgeries responsibly. My freedom also depends on my own sense of my worthiness to act—my belief that I was properly trained, that I know what I'm doing, and so on. So the extent to which my agency is free turns on how I am identified both by others and by myself.

Our identities are shaped in part by what our actions say about us, but whether we will be seen as the sorts of people who can be held morally responsible for what we are doing in general, or as competent to perform certain sorts of tasks, has as much to do with the norms of those who assess our actions as with our ability to understand and act on those norms. This consideration, I've argued, suggests that normative competence is interpersonal, not just a capability residing in an individual. Because my acts fully express who I am only if that expression receives appropriate uptake, my being normatively competent requires the cooperation of others. Conversely, if who I am is seen as morally sub- or abnormal, whether by me or by those others, I cannot act freely.

After I secured the link between identity and agency that is presupposed by the concept of the counterstory, I explored the narrative approaches to ethics taken by other moral philosophers. Like them, I believe that narratives figure prominently in the moral life: they cultivate our moral emotions and refine our moral perception; they make intelligible what we do and who we are; they teach us our responsibilities; they motivate, guide, and justify our actions; through them, we redefine ourselves. But whether and how these moral purposes can be fulfilled through the narrative means that these philosophers propose depends heavily on the narrative agent's social position. It also depends on what levels of narrative and normative competence the agent has attained, on whether her biography can credibly be plotted as a quest narrative, and on whether literature is enough like life to be the best training ground for reinventing oneself or for delicately nuanced feats of moral virtuosity.

The examination of Nussbaum's, Rorty's, MacIntyre's, and Taylor's work contributes to my own project in three ways. First, it offers assurance that at least some narrative approaches to ethics are fruitful; stories do serve a number of moral purposes and it seems right that they should. Second, in pinpointing the problems raised by these particular approaches, the examination helps us get clearer about some of the moral tasks stories aren't quite up to, or can do only under certain conditions. Third, the examination demonstrates the need to be clear concerning just what sorts of stories we are talking about when we make claims about the moral purposes to which stories can be put, and the need to take careful account of certain general features of stories if we are to make claims of this kind at all. We saw how the lack of specificity with regard to the fiction we ought to read raised the problem of corruption for Nussbaum and Rorty, and how too narrow a view of an acceptable plot for a life-story raised the problem for MacIntyre and Taylor of ruling out a number of different kinds of stories that do in fact seem to be identity-constituting for many people.

In this chapter, I'll use a three-part argument to defend the claim that personal identities are narratively constructed. In part one, I'll develop the idea that identities are constituted from the first-person perspective through the loosely connected stories we weave around the things about us that matter most to us: the acts, experiences, and characteristics we care most about, and the roles, relationships, and values to which we are most deeply committed. In the course of this narrative construction, we draw on stock plots and character types that we borrow from the familiar stories embodying our culture's socially shared understandings—the stories that I have been calling master narratives. Equally necessary to our identities is the narrative activity that takes place from the third-person perspective: other people weave the things about us that matter most to *them* into stories that also constitute our identities. Important too is our membership in various social groups, whose identities are themselves narratively constructed.

In part two I'll work out the constraints on a self-constituting narrative. Since not just any story contributes to an identity, it's necessary to consider the various ways in which stories claimed to be identity-constituting might or might not be *credible*. The three criteria for the credibility of the stories—their explanatory force, their correlation to action, and what I will call their heft—allow us to judge whether it's reasonable to believe that a given story is in fact identity-constituting. Setting out these limits for the credibility of an identity-constituting story lays some of the groundwork for the later task (in Chapter 5) of evaluating a counterstory.

In part three I'll explain why my own stories about who I am don't automatically trump other people's stories about me, even though it might be supposed that I have more authority over my identity than others do. I'll offer epistemic, practical, and conceptual grounds for why others' stories are sometimes better representations of who I am than are my own. When these grounds give rise to differences between first- and third-person narrative constructions of someone's identity, the criteria for the credibility of self-constituting stories allow us to judge which is the better story. In addition, though, I'll offer a moral ground—

respect for personal self-determination—for according a certain amount of privilege to narratives from the first-person perspective.

## The Narrative Constitution of Identities

### WE ARE WHAT WE CARE ABOUT

Personal identities consist of a connective tissue of narratives—some constant, others shifting over time—which we weave around the features of our selves and our lives that matter most to us. The significant things I've done and experienced, my more important characteristics, the roles and relationships I care about most, the values that matter most to me—these form the relatively stable points around which I construct the narratives that constitute the sense I make of myself. The (backward-looking) stories of my connection to these things over time are explanatory: they explain to me who I am and it's this that is my own contribution to my personal identity. But my identity is also constituted by the stories other people construct around the things about me that seem most important to *them*. From neither the first- nor the third-person perspective are the stories that constitute an identity entirely original; many contain stock plots and character types that are borrowed from narratives that circulate widely in the culture.

*Acts, experiences, and characteristics.* Let me begin my account of the narrative construction of personal identities with an examination of how they are created from the first-person perspective. In one of the most interesting and useful recent discussions of this, Marya Schechtman observes that the question whether a person at one point in time is still the same as the person at an earlier point in time—which she dubs the "reidentification question"—is not what most of us are interested in when we think about who a person is. Instead, we want to understand how the person thinks, feels, and acts, what matters to her, how she sees herself. Schechtman calls this conception of personal identity the "characterization question"—the question about the set of actions, experiences, and characteristics that contribute to someone's self-understanding. On Schechtman's account, the characterization question is an attempt to get at the relationship between persons and intuitions we have concerning four basic features of personal existence—moral

responsibility, self-interested concern, compensation, and survival—
about which we typically care a great deal. She argues that although
these four basic features have a temporal dimension, they ought not to
be confused with the reidentification question, since they have a different logical form. Unlike the question of whether one is still the same
person at two different points in time, which demands a yes-no answer,
the characterization question admits of degrees. "All of the characteristics that are part of a person's history are presumed to contribute to
making up her identity. Some, however, play a more central role than
others and are more truly expressive of who she is" (77).

Assignments of *moral responsibility*, Schechtman claims, centrally
involve judgments not only about whether the person now being punished actually did the deed, but about the degree to which doing the
deed expresses one's identity (Schechtman 1996, 80). Whether a particular action is something that merely occurs in my history or something
that flows naturally from features absolutely central to my character is,
on Schechtman's view, directly relevant to the degree to which I am responsible for what I do. I am, for example, less responsible for tripping
on a rock and inadvertently knocking someone down than I am for willfully pushing someone out of the way. Conversely, if I fail to take responsibility, say, for the care of my frail elderly mother merely because
I would find it depressing and inconvenient to do so, that also characterizes me in a certain way.

*Self-interested concern*, conceived as the concern a person has with
her future well-being, includes the desire to avoid unnecessary pain, to
make a difference in the world, to pursue one's goals (Schechtman 1996,
81). Some of these desires, however, are more fundamental to our sense
of ourselves than others, and so are on Schechtman's view more truly
our own. While we all care to some extent whether our lungs remain in
good working order, for example, this is of particular concern to me if I
am a singer, since the state of my lungs has a direct bearing on my ability to pursue my career. When I become too old to sing well, however, I
might care more about the lungs of the younger generation of singers
than I do about my own. Since the degree to which we care about fulfilling any desire we consider important and worthwhile is typically a
function of how strongly we identify with that desire, facts about characterization enter into any account of self-interested concern.

As Schechtman sees it, *compensation* too is linked to the characterization question, since whether a person is actually compensated in the
future for some present pain depends on how much the person identi-

fies with the future reward (Schechtman 1996, 86). The question is not simply whether the person who gets the new car is the same person who took a second job to pay for it, as reidentification theorists have supposed, but whether the person cares enough about owning a new car so that it counts as compensation for the sacrifice she made for it. Because compensation is bound up with the question of what is worth giving up for something else, it cannot be explained without appealing to a person's values and commitments, and these contribute to an understanding of who the person is.

Finally, Schechtman argues, the kind of *survival* that is most important to us—psychological continuation—also admits of degrees and is linked to facts about characterization (Schechtman 1996, 87). That psychological continuation admits of degrees can be seen by thinking of the varying extents to which personality change is associated with disease, torture, drug addiction, cult membership, spousal abuse. That it is linked to facts about characterization becomes apparent when we consider that the degree to which a person *survives* disease, abuse, or addiction bears some relationship to the degree to which her current actions, experiences, and characteristics remain what they were earlier. "I am no longer the same person I was before the assault." "I died in Auschwitz." Or, said of a person suffering from Alzheimer's disease: "She's not herself anymore."

For Schechtman, then, Who am I? is a question that can be answered in terms of overlapping complexes of *actions, experiences,* and *characteristics* that vary in terms of their centrality (Schechtman 1996, 77). We arrange our depictions of such of these elements as matter most to us into the stories of our lives that constitute our self-concepts. On Schechtman's view, it is the act of weaving stories of one's life that makes an individual a person, and a person's identity "is constituted by the content of her self-narrative" (94)—by what she holds herself responsible for, what concerns she has for her future well-being, what counts as compensation for her, to what degree she remains who she once was.

According to Schechtman's "narrative self-constitution view"—a view with which I am in basic agreement—the construction of an identity-constituting autobiographical narrative does not have to be self-conscious. The autobiographical plotline is an organizing principle of our lives, often implicit rather than explicit. The sense of one's life as unfolding according to the logic of a narrative "is the lens through which we filter our experience and plan for actions, not a way we think about ourselves in reflective hours" (Schechtman 1996, 113). While I possess the ability to construct a representation of my past, I am only occasionally its narrator, though I am, of course, the protagonist and consistently the focalizer of this story. By selectively depicting and characterizing the acts and events of my life that are important to me, by characterizing *myself* in terms of the features of my body and personality that I care about, by plotting these various elements in ways that connect my stories to other stories and that give my stories their overall significance, I come to an understanding of who I am.

The plotline of an identity-constituting narrative, says Schechtman, must be that of a "conventional, linear narrative" if the story is to be identity-constituting for persons (Schechtman 1996, 96). Her reason for insisting on this is that she believes the traditional, linear narrative is the only one employed by individuals "like us": individuals for whom moral responsibility, self-interested concern, compensation, and survival are basic features of existence. Indeed, she claims that beings who arranged their experience in nonlinear ways would be unable to "make plans, engage in long-term commitments, or take responsibility for the past" (101). Such beings, she supposes, couldn't be recognized by us as *persons*, as their self-conception would be too different from ours to fit under that category.

Schechtman insists on the linear plotline because she fears that without it, we can't make sense of the four features. It's not easy, though, to see why Schechtman is worried about this. She seems to take it as self-evident that individuals "like us" have one identity-constituting story that takes a "standard" linear form; and then she reasons that because "those whose self-conceptions take a form sufficiently different from our own cannot lead the kind of lives we live" (Schechtman 1996, 99), the linear form of self-conception must be necessary to anything we would recognize as a person. However, if it turns out that an identity is constituted, not by a *single* story with a beginning, middle, and end, but by a tissue of *many* such stories, then the link between personal identity and the four features does not take a linear form. Indeed, the cluster of identity-constituting stories might not have any particular form at all. It's even possible that different narrative configurations might entail different ways of understanding the four features.

In my discussion of Taylor and MacIntyre I rehearsed some of my objections to the claim that human lives must be depicted in terms of a unified, linear plot. It's doubtful that anyone could actually live out all of one's life according to such a plot, and it surely seems as if many people do not. Because identities change over time, the stories that constitute them often appear to be a hodgepodge of narrative fragments, some giving meaning to very localized experiences, others forming a kind of umbrella tale that pulls together a number of local stories but possibly leaves an equal number out of account. In bits of some people's stories, the plot intertwines with the stories of others but goes nowhere in particular, and there might or might not be connections among the narrative strands that constitute the histories of our relationships to the various things we care about. The story that is constructed around a deeply significant event may have an iterative chronology, looping back repeatedly through time as the event is characterized from different angles. Some of the stories that constitute a person's identity may be deeply at odds with one another—think of an immigrant who belongs to two very different cultures and simply moves between them without any thought that they must somehow be reconciled[1]—while others might be contained one within the other and so be part of the same larger narrative strand.

Because a great many stories and fragments of stories are apt to constitute an individual identity, I think it quite misleading to talk about "*an* identity-constituting autobiographical narrative," as if these came one to a customer. It's also misleading to refer to the tissue of stories that together constitute a personal identity as a single story—as, perhaps, "the overarching story." The cluster might, in some instances, best be understood as an epic, which is a series of stories strung together like the beads of a necklace, but that isn't the only possible arrangement. The tissue of tales is at least as likely to take a nonlinear form, whereby fragments of stories are incorporated into larger stories, some of which might run through the whole of a person's life while others most certainly do not, and some are connected by one common theme while others have a different theme in common. The better to bear in mind the untidiness of these accumulations of "overlapping fibres," I'll continue to speak of stories in the plural as the stuff of which identities are made.

*Roles and relationships.* The stories we weave around the acts, experiences, and personal characteristics we care about most, then, allow us

---

1. Or think of someone caught between two such incompatible cultures as Hispanic and lesbian. See Lugones 1990.

to make sense, in our own lives, of moral responsibility, self-interested concern, compensation, and survival. But we can't fully make sense of Schechtman's four features of existence without also weaving identity-constituting stories around our more important roles and relationships. Roles and relationships can be so central to our narrative self-conceptions that Christine Korsgaard numbers them among our "practical identities":

> The conception of one's identity in question here is . . . a description under which you value yourself, a description under which you find your life to be worth living and your actions to be worth undertaking. So I will call this a conception of your practical identity. Practical identity is a complex matter and for the average person there will be a jumble of such conceptions. You are a human being, a woman or a man, an adherent of a certain religion, a member of an ethnic group, a member of a certain profession, someone's lover or friend, and so on. And all of these identities give rise to reasons and obligations. Your reasons express your identity, your nature; your obligations spring from what that identity forbids. . . . Some parts of our identity are easily shed, and, where they come into conflict with more fundamental parts of our identity, they should be shed. The cases I have in mind are standard: a good soldier obeys orders, but a good human being doesn't massacre the innocent. (Korsgaard 1996, 101–2)

As Korsgaard's examples indicate, quite a few of our practical identities arise from our social roles and our relationships to other people, so these too serve as answers to the characterization question. My own understanding of my relationships with my daughters and sons, for example, is a crucial component of who I take myself to be, and as these are relationships that have endured over time, I can best capture their temporal dimension by representing them in narrative form. The stories of the time when each child was born, when we lived in a tiny house together, when I unfairly punished this one, when disaster befell those two, when I made choices that hurt them and did loving things that helped them along—these are the lenses through which I filter the life I've shared with my children. They are the backward-looking stories that constitute my understanding of who I have been in relation to them, but at the same time, these backward-looking narratives create the field of action in which I can construct the forward-looking stories that guide my future relations with them.

*Commitments.* An important thing to notice about roles that are more than fleeting and relationships that go on over a long period of time (as opposed to a shipboard flirtation, for example) is that they require substantial levels of *commitment* or they can't be sustained. For many roles and relationships, the commitment has to go both ways: I have to be committed to the people with whom I want to be in relationship, and they have to be committed to me in some degree at least if there's to be a relationship at all. Other sorts of commitments—to ideas and causes, to moral or aesthetic values, to the projects we personally find most worthwhile—don't typically require this kind of reciprocity, although a fair amount of cooperation on the part of others may be required if a person is to act on her commitments.

For Marcel Lieberman (1998), our more important commitments are the fixed points that are narratively connected to form our moral identities. He distinguishes between "intention-like" commitments, "which might be thought of as a steadfast determination in the sense that one has settled upon one course of action and is determined to see it through" (5), and "substantive" commitments, which might be thought of as fidelity to a value or a person that endures over a considerable portion of one's life. It's our substantive commitments— "the commitment one has to political causes, for example, or to moral principles, ideals, and even other persons" (4)—that are, in Lieberman's view, identity-constituting. He calls these "the constancies around which we construct and, I would add, narrate our identities. These narrative constructs of our identities, and the narrative form of self-understanding, aim to *make sense* of our actions and of who we are" (175).

The intention-like/substantive distinction is a valuable one, because we surely don't want to say that a commitment to meeting a friend for lunch or, to take one of Lieberman's own examples, to giving up our Saturdays to learn German, must be identity-constituting. It's only the commitments we care about most that contribute to our sense of who we are. The activity of constituting one's identity by acting on one's substantive commitments is *narrative* in two respects. First, it is narrative because a substantive commitment is the story of a person's relationship to a value over time. It functions as a plot structure that puts an axiological spin on the history of a person's actions. The depiction of a particular event (picking up a piece of paper, for example) can take its significance from being juxtaposed with descriptions of other events, persons, or places that have been characterized in certain ways (the location is a path in a public park, the paper was dropped by a stranger, the protagonist has often picked up paper here before) which together add up to a particular person's being committed to some value (keeping the park beautiful), which contributes to her identity. The commitment to a beautiful park might in turn be a part of a larger story of the person's commitment to her home town. Just as the events surrounding Hamlet are cast as tragic by the plot Shakespeare used when he retold the ancient story, so, in the tiny story I just told, the plot casts the elements as a commitment to civic beauty.

Second, a substantive commitment is narrative because it requires the moral agent to create a backward-looking story by characterizing her past actions and the events in her life in terms of what she cares about or has cared about, and then to set those commitments into the forward-looking story of how she hopes to go on from here. The backward-looking story makes intelligible to her where she's been and what her actions say about what's mattered most to her; the forward-looking story allows her to confirm what she cares about, to own that she never did care as much as she thought, to acknowledge that she ought to care more, or to renounce what she cares for but shouldn't—and henceforth to act accordingly. In the course of all this narrative activity she both defines and constitutes her moral identity.

So far, so good. But Lieberman then goes on to insist that we can't make sense of who we are in terms of our substantive commitments unless we can give a rational rather than a causal explanation for holding the commitments we do. "The coherent story we develop regarding the transition from one fixed point to another rests on *the reflective inquiry that takes place regarding our reasons for having certain commitments and how they fit, or failed to fit, with our . . . self-conception*" (Lieberman 1998, 180, italics in original). He argues that, in regarding human actions as if they were events like any other, causal explanations deny the importance of the first-person point of view and so fail to capture the meaning of what one does from one's own perspective. What is required to make sense of an action, Lieberman believes, is to ask how the agent herself understands what she is doing, and he thinks she must understand this, not in terms of causes that propel her to do what she does, but in terms of the reasons she can give for valuing what she values— she must be able to offer a normative justification for her commitment.

I'm not so sure he's right. Consider the case of Dr. DeSoto.[2] In

2. I'm indebted to James Lindemann Nelson for coming up with this counterexample.

William Steig's eponymously titled children's story, a clever dentist who happens to be a mouse makes it a policy never to treat animals who are not mouse-friendly. But one day a fox, suffering piteously from a rotten bicuspid, pleads for help, and Dr. DeSoto hasn't the heart to turn him away. Under the anesthesia, however, the fox mutters, "How I love them raw . . . with just a pinch of salt . . . and a dry, white wine." The fox leaves the office with an appointment for the next day, when he will be fitted with a new tooth. Although Dr. DeSoto is badly shaken by the fox's unconscious revelation, he is determined to carry out his commitment to completing the work. "When I start a job, I finish it," he declares. "My father was the same way." It's not clear whether this remark should be thought of as a premise in an argument having to do with his father's general moral reliability, where the unstated conclusion serves as a normative justification for the value of finishing what he starts, or whether Dr. DeSoto is simply explaining his behavior in causal terms: "my father was the same way." The fact that the remark *could* be interpreted as a causal explanation, however, is enough to make my point: even if we regarded it as causal, the explanation makes it plainly intelligible that the mouse is cleaving to a commitment. If I'm right about this, then not all commitments require rational reflection. Even one's substantive commitments—in this case, the commitment to finishing what one has begun—needn't necessarily be grounded in reasons for why we value what we do. Sometimes we don't *have* reasons. When we don't, a causal explanation is enough, it seems, to show us how a commitment fits in with our sense of who we are.

In any case, as Harry Frankfurt has argued, often our identity-constituting commitments *are* our reasons for acting. A mother who is faced with abandoning her child but finds that she simply can't do it, for example, is probably acting not for reasons of duty but because she cares about the child and about herself as its mother. "Especially with respect to those we love and with respect to our ideals," Frankfurt writes, "we are liable to be bound by necessities which have less to do with our adherence to the principles of morality than with integrity or consistency of a more personal kind. These necessities constrain us from betraying the things we care about most and with which, accordingly, we are most closely identified. In a sense which a strictly ethical analysis cannot make clear, what they keep us from violating are not our duties or our obligations but ourselves" (Frankfurt 1988, 91).

## WE ARE WHAT OTHER PEOPLE CARE ABOUT

If a person's identity "is constituted by the content of her self-narrative," and that content comprises those features of our lives and ourselves that we care most about, there is also an extent to which our identities are constituted by the content of *other* people's narratives—the features of our lives and ourselves that *they* care most about. As Alasdair MacIntyre rightly reminds us, "we are never more than coauthors of our life narratives" (MacIntyre 1984, 213). When we are children, we live inside the larger narrative that is our family's history, and the stories our parents and grandparents tell us about their own and our other relatives' lives add to our sense of ourselves (Minuchin 1974). When we go to school we learn the history of our culture, and this too produces in us an awareness of ourselves as members of various social groups. And if we belong to a social group that is generally despised, the master narratives that are told to explain our inferiority and keep us in our place contribute to our identities—as do the narratives we tell to resist our oppression.

A personal identity thus requires social *recognition*. Identities are not simply a matter of how we experience our own lives, but also of how others see us. My conception of myself as a skilled office manager who knows the firm from inside out goes nowhere if the new CEO thinks of me as the faithful old retainer who ought to be pensioned off. Here the question isn't merely whose view of me will prevail, but whether my sense of who I am can be kept in place. Because the new CEO has the power to assign me to a marginal role in the office or to make things so unpleasant for me that I prefer to retire, my capabilities will find no expression once he constructs a social context that denies them an outlet. At that point, even if my commitment to my job is absolutely central to my identity-constituting self-narrative, I can no longer incorporate it into my ongoing story. The CEO's identifying me as the faithful old retainer thus has a direct impact on the identities that are now open to me. Because roles and relationships are necessarily social and interpersonal, they require the cooperation of others—they aren't just up to us to enjoy at will.

Who we can be is often a matter of who others take us to be. Many practical identities require more than one person for their construction and maintenance. Your identity as a competent adult crucially depends on others' recognizing you as such. Your identity as a white person hinges on the acknowledgment of others that you are indeed white. And your identity as a wife is thrown into devastating confusion if your husband decides he no longer wants to be married to you. In all these instances and many more, a key component of identity is the people around you, who must recognize that the identity is properly yours. Indeed, often these others keep one's practical identities in place by themselves taking up reciprocal or related roles and identities. How others must recognize someone and the extent to which they must do this varies considerably across persons, but not even the most powerful or the most socially isolated of us is in sole charge of who she gets to be.

To some extent, then, our identities depend on who other people are in relation to us. But that isn't the only way in which others have an impact on our identities. Just as we construct self-constituting stories around the aspects of ourselves and our lives we care most about, so *others* construct identity-constituting stories around the aspects of ourselves and our lives *they* care most about. Sometimes these stories center on the same features that we care about too, and sometimes they don't. And sometimes these others interpret a feature of our lives very differently from the way we interpret it, which is to say that they construct different stories, with different plots and from different points of view, around that feature. It's in precisely this way that the office manager and the CEO have parted company over the office manager's identity: she takes one of her characteristics—that she's worked for the company a very long time—to express something quite positive and valuable about who she is; the CEO tells a different story about that and thus identifies her in a negative way.

## Narrative Recognition via Master Narratives

Whereas so far we have been speaking of an identity as narrative primarily in virtue of its form—I make sense of myself or others by arranging what I care about into a story—identity is also narrative in virtue of the already existing stories and fragments of stories with which we identify ourselves and one another. To explain what I mean, let's return to the idea that the relationships among the elements of a story can be established through allusive nods to other stories. Novels, films, and plays are peppered with such allusions, but they also serve as shorthand for characterizing actual people. So, to give a trivial example, if I know you're a Monty Python fan and I want to offer you a quick sketch of my revolting cousin, I might say, "He learned his table manners from Mr. Creosote." By treating Mr. Creosote as a referential character in this scrap of a story about my cousin, I create a rough portrait of who I understand my cousin to be.[3] The connection between existing stories and identities goes much deeper than literary or cinematic allusion, however. We commonly identify people—including ourselves—by associating them with narratives, whether idiosyncratic or culturally shared, seeing both ourselves and others in terms of the plot templates and character types we've known all our lives.

Richard Nisbett and Lee Ross have written of these fragments of well-known stories in connection with their explanation of human interpretive activity. On their view we make use of a number of strategies that allow us to "go beyond the information given" as we try to make sense of the world (Nisbett and Ross 1980, 261). One such heuristic—dubbed the "representativeness heuristic" by Amos Tversky and Daniel Kahneman—involves the use of two types of "schema": event-schemas, or "scripts," and person-schemas, or "personae" (Nisbett and Ross 1980, 278). A schema can be thought of as a category that forms an important basis for inference. That is, once the interpreter has categorized an event or person as being of a certain type, she readily assigns to it or to him or her a number of characteristics in addition to those she perceives directly, inferring (usually correctly) that these characteristics are in fact present.

A "script" categorizes a causal sequence of events (Nisbett and Ross 1980, 280). It can be compared to a cartoon strip consisting of a number of recognizable scenes. So, for instance, the "restaurant script" contains "entering," "ordering," "eating," "paying," and "exiting" scenes, and because these are all very familiar, the interpreter needs to observe just one of them in order to infer with a high degree of accuracy what happened earlier or will happen next. The event-schema can be thought of as a stock plot in miniature, a story cliché that's an old cultural or personal standby.

"Personae" are, of course, the dramatis personae who populate the script. "Indeed," write Nisbett and Ross, "to specify the characters is often sufficient to convey much of the action of the script (for example, 'the prostitute with the heart of gold and the scholarly but naïve young man' or 'the crusty but benign older physician and the hot-headed, idealistic young surgeon')" (Nisbett and Ross 1980, 281). Some personae are the products of our own personal histories, as when we expect a

---

3. No actual cousin was harmed in the telling of this story.

stranger to behave like Aunt Mary because she looks a bit like Aunt Mary. Others are characters drawn from master narratives—the stories circulating in our culture that embody socially shared understandings—whether these be mythological (the earth-mother, the simpleton), cinematic (the rebel without a cause), or literary (Frankenstein's monster). "In each instance the persona constitutes a knowledge structure which, when evoked, influences social judgments and behaviors" (281). Personae can be thought of as stock characters, person-clichés.

The *connective* feature of master narratives allows them to be linked in various ways to our own self-constituting stories. Their *interpretive* feature allows them to be used both for characterizing the actors in our stories and for arranging what we care about into a plot. The flat characters in the stories that constitute our identities are particularly likely to be associated with the personae peopling some master narrative or other, but even the round characters who develop and grow along with the protagonist (our children, friends of long standing, spouses, perhaps parents) are apt to take some of their coloring from the personae of narratives known to us all. Similarly, the plots we employ to structure the elements of our own stories are often either borrowed directly from master narratives or serve as variations on those familiar themes.

Many people we need or want to identify, however, are not a part of our identity-constituting stories. As we construct narratives that feature the things about *them* that matter most to *us*, master narratives once again come in handy. Sometimes we weave them into our own storytelling, borrowing a plot here and a character there as we construct our understanding of another person; at other times, master narratives allow us to recognize others directly, without our having to engage in any other narrative activity at all. In this way, master narratives serve as a kind of shortcut that saves us the trouble of having to create a story out of whole cloth.

We aren't always explicitly aware of it when we draw on these fragments from the master narratives to identify ourselves and one another, but such narrative recognition occurs commonly enough. At some point in your life, you may have made sense of your relationship with a mentor by plotting the episodes of that relationship according to the stock initiation script that structures everything from "The Sorcerer's Apprentice" to Dante's *Divine Comedy*; the story then becomes a piece of your identity-constituting autobiography. A rider on the subway looks at the beefy man with the baseball cap and rolled-up sleeves sitting across from him and pigeonholes him as a redneck, with an unconscious assist, perhaps, from the movie *Deliverance*. You help a stranger in need and she identifies you in biblical terms: you are a good Samaritan. There are days when I think my own understanding of my teaching role is compounded almost entirely of absent-minded professor jokes and *Goodbye, Mr. Chips.* Master narratives like these constitute the identities of social groups as well as individuals, and members of the group draw a part of their identity from how the group identity is narratively constructed.

As we make use of the standing stories of our culture, sometimes employing them in isolated acts of recognition, sometimes incorporating fragments of them into stories we've created, the norms of the master narratives tell us how we are supposed to understand the people (including ourselves) to whom we apply them. Often the narratives embody these norms in such a natural-seeming way that we aren't aware of their prescriptive force at all, since their normative content is typically presented as description that makes no evaluative demands on us.

"Culturally entrenched figurations," Diana Tietjens Meyers observes, "are passed on without obliging anyone to formulate, accept, or reject repugnant negative propositions about any group's standing or self-congratulatory positive propositions about one's own" (Meyers 1994, 53). In a similar vein she argues elsewhere, "To some extent, people are captives of their culture's repertory of figurations. It takes a conscious effort to become aware of and to criticize ubiquitous figurations, especially those that are integral to a cultural worldview, and it takes a great deal of assiduous self-monitoring to begin to extricate one's thinking from these figurations" (Meyers 1997, 239). Meyers writes of these figurations in the context of the role they play in "culturally normative prejudice" (Meyers 1994, 51), so she is speaking of *pernicious* cultural scripts and personae, rightly emphasizing the power that these narrative fragments have over our imaginations. It's worth pointing out, however, that it's neither possible or desirable to extricate one's thinking to any great degree from *all* the clichés of one's culture, since these are the understandings we share in common. If a person were to dissociate herself from them completely, she would no longer be able to understand either herself and the people around her or the workings of her society.

GROUP IDENTITIES

The notion of narrative recognition, by which we help ourselves to bits of the master narratives in the cultural repository, obviously applies to groups of people at least as much as it does to individuals, because master narratives characterize people categorically rather than singly. They tell us that young doctors *as a type* tend to be hotheaded and idealistic, that sexy blondes *as a group* tend to be dumb but calculating, that Irishmen *on the whole* tend to be drunks and poets. These personae trail behind themselves, like comet's tails, long and complicated stories of socially cultivated and reinforced attitudes toward certain sorts of people. That these story fragments figure into our narrative practices of personal identification points to yet another element that enters narratively into our understandings of ourselves and others. To our commitments, and to the acts, experiences, characteristics, roles, and relationships in general that matter most to us, we may now add an especially important, particular sort of relationship: our membership in *social groups*. These too figure into our self-concepts and weight the ways others will or won't tend to see us.

Iris Marion Young distinguishes among three sorts of groups, not all of which are identity-constituting. An *interest group* is "any aggregate or association of persons who seek a particular goal, or desire the same policy, or are similarly situated with respect to some social effect—for example, they are all recipients of acid rain caused by Ohio smokestacks." An *ideological group* is a "collective of persons with shared political beliefs," such as Nazis, feminists, or antiabortionists. A *social group* is a "collective of people who have affinity with one another because of a set of practices or way of life; they differentiate themselves from or are differentiated by at least one other group according to these cultural forms" (Young 1990, 186). While interest groups might be venues which allow us to act on commitments that are so deeply held that they constitute our self-understandings, I'd argue it's the commitment itself, and not the group, that contributes to one's identity. So, for instance, if I am a peace activist making common cause with other activists, I derive my identity as an activist not so much from my solidarity with the others as from my championship of peace. The social groups with which we identify, on the other hand—the Cuban-American community, the white European community, the community of Orthodox Jews—are directly identity-constituting in that they both contribute to our sense of who we are and maintain us in that identity. Between these two lie ideological groups, which might for some people function like an interest group and for others like a social group: an ideology such as feminism can commit one to seek a particular goal or policy (criminalizing marital rape in all fifty states, for example), but it can also become a way of life that structures the sharing of housework and child care, how one thinks about one's work, and so on. To the extent that the ideology shapes one's daily practices, it too can be identity-constituting.

Although social group identities, like personal identities, are narratively constructed, the stories that my group tells to distinguish itself from your group are frequently different from the ones your group tells to distinguish itself from mine. Both sets of identity-constituting stories are shot through with fragments of the socially shared stories that function as master narratives for each particular group, but my group's master narratives might be unknown to your group, and your master narratives might not circulate within my group either. If a social group is a minority group embedded within another, culturally dominant group, the dominant group is apt to dismiss the master narratives of the minority group even when they are known within the larger group. But while the dominant group is unlikely to take up the scripts and personae of the minority group, there is often considerable uptake of these story fragments by the individuals who belong to the minority group. It's through the master narratives of the group that social group identity contributes to the identities of its individual members.

Social group identities, like the personal identities that are partly constituted by them, are dynamic. Some of their features change, mostly gradually but sometimes catastrophically. A social group's identity can be affected catastrophically by a social revolution or by famine, or gradually by assimilation into another group or by the technological obsolescence of its way of life. Personal identities can undergo catastrophic change via religious conversion, sudden wealth, the birth of a child, or a mental or physical trauma. More gradual changes are the effect of age, education, intimate relationships, or travel. It's precisely these changes over time, which are central to the concept of personal and group identity, that require us to make sense of ourselves singly and collectively in narrative terms.

In sum, then, personal identities are constructed through the stories that concern the things we ourselves care most about, the things about us that other people care most about, and the things that we and others see as most important about the social groups to which we belong. So it turns out that a person's identity is only partly constituted by what she holds herself responsible for, what concerns she has for her future well-being, what counts as compensation for her, to what degree she remains who she once was. Although these contribute to the content of her self-narrative, there are other first-person elements, including explicitly self-evaluative judgments: what virtues the person sees as possible and important to cultivate in herself in the future, what marks she gives

herself for her conduct in the past. Then there are the narratives and
narrative fragments of others, both individuals and social groups, which
also contribute to the overlapping fibers of the stories that identify her.

## Constraints on Identity Construction

### WHAT STORIES COUNT?

Clearly, not just any story that serves as a basis for my self-understanding is identity-constituting. If it were, I could be whoever I liked.
Rorty comes perilously close to this position in his description of ironist self-invention; and as I've already noted, the constraint he imposes
on self-invention—that the ironist project be confined to the private
sphere—is seriously inadequate, since the bulkhead dividing the private
from the public isn't nearly as watertight as Rorty seems to think. The
difficulty with Rorty's position, however, isn't just that the private
sphere contains other people who will be affected by who you are—it's
also that who you are isn't simply a function of your poetic imagination. Personal identities are always meaning-systems, but not just any
meaning-system counts as a personal identity. What, then, are the limits on the narrative constructions that constitute us?

Both Lieberman and Schechtman offer candidates for constraints on
self-constituting autobiographical narratives. Lieberman's first constraint is that we must regard the substantive commitments around
which we narratively construct our identities to be "objectively valid,"
to have "objective merit" (Lieberman 1998, 176). He imposes this constraint because he thinks that if we value something so much that the
story of our commitment to it is self-constituting, we have to believe
that our reasons for valuing it are equally binding on others—that others ought to value the thing as much as we do. If we didn't believe this,
he thinks, we couldn't hang on to the commitment. Even for commitments that *don't* form a part of the agent's identity, Lieberman argues,
the agent must always believe that others could at least understand the
reasons she gives for why she values the thing she's committed to, although they needn't care about it themselves. But he contends that in
the case of substantive commitments, the agent must also believe that
the value's goodness and rightness are such that all other rational persons ought to embrace it. "Strong objectivity, which I shall argue is associated with substantive commitments, does not only require that
one's reasons or values be intelligible to others, but also that they hold

for other persons generally" (129). "These objective values purport to capture certain facts about human nature or the human good, and consequently can be said to be values for anyone who is not influenced by personal prejudice or short-sightedness, or is limited by an unwillingness to step outside the personal point of view" (174).

One difficulty with this view is that, as I've already pointed out, we mightn't *have* any reasons for holding our deepest commitments. However, if in fact we do have reasons, Lieberman's demand that they be intelligible to others is surely legitimate, since "reasons" that are so idiosyncratic as to be intelligible only to the person herself aren't reasons at all. The constraint that the reason be seen to be equally *binding* on all other persons, though, is too strong. It would seem to require the agent to believe that any substantive commitment she reflectively endorses ought also to be a substantive commitment for everyone else. But in that case, the agent would have to believe that substantive commitments are always obligatory and never discretionary. I couldn't, for example, devote myself to becoming a doctor, to use Lieberman's own example of a substantive commitment, unless I believed that everyone else ought to devote themselves to becoming doctors as well.

Clearly, this result can't be one that Lieberman intends, so perhaps he merely means something like, "If I have reflectively endorsed my substantive commitment to being a doctor, I have to believe that the values that led me to want to be a doctor, such as the relief of suffering, the good of human health, and the like, are values whose goodness and rightness should be acknowledged by everyone across the board." But on this reading, objective validity no longer functions as a constraint on an identity-constituting story, since the values to which we are now appealing lie at such a level of abstraction that we've lost the distinction between an "intention-like" commitment (such as the commitment to taking German lessons, which is on Lieberman's view not identity-constituting) and a "substantive" commitment (such as the commitment to becoming a doctor, which is). If I become sufficiently abstract, after all, I can take my "intention-like" commitment to learning German to be grounded in the value of getting an education, which I would presumably think others ought also to endorse, or my commitment to watching *The X Files* on television every week to be grounded in the value of imaginative fantasy, which presumably everyone ought to endorse as well. The difficulty is that then everything becomes a substantive commitment, but surely this too is not what Lieberman intends.

Lieberman's second constraint on narrative self-construction is that

the story be not only continuous but also coherent, "which means that
we cannot have, as it were, two *different* stories running at the same
time. . . . We want a *single* story which offers the best account across
the greatest number of explanatory dimensions. A unified story gives
rise to a unified identity" (Lieberman 1998, 176). Lieberman insists on
this constraint because he is concerned to block the sort of move Rorty
makes when he confines ironist self-invention to the private sphere, as
this permits the ironist to create one sort of story of who she is in private, and a radically discontinuous story about who she is in public. "It
is only through a *unified* theory of the self, one that has wide explanatory power," he contends, "that one reaches a stable, unified identity"
(176).

The question, though, is whether a unified theory of the self actually
does produce stability. Arguably, Lieberman has got it the wrong way
round: the greater the unity of an identity, the more *precarious* it is, because any stray or recalcitrant element that can't be made to conform
to the unified whole destabilizes it. A unified theory therefore has either to ignore the elements that don't fit or deny their existence. For
that reason, it might have considerably *less* explanatory power than a
theory of the self that acknowledges warring elements, inconsistencies,
and diversity. In any case, the demand that an identity-constituting
story must always possess "wide explanatory power" is excessive, since
there is seldom any need to understand a person fully and completely.
To return to Lieberman's own example, wide explanatory power isn't
required for making sense of someone's devotion to becoming a doctor.
Here, local explanatory power is quite sufficient for understanding
what the person is doing. No further intelligibility is gained by setting
this commitment into the context of the person's life from start to finish. As Walker declares, "There's just no plausible move in general
from making sense of an action in some narrative context to needing to
see it against the backcloth of an entire life" (Walker 1998, 148).

Schechtman likewise puts two important constraints on identity-
constituting autobiographical narratives, although they are not the
same as Lieberman's. The first is the requirement that even if the narrative we use to organize our lives is implicit, it cannot be entirely hidden from us. As Schechtman puts it, "An identity-constituting narrative [must] be capable of local articulation. This means that the
narrator should be able to explain why he does what he does, believes
what he believes, and feels what he feels" (Schechtman 1996, 114). This
constraint amounts to the claim that while the person needn't be able

to narrate the whole of her self-constituting autobiography, she must be able to narrate bits of it. When, for example, others are puzzled by what the person is doing and call her to account, the person must be able to put the part of her story that explains her actions into words or other sign-systems. If she can't, says Schechtman—because, say, whatever it is that prompted her behavior is buried deep in her unconscious—then that trait isn't fully identity-constituting.

Schechtman asks us to think of a man who sincerely believes he loves his brother, but frequently acts toward him in ways that suggest hostility. Because he is unaware of this hostility, she argues, it is not fully integrated into his life and so is attributable to him to a lesser degree than the parts of his autobiography that he can turn into words (Schechtman 1996, 119). But something's amiss here. She's surely right to suppose that an autobiography couldn't very well be self-constituting if the subject can turn *none* of it into a narrative. But if a person is hostile, we may attribute hostility to him independently of whether he understands that he is hostile. What a person knows of himself determines a good deal of how he will make sense of his life, but what he needs to make sense of may be strongly determined precisely by the fact that there are things about himself he doesn't know.

To see this, we need only to consider Sophocles' tragedy *Oedipus the King*. Through no fault of his own, Oedipus lacked certain crucial pieces of information about himself, and as a consequence, he acted in ways that turned him into a kind of moral chimera. Like the Sphinx whose riddle he solved, he ended up a hybrid thing, a parricide, Jocasta's son as well as her husband, the begetter of his own siblings. As the play unfolds, it becomes clear that it's his ignorance regarding who he is that precipitated the events he must now, as King of Thebes, come to understand. Oedipus *is* a parricide, father to his sisters, husband to his mother, even though he can't possibly articulate the stories that constitute his identity in these ways. In claiming that what we can't articulate about ourselves isn't as fully self-constituting as what we can, then, Schechtman fails to acknowledge that one's identity isn't simply a function of one's self-knowledge.

The second of Schechtman's constraints is that identity-constituting narratives "cohere with reality," so as to allow for the possibility that people can be psychotic, mistaken about the facts, or guilty of interpretive inaccuracies (Schechtman 1996, 119). While minor errors of fact or interpretation don't seriously compromise one's self-conception, "seeing the facts as having implications wildly different from those others see makes taking one's place in the world of persons virtually impossible" (127). To observe the reality constraint, then, "one needs a self-concept that is basically in synch with the view of one held by others. Personhood, it might be said, is an intrinsically social concept" (95).

Schechtman is surely correct to argue that a theory of personal identity has to accommodate the possibility that one may be mistaken or delusional in one's beliefs about who one is, but something is wrong with the standard she proposes for evaluating how closely a self-conception adheres to reality. The grip of reality on my self-understanding can't reliably be tested by checking whether my self-concept is basically in synch with the view of me held by others. Couldn't the view held by others be mistaken, bigoted, or hostile? If most people think that I am intellectually and morally below par because I am black, or that I am a thief or a cheat because I am a Gypsy, or a monster because I don't fit neatly into the disjunctive categories of male or female, then there are good reasons for me to resist the idea that how others see me constitutes the reality to which I must conform. The reality constraint as Schechtman understands it seems to suppose that the question of who gets to say what is real about me has already been settled, by majority vote, but that implies that others' understandings of me could never be challenged.

## The Credibility Constraint

Lieberman's notion of objective validity and Schechtman's reality constraint are both attempts to get at something important, namely, that identities are more than merely subjective self-understandings. And Schechtman is also right to insist that self-constituting stories must at least sometimes be capable of local articulation. Nevertheless, it appears that there are problems with all four of the candidates that have been proposed as constraints on the autobiographical narratives that constitute our identities. Some won't do at all, and others require considerable modification before they can be made to function properly. I want, therefore, to start fresh, by exploring the various ways in which narrative constructions of identity might or might not be *credible*, according to ordinary standards of what it's reasonable to believe. Thinking about a story's credibility allows us to stay focused squarely on the idea that a personal identity is a system of meaning—a semiotic representation of the things that contribute importantly to one's life over time—and to consider whether the story can reasonably be seen as a part of that system. In this way we can circumvent the difficulties that arise from insisting on only one story per identity, on the ability to articulate any story that is fully identity-constituting, on "objectivity" or "reality" as Lieberman and Schechtman understand these terms. Let me propose three criteria—strong explanatory force, correlation to action, and heft—for judging the credibility of a self-constituting story.

*Strong explanatory force.* I observed earlier that the backward-looking stories that contribute to a person's identity are explanatory stories. But what exactly is it that they explain? In the most general terms, they explain the person to herself and to others, allowing them to understand, for example, the connection between who she is and what she holds herself responsible for, or why it's important to her to finish what she starts, or how her relationship with her father continues to play itself out in her marriage. These narratives might also explain why she's so dissatisfied with her life, or why other people are treating her so badly, or what it was about her that brought her to this particular pass. The narratives' depictions of her life up to now, and of the other lives with which hers is enmeshed, let her and those around her see why she tends to respond to people in the way she does, why she can be counted on in certain sorts of situations, why she keeps getting passed over for promotion. If these explanations meet the standard epistemic criteria for evaluation—being consistent with the data, being coherent, and being sufficiently broad in scope (Longino 1993, 112)—they are candidates for inclusion among the stories that constitute the person's identity.

But the mere fact that a narrative meets the standard criteria for evaluation doesn't mean that it's identity-constituting, as several stories that are mutually incompatible might all meet these criteria. Identity-constituting stories are those that don't just take the evidence into account—they're the ones that fit the evidence best. The standards for evaluating them are "standards of theory construction like simplicity and elegance and verifiability," which, in Ronald Dworkin's words, "reflect contestable and changing assumptions about paradigms of explanation, that is, about what features make one form of explanation superior to another" (Dworkin 1986, 53).

Suppose, for example, that I am a professor at a university and have invested a great deal of time and energy over the last five years in mentoring a young colleague in my department. Suppose too that I see the history of my relationship to my colleague as a part of a larger story of who I am professionally, and that I take very seriously my responsibility to help the junior members of the profession to start making a name for themselves, to establish good relations with the university administration, to get tenure, and so on. So I have lunch with my colleague once a week, invite her regularly to my home, drop by her office occasionally for a chat, and in general do what I can to smooth her path. I make sense of what I am doing by weaving the episodes of our interactions into a story that puts a particular interpretive spin on them: the story depicts me as a good citizen of the academy. In this way it explains me to myself; it contributes to how I understand myself professionally.

Now let's suppose that my young colleague incorporates the very same data into her own, radically different story of who I am. According to the plot through which *she* characterizes our interactions, I've lusted after her ever since she arrived on campus, and taken advantage of the fact that she is untenured to pressure her into accepting invitations that she can't very well refuse. She can't even escape me by retreating to her office, because I insist on dropping in, uninvited, and making a nuisance of myself there as well. Her story contributes to her understanding of who I am by casting me as a sexual predator who abuses my position of power within the department: it depicts me as a bad citizen of the academy.

Now, one of these stories has got to go. As they flatly contradict one another, they can't both contribute to the narrative construction of my identity. It's possible, of course, that if each were modified slightly they might both be true. People's motives are often mixed, so perhaps I entertain salacious thoughts about my younger colleague at the same time as I genuinely want to help her. On the other hand, it's equally possible that one of these stories represents me accurately while the other doesn't. The task is then to decide which of the two contending narratives to choose. The connective feature of stories can be of assistance here, since either story lets us draw connections to other stories that constitute my identity. If my colleague's third-person narrative finds no thematic echoes in those other stories (we could suppose she asks around the department and learns that none of the graduate students or junior faculty I've mentored before have any stories about me that resonate with hers), then her story probably doesn't explain very much after all. If, on top of that, the story I tell from my own perspective does clearly connect to themes of conscientiousness and care in my professional role and in the other aspects of my life, then we are justified in concluding that my story has the stronger explanatory force. A story credibly contributes to a person's identity, then, if it offers the *best* available explanation of some aspect of who she is.

*Correlation to action.* Second, since acts express a person's identity, we have reason to believe a story is identity-constituting only if there is a strong correlation between it and the person's actions. Without such a correlation, the story must be ruled out. The action criterion allows us to disqualify adolescent daydreams and deliberate or delusional fantasies, but it also sheds light on cases where a person is unconscious of the beliefs or intentions that motivate her. In the instance of the man who protests that he loves his brother but is unconsciously hostile toward him, we can identify the man as hostile because we can see what he does that expresses his hostility, even though the man's own story of his relationship to his brother is one of admiration and affection. The man's actions, we say, speak louder than his words.

Just as the action criterion insists on a strong correlation to past action (which allows us to screen out as incredible a psychotic's story of having been conquered by Wellington at Waterloo), so it also requires a strong correlation to future action. A credible backward-looking story must *explain* the person's actions, while a credible forward-looking story must *structure the field* of the person's actions so that she can continue to act in accordance with who she understands herself to be.

To see how the forward-looking story must correlate to action, think of the artist Gauguin, as Bernard Williams discusses him in "Moral Luck." Williams's Gauguin "turns away from definite and pressing human claims on him in order to live a life in which, as he supposes, he can pursue his art" (Williams 1981a, 22). The story by which he constitutes himself as a painter, which involves abandoning his family and going to Tahiti, guides his further actions. In the light of that story, it makes sense for him to go on in certain ways—indeed, it shows him that he *must* go on in certain ways. Presumably Gauguin's indignant wife and hapless children do not, at least initially, find the painter story credible: the husband and father they know isn't a painter, hasn't sold any of his work, hasn't yet acted in any of the ways that would correlate with such a story. The story (to revert to Schechtman's language) just doesn't cohere with reality. But what Gauguin is doing with the story is *creating* the reality that makes the story credible. If he's lucky, he'll become the painter he sets out to be. Others might then be able to make sense of his life in Tahiti in terms of the story he constructs around his painting. That the credibility of some identity-constituting stories rests on how well they structure the person's field of action points to an important difference between a story told from the first-person perspective and one told from the third-person point of view—a difference to which I'll return shortly.

*Heft.* Finally, a story is credibly a contribution to a person's identity if it possesses the right amount of heft. The criterion of heft underscores the idea that identity-constituting narratives are woven around the features of people's lives that they, or some of the rest of us, care about most. The story of someone's commitment to Roman Catholicism, for example, might figure so prominently in her life that she could quite truthfully claim, "I couldn't have an abortion and still be me." If having an abortion would be a betrayal of the moral and religious values she cares about most and with which, accordingly, she is most closely identified, then the claim that the story of her Catholicism is identity-constituting is a credible one.

It's important to note that a story about something quite trivial could credibly be considered identity-constituting if, for the particular person, the thing weren't trivial at all. A man who took great pride in his long hair and had worn it that way for many years might incorporate into his self-understanding the story of his commitment to keeping it long, while strangers too might identify him primarily in terms of the narrative personae associated with long hair, such as "hippie," or "God." For most of us, the length of our hair doesn't affect who we are, but this man cares enough about it so that it forms a fixed point around which he credibly constructs an identity-constituting narrative.

In effect, then, like the action criterion, the heft criterion serves to rule out certain stories from consideration altogether. If a story is important to no one from either the first-person or the third-person perspective, it isn't even a candidate for inclusion in the set of stories that make up a personal identity. The more interesting problem for the criterion, however, arises when there is a difference of opinion between the two perspectives about how much heft to assign a story. In cases of this kind, the depictive feature of stories helps us to determine what counts as the "right amount" of heft. If a story is to depict a person accurately, it's got to get the proportions right. It can't gloss over the person's failings, or be weighted in favor of culturally normative prejudices that are morally degrading. It can't unfairly exaggerate one feature to the exclusion of others, and it can't take refuge in such homogenizing platitudes as "everybody's really nice once you get to know them" or "it takes two to tango." And finally, even if the narrative does not distort the proportions and so can be taken to be a credible representation of some aspect of who the person is, the fact that it is then part of a connective tissue of self-constituting stories means that it must be weighted accurately with respect to the *other* narratives that also contribute to the person's identity.

A story could therefore partly constitute my identity if it concerns something *I* don't care about in the least, but other people do. Suppose I were totally indifferent to the fact that my social skills were abysmal, in consequence of which my appalling and habitual rudeness to others never figured into any of my self-constituting narratives. But suppose further that these others plotted my disgusting displays of indifference to them into a narrative that constitutes me as a boor. The criterion of heft can then be used to adjudicate whether my story or the story of others is the more credibly self-constituting. My self-portrait is arguably out of proportion, much as if I had drawn one of my eyes or half of my mouth too small, and because the third-person portrait does a better job of representing these features, we may judge that it is the more credible depiction of me.

On the other hand, just because others care enormously about some feature of me doesn't necessarily mean that their narrative understandings credibly contribute to my identity. Many Europeans of Jewish ancestry living in France in the 1930s attached no significance to their familial history, identifying themselves as, say, French Catholics instead. But a decade later, in Vichy France, that familial history was of paramount importance, not only to those in authority, but to many of the person's neighbors and coworkers as well. Because the French people in general had the state-backed power to impose their own views of who a person of Jewish ancestry "really" was, the genealogical stories linking the person to, say, a Jewish grandmother were suddenly taken to be identity-constituting, with the result that the person might be deprived of his job, forced into hiding, or sent off to a concentration camp.

In this instance the story that purports to constitute the person's identity is arguably *not* credible. It effectively blocks the person from continuing in his previously established identity, viciously declaring that people with a certain ancestry are dangerous to the state or of so little value that they may be sacrificed to appease the Nazi occupiers. Moreover, it takes no account whatsoever of what this person's actions say about who he is. It even denies the person presumptive standing to offer a contending story about what his actions say about him. In this scenario, the mere fact that the story possesses heft for the others who identify the person is insufficient to render it identity-constituting. Since the story is unfairly weighted in favor of a cultural prejudice that morally degrades the person, we may judge that it is not a credible constituent of the person's identity.

The Vichy example is complicated in that the third-person perspective constructs the Frenchman's identity according to the requirements of an abusive, anti-Semitic power system. The Vichy officials assigned great weight to a person's Jewish ancestry, not so that they might better understand who the person was, but so that they could carry out their own appalling political agenda. The heft criterion rules out these stories on the grounds that they assign undue weight to the Jewish grandmother in the Frenchman's family tree, but the stories are also ruled out by the constraints of morality, which forbid us to slander individuals or oppress social groups. Damaging a person's identity by weaving hateful stories around his ancestry not only deprives him of opportunities and constricts his freedom of agency, but, in Vichy France at any rate, could also cost him his life. The moral constraints on identities are independent of the constraints on credibility, but it's worth pointing out that stories that constitute damaged identities are never credible, because by distorting and deforming the identity, they violate the heft criterion.

Now, it might be objected that we don't ordinarily evaluate pictures according to whether they get the proportions right. In fact, photographic fidelity to the subject is often taken as the sign of a *bad* picture—it shows a failure of creativity and imagination, and in clinging to the surfaces, it misses the deeper truths. But the aesthetic criteria we employ when assessing a narrative as a work of art are just as irrelevant here as, arguably, they were for Michael DePaul's Billy, who hoped to correct his naïveté about women by reading novels that would give him the proper formative experiences. What we are after, in the narratives that constitute selves, is not art but *accuracy*. For that reason, I'm going to insist that if a narrative is to be credible as a part of a person's identity, it must depict the proportions faithfully. To the fullest extent possible, we want to understand the person as she actually is, not tip the scales either for or against her in the pursuit of aesthetic or self-serving or political ends.

## Who Gets to Say Who I Am?

### THE "NO-TRUMP" VIEW

The credibility constraint suggests a number of reasons why my own self-constituting stories don't automatically trump other people's stories about me. For one thing, self-knowledge is fallible, so there are gaps and distortions in my understanding of who I am. This is an *epistemic* consideration. But there are also *practical* reasons why other people's stories about me are sometimes more authoritative than my own: who I am depends to some extent on who other people will let me be. And finally, there are *conceptual* grounds for denying that I hold trumps: my identity is always contingent in part on others, because personal identities are necessarily social or interpersonal. In what remains of this chapter, I espouse a "no-trump" view of personal identities, arguing on epistemic, practical, and conceptual grounds that I cannot be the sole arbiter of the stories that constitute me. But then I'll return to Bernard Williams's Gauguin to argue that there is a moral reason for privileging certain first-person narratives despite the "no-trump" view.

### EPISTEMIC CONSIDERATIONS

One reason why my self-constituting autobiography isn't definitive is that, as John Hardwig has pointed out, autobiographies are epistemically suspect. The widespread presumption that we have more authority over our identities than others do is, as he puts it, "palpably naïve" (Hardwig 1997, 52). In the first place, our self-understandings are plagued by *ignorance*. I might, for instance, not know why I was fired from my first job or what my children really think of me, and while these stories might be of central significance to who I now am, I'm in no position to supply them. "There are many things that we do not know about events in our lives. What I do not know cannot figure in my autobiography, however important it may be to my life" (52–53).

Second, we are capable of major *mistakes* about our motives, intentions, and beliefs. I might think that I have my drinking under control and so fail to incorporate into my self-conception any sense that my need for alcohol is dictating almost everything I do. "The rage I feel is unnoticed, my desire for revenge unexperienced, and consequently my account of what I was up to is . . . not only fallible, not only faulty or flawed, but fundamentally wrong and wrong-headed" (Hardwig 1997, 53).

Third, we are all prone to *self-deception*. We see ourselves as fearless when in fact we are cowards; we think Dad is doing fine when in fact he is in the early stages of Alzheimer's. Because we want to appear to ourselves in a favorable light—or we want to be justified in the belief that we are guilty and deeply flawed—we may, without realizing it, plot our stories in such a way as to force an interpretation of the data that just isn't plausible. And because we sometimes have a strong need to believe that the people we care most deeply about are safe from disaster, we may unconsciously attempt to keep them safe by plotting equally implausible stories about them.

Finally, we sometimes tell ourselves flat-out *lies* about who we are. Here, there is no trick of the unconscious that moves us to construct fairy tales—when enough rides on it, we are all capable of insisting to ourselves that we didn't really do or suffer something when we know perfectly well we did. And if we continue to insist on the lie, we may in time come to believe it. Sometimes we lie to ourselves because the truth is too painful; sometimes we're simply too stubborn to admit we were in the wrong. Whatever the reason, deliberate mendacity is a common enough phenomenon to warrant further suspicion of our self-constituting autobiographies.

Just as we ourselves aren't always the best judges of our own self-narratives, however, neither are the others who constitute us narratively. My ex-husband, for example, probably doesn't see me very clearly, and for very different reasons, my current husband probably doesn't either. People who are overfond of me are apt to discount the negative elements in my stories that importantly contribute to who I am, while those who are biased against me or my social group are also bound to have a distorted understanding of my identity. So while it makes sense, on epistemic grounds, to doubt that I know more about me than anyone else does, it's worth pointing out that because these others are sometimes also ignorant, mistaken, self-deceived, or mendacious, they too are only indifferently reliable authorities regarding who I am.

It seems, then, that even when everyone around me puts a narrative construction on me that is sharply at odds with a story through which I claim to constitute myself, the inference that *my* story must be the one that's epistemically suspect isn't licit. I'm not the only one whose beliefs about myself could be seriously flawed. When differences in people's epistemic states produce a disagreement about which of two contending narratives should be regarded as identity-constituting, the three credibility criteria can work together to provide the standards for assessing which is the better story.

## PRACTICAL CONSIDERATIONS

To explain the practical reason why my narrative self-conception doesn't always trump others' sense of my identity, let's return for a moment to the story of the skilled office manager whose new CEO identifies her as a faithful old retainer. Fearing that she is likely to prove obstructionist or set in her ways, the CEO either marginalizes her or makes her life so miserable that she has no choice but to retire. When individual others or social forces bring it about that a person can no longer act on a particular identity, then no matter how fundamental her commitment to the value around which that identity centers, and no matter how centrally the story of that commitment figures into her self-constituting autobiography, the identity is not hers. She cannot claim an identity that has no outlet for its expression.

Virginia Woolf makes this point quite forcefully in *A Room of One's Own*, where she imagines what would have happened had Shakespeare had a wonderfully gifted sister named Judith. Unlike her brother, Judith is not sent to school, and when her parents catch her writing plays and sonnets, they scold her for inattention to her household duties. She is married at sixteen to a wool-stapler but, driven by the force of her gift, runs away to London. There she quickly discovers that no theater will permit her to learn her craft, since no woman could possibly be an actor, and even if she could teach herself to be a dramatist, she cannot command the theater, the actors, and the financial backing that would allow her to put her scripts into production. Since she is barred from earning her living, she is forced to accept the protection of an actor-manager, and quickly finds herself pregnant by him. Thus thwarted at every turn by a society that does not permit women to be playwrights, she kills herself in despair (Woolf 1929, 48–50). Woolf's point was that women need material and social support if they are to become major literary figures, but another point emerges from her story as well: because Judith couldn't act on the "genius playwright" identity, she never was or would be a genius playwright.

Judith Shakespeare had the bad fortune to be born into the wrong century, when it just so happened that one of her practical identities—"woman"—was taken by the people around her to preclude the "playwright" identity. There was no necessary incompatibility between these two practical identities; in other times and places they arrange these matters differently. But because her ability to constitute herself as a playwright was directly contingent on others' cooperation and on the social factors that are conducive to that cooperation, her own unaided efforts were no match for the sustained, universal hostility she encountered in pursuit of her self-constituting project. Much of who we can be depends contingently on other people: on the families we happen to be born into, whether we are orphaned at an early age, the social groups we find ourselves a part of, the reckless driver who left us paralyzed, the kind and quality of the education we receive, the voters who elected us. These people determine the set of possible identities that are open to us.

The difference between the contingencies constraining the skilled office manager and Judith Shakespeare, of course, is that the one was able to establish and maintain a particular practical identity for many years before it was closed off to her, while the other never got her identity off the ground. So it will always be true of the office manager that she *was* an office manager, even though by chance she can now no longer maintain that identity. In both cases, however, who these people are—and are not—hinges significantly on their contingent relationships with other people.

If the discordance between a first- and a third-person identity-constituting narrative is practical in nature, the criterion that is most likely to be useful for assessing which of the stories is more credible is the one requiring the story to be strongly correlated with action. The narrative terms in which Judith Shakespeare's parents, husband, and "protector" constitute her identity are thus the more credible ones, because to some extent she does act on those stories, though try as she might she cannot act on her own.

## CONCEPTUAL CONSIDERATIONS

Finally, there is something in the very concept of 'identity' that gives us a reason why our own self-constituting stories don't automatically trump the narratives other people use to recognize us. A personal identity, I've argued, is a meaning-system that narratively represents, from one's own perspective and from that of others, the things that contribute importantly to one's life over time. As such, it cannot be intelligible only to me. To suppose that it could is to treat an identity as a kind of private language whose rules and syntax need not be accessible or meaningful to anyone else. That supposition misses the fundamentally social nature of systems of meaning. Since my identity arises from the interaction of the narratives that constitute my self-conception with the narratives that constitute others' understanding of me, my view doesn't automatically prevail. The assumption that I alone get to say who I am suffers from the same conceptual difficulties as Humpty Dumpty's assumption that he alone gets to say what a word means:

"But 'glory' doesn't mean 'a nice knockdown argument,'" Alice objected.

"When *I* use a word," Humpty Dumpty said, in rather a scornful tone, "it means just what I choose it to mean—neither more nor less."

"The question is," said Alice, "whether you *can* make words mean so many different things."

"The question is," said Humpty Dumpty, "which is to be master—that's all." (Carroll 1978, 171)

Humpty Dumpty's mistake lies in his failure to recognize that languages are social practices that can't just be changed on an individual whim. Because the narratives that construct a personal identity likewise have relatively fixed social meanings, I can't change these on a whim, either. If the stories by which I constitute my identity are to permit me to make sense of who I am, they must also permit others to make sense of this.

At this point, of course, we've come full circle, to the reason why we need constraints on identity-constituting stories in the first place. I can't just be whoever I want, like Rorty's self-inventing ironist, because who I am must to some extent be contingent on the social practices that make certain roles and relationships possible, on the master narratives—not of my own making—that let me and those around me make sense of the form of life that we inhabit, and on other people who either will or won't cooperate to keep my identity in place.

In sum, then, there are epistemic, practical, and conceptual reasons why first-person, self-constituting autobiographical stories don't always hold trumps. When these stories conflict with third-person narratives, the criteria of strong explanatory force, strong correlation to action, and heft allow us to apply the credibility constraint, which in turn lets us judge which story should be regarded as identity-constituting. But there is one final consideration that tips the presumption of neutrality between the first- and third-person narratives back in the direction of the first-person point of view, at least for some identity-constituting stories.

## THE FREEDOM TO SHAPE MY LIFE

While it's true that the actions that express who I am require uptake on the part of others for their completion, it's also true that these others stand in a different relation to my acts from me. I initiate them; I intend and endorse them; I bring it about that my past actions come to mean something, or something different, in light of my further actions; I am responsible for much of what I do. Indeed, it's because I am the person most closely identified with my actions that they reveal who I am. For these reasons, if the backward-looking stories I weave around what I've done are acceptable according to the credibility criteria, then they should be acknowledged to have a certain authority over others' equally acceptable but different stories about who I am.

Further, the backward-looking stories by which I claim to constitute my identity are often connected to the forward-looking stories by which I hope to construct my identity in the future. So, we may suppose, Williams's Gauguin, in the throes of choosing for himself whether to stay in France or go to Tahiti, doesn't say, "From here on I value painting, though I never cared about it before." Instead, he probably says, "Here is something I have cared about so much that I must now make a commitment to it. It was always important to me—more important, I now see, than my wife and children." As he engages in this narrative act of strong moral self-definition, he draws on his own understanding of what he's done to structure the field of his future action. If the backward-looking stories by which he makes sense of his past are as credible as other people's competing stories about his past, his stories should be considered more authoritative than theirs because of the use he is still making of them.

And finally, Gauguin's forward-looking self-constituting stories ought in any case to be acknowledged as having a certain authority, regardless of whether or how they are connected to his backward-looking stories, because he has the moral standing to make life-shaping choices for himself alone. It is, when all is said and done, *his* life, and he must make the best of it. His future is ordinarily of greater concern to him than to anyone else, and surely it matters more to him than to others whether he wasted his life or lived it well. So his forward-looking stories carry more weight than do the forward-looking stories his wife, friends, or children tell on his behalf. These others cannot live out his future for him. Later on, when events have borne out Gauguin's forward-looking stories or revealed them—and him—to be a failure, the credibility criteria might be invoked to judge whether these stories actually constituted him, but from those points in time when the stories are genuinely forward-looking, they ought to be accorded more authority than those that others tell for him.

None of this says anything about how identities are constructed in other cultures; I am not making universal claims about the primacy of the first-person point of view. I am, rather, setting my account of personal identity within the context of existing moral understandings— among them, respect for autonomy, notions of personal responsibility, and individualist conceptions of moral agency—that are widely shared in westernized, postindustrial societies. In the form of life characterized by those moral understandings, individuals are held to account for how they conduct themselves; we are expected to lead our own lives, not the lives of others. These considerations are not dispositive, but because of their prominence in our culture, they do tip the balance back so that it slightly favors the first-person perspective.

The account I've offered of how personal identities are narratively constructed has, I hope, established some grounds for conceiving of an identity as the sort of entity on which a counterstory might have a practical effect. In the fact that oppression can damage my identity lies a threat to my freedom of agency. In the fact that more credible stories of who I am can be constructed lies the possibility that the damage might be repaired. It's to these matters that we now turn.

# 4 Identities Damaged to Order

The effort really to see and really to represent is no idle
business in face of the *constant* force that makes for
muddlement.

— Henry James, *What Maisie Knew*

I've argued that personal identities are complicated narrative constructions consisting of a fluid and continual interaction of the many
stories and fragments of stories that are created around the things that
seem most important, from either the first- or the third-person perspective, about a person's life over time. They are therefore structures of
meaning, ways of understanding who we and others are. I've also argued
that these narrative constructions draw in part on master narratives:
the widely circulated stories summarizing the socially shared understandings that make communal life intelligible to its members. I
claimed that the stock plots and readily recognizable character types of
master narratives characterize *groups* of people in certain ways, thereby
cultivating and maintaining norms for the behavior of the people who
belong to these groups, and weighting the ways others will or won't
tend to see them.

Identities can be damaged and made incoherent or painful in all kinds
of ways that have nothing to do with unjust social group relations, but
in this chapter I want to focus on those relations, exploring their destructive impact on how we understand who we and others are. In particular, I want to show how the master narratives used by a dominant
group to justify the oppression of a less powerful group distort and falsify the group's identity by depicting the group—and therefore also its
members—as morally subnormal. Because group identities, like personal identities, are complex narrative structures of meaning, I'll argue
that oppressive master narratives cause *doxastic* damage—the damage
of distorting and poisoning people's self-conceptions and their beliefs
about who other people are. I shall therefore draw on a contemporary
account of oppression that conceptualizes it in cultural rather than
purely in economic or social-structural terms, as it's the cultural aspect

of oppression that allows me to get at oppression's doxastic impact on identity. I want to confine myself here to only one facet of the epistemology of oppressive group relations—the one that has to do with the narrative understandings that, as I've been arguing, constitute personal identities. So I won't be addressing oppression per se. People's beliefs are not the sum total of oppression, or even its most important constituents. The abusive power relations that constitute group oppression arise also out of material, political, and institutional arrangements and practices and are not simply a function of "what people think." But people's beliefs do bear directly on the construction—and misconstruction—of personal identities, and it's that aspect of oppression that concerns me here.

Once I've isolated certain features of abusive power arrangements that bear directly on the construction of oppressive identities, I'll argue that the identity of a subgroup in an unjust power relation is damaged when the stories that constitute that identity from the dominant group's perspective depict the subgroup as fit only for the dominant group's purposes, or as undeserving of moral consideration, or as morally intolerable. Sometimes too the stories have to make concessions to a subgroup's unwillingness to accept the dominant group's norms, so that the story shifts its shape to cast the subgroup's unruliness in morally degrading terms. All of these various sorts of narrative depictions can be present at the same time, or they can be present in different combinations in differing degrees, and because they are the dominant stories, they tend to crowd out, distort, discount, or make unavailable alternative stories that the subgroup might tell from the first-person perspective. Individuals who belong to the subgroup then suffer the harm I have been calling deprivation of opportunity: they cannot avail themselves fully of the goods that are on offer in the society that they inhabit as a subgroup. Damage to the subgroup's identity from the first-person perspective is inflicted when the members of the subgroup accept the dominant group's stories of who they are, or take the norms of the dominant group as the unstated standard against which they are to measure themselves. There may then be a significant overlap between the morally degrading third-person stories that constitute the subgroup's identity and the stories that are told from the first-person perspective. Individuals who narratively constitute their own identities from the dominant, third-person point of reference suffer the harm that I have been calling infiltrated consciousness. Either sort of harm is a compound harm, consisting, first, of the respect-harm of failure to acknowledge the person's moral worth and, second, of the practical harm of diminished moral agency that arises from this failure.

## The Five Faces of Oppression

Although there are a great many ways in which identities can be degraded, distorted, or rendered unintelligible, oppression's impact on identity is perhaps particularly worth studying in that its damage is systematic, depicting not only individuals but entire social groups in ways that elicit disrespectful treatment of them. The term "oppression" names a number of different social phenomena that arguably can't be reduced to any one social system. Oppression manifests itself in a number of ways, and these manifestations work singly and in combination to produce faulty narrative understandings of who some people are. What all oppressions have in common, though, is that they consist of unjust structures of power that operate to restrict the freedom of agency of certain people in virtue of their identities as members of particular social groups. While there are psychological and economic analyses of oppression dating back to Hegel and Marx,[1] there seem to be few accounts that focus on social group relations in contemporary postindustrial societies. Since social groups are key to the examination of oppression's impact on identity, I will help myself to an analysis that does a particularly good job of theorizing oppression in social and cultural terms—Iris Marion Young's *Justice and the Politics of Difference*.

As Young defines it, oppression refers to structural phenomena that immobilize or diminish a social group, and it consists in everyday, systematic constraints that keep people in the group from developing and exercising their capacities and expressing their needs, thoughts, and feelings (Young 1990, 42, 40). Because Young is dissatisfied with so abstract a definition, yet thinks it impossible to formulate a single set of criteria that describe the condition all oppressed groups share in common, she argues that the term names a family of concepts and conditions, each of which represents a different "face" of oppression. The five faces she identifies are exploitation, marginalization, powerlessness, cultural imperialism, and violence.

1. In addition to Marx's *Capital* and Hegel's *Phenomenology of Spirit*, some better-known accounts are Alexandre Kojève's *Introduction to the Reading of Hegel*, Louis Althusser's "Ideology and Ideological State Apparatuses," Herbert Marcuse's *One-Dimensional Man*, and Judith Butler's *The Psychic Life of Power*.

*Exploitation.* Following Marx's lead, Young understands exploitation as "a steady process of the transfer of the results of the labor of one social group to benefit another" (Young 1990, 49). According to Young, however, the injustice of some people's having vastly more wealth than others consists not merely in an inequity of distribution, but in an unjust social structure, which dictates how the products of some people's work are to be appropriated by other people. Young argues that while women are exploited in the Marxist sense to the degree that they work for wages, they are also exploited by corporate and domestic institutions which, while failing to acknowledge or even to notice it, require women "to benefit men by releasing them for more important and creative work, enhancing their status or the environment around them, or providing them with sexual or emotional service" (51). Similarly, African Americans as a group are exploited because the labor market tends to reserve unionized, well-paying, interesting jobs for whites, on the assumption that African Americans and members of other nonwhite racial groups ought to be the servants or assistants of people who enjoy race privilege. While social *processes* unfairly transfer the fruits of one group's labor to another, and social *institutions* allow the few to acquire wealth while the many are constrained from doing so, these social and institutional forces generate expectation-inducing *beliefs* about who certain people are—beliefs that fuel the injustice of these processes and institutions. Exploitation causes groups of people to be identified primarily in reference to other people, requiring them to be the means to these others' ends.

*Marginalization.* This face of oppression refers to the unjust exclusion of particular social groups from useful participation in social and economic life. The marginalized are the groups of people the system of labor can't or won't use. "In the United States," Young writes, "a shamefully large proportion of the population is marginal: old people, and increasingly people who are not very old but get laid off from their jobs and cannot find new work; young people, especially Black or Latino, who cannot find first or second jobs; many single mothers and their children; other people involuntarily unemployed; many mentally and physically disabled people; American Indians, especially those on reservations" (Young 1990, 53). These and other groups are denied the "cultural, practical, and institutionalized conditions for exercising capacities in a context of recognition and interaction" (55), and as a consequence they may suffer extreme material deprivation and in some cases even extermination. Forced to live on the margins of a society that offers them no meaningful place, they must either affirm their group identity in the face of opposition, become assimilated and so lose some important part of their identity, or struggle with the stigma that is attendant on their identity. Sometimes they must do all of these at once. Marginalization breeds identity-constituting narratives that depict certain groups of people as unwanted or undesirable, and puts undue pressure on subgroups' own understanding of who they are.

*Powerlessness.* Just as the class division between capitalist and worker reveals the structure of exploitation, so, according to Young, the class division between professional and nonprofessional reveals the structure of powerlessness. The condition of powerlessness may be described negatively: the powerless lack "the authority, status, and sense of self that professionals tend to have" (Young 1990, 57)

For one thing, where professionals acquire symbolic and conceptual knowledge that allows them to advance in a career and to attain continually higher levels of social recognition, nonprofessionals must work in jobs that tend to go nowhere in particular and lack status. Second, where professionals enjoy considerable autonomy in their work, nonprofessionals must answer to professionals and are continually supervised by them. And third, because professionals and nonprofessionals tend to live in different neighborhoods, have different tastes, and often different health and educational needs, the privileges of the professional extend beyond the workplace to nearly all aspects of social life.

Young calls the professional's way of life "respectability," pointing out that the norms of respectability in U.S. society are specifically associated with professional culture. As a rule, professionals expect and receive more respect than nonprofessionals get; they are, for example, far less likely to have to pass a drug test as a condition of employment and their neighborhoods aren't as heavily policed. Because professionalism commands respect, "nonprofessionals seeking a loan or a job, or to buy a house or a car, will often try to look 'professional' and 'respectable' in those settings" (Young 1990, 58). Powerlessness is a product of institutions and social structures, but the forces producing it generate identity-constituting narratives that mark nonprofessionals as not entitled to privilege and as appropriate targets for disrespectful treatment.

*Cultural imperialism.* While exploitation, marginalization, and powerlessness are largely a matter of concrete power relations stemming from the economic arrangements that determine who gets to work, what kind of work they get to do, and who is supposed to work for whom, cultural imperialism refers to the power relation that obtains when a dominant group's shared understandings render the understandings of other groups invisible at the same time as they stereotype the groups and mark them as abnormal. "Cultural imperialism involves the universalization of a dominant group's experience and culture, and its establishment as the norm" (Young 1990, 59). The dominant group takes its own experiences, achievements, and values to be representative of human nature per se. To the extent that other groups differ from it, then, those groups must consist of defective human beings. It's often habitual and unconscious fears and aversions that drive people in the dominant culture to identify subgroups as deviant rather than merely different, but an element of moral censoriousness regarding people who do not conform to the norms of the dominant group can also be present in the identities that are constructed through cultural imperialism. In identifying those outside the dominant group as deficient or defective, the group affirms its own sense of who it is.

*Violence.* Members of many subgroups live in fear of attacks that are motivated by nothing but the desire to humiliate, hurt, or destroy them. Young includes the less severe practices of harassment, intimidation, and ridicule in this category as well, when their sole purpose is to humiliate or degrade people belonging to social groups that do not fit the dominant norms (Young 1990, 61). Violence of this kind is systemic because it is directed at people simply because they are members of a despised group. It is social because people often band together to do it (in gang rape, for example) and because there are rules about when the target of the violence has asked for it (he got uppity, she was in the wrong neighborhood). And although there is a limit beyond which it is not tolerated, up to that limit it *is* tolerated. People know it will happen again, frequently, and so they become inured to it. Its perpetrators often receive light punishment or none at all, particularly if they are in positions of authority (62). Hate-motivated violence, directed at people just in virtue of their group membership, can catastrophically damage their understanding of who they are, shattering their sense of self and sometimes undoing an entire lifetime of self-respect. Violence can also alter other people's understanding of who the person is: the rape victim is taken to be defiled, the ridiculed person is seen as ridiculous. As Susan Brison has argued, if victims of violence are to regain an integrated self, they must be able to tell their identity-constituting stories of what was done to them, but just as important, the stories must be heard by caring others who are able to listen (Brison 1997, 25, 29).

In each of its five guises, then, oppression is capable of inflicting damage on the identities of subgroups and, through them, on the individual members of the group. Exploitation can impose the "servant" identity on a group of people, and the stories by which that identity is constructed can change their shape to accommodate individuals who refuse to be exploited: they aren't team players, they lack a work ethic, they have a chip on their shoulders. Marginalization can label people as worthless, and since identities are narratively constructed in part around people's social roles, being denied access to many such roles unfairly limits who a person can hope to be. Powerlessness identifies groups of people as neither respectable nor worthy of respect, and where this identity is contested, that very contestation can be figured as a further indication that the person is disreputable. Cultural imperialism insists on conformity to the norms of the master narratives that constitute the dominant group's identity, setting the standards for who people must be. And violence can shatter a person's identity at the same time as it destroys the trust in others that is crucial for constructing the forward-looking stories that constitute the person's understanding of who she now can be.

## Currents, Crosscurrents, and Eddies

The five faces of oppression can work singly or in concert to force groups of people to lose or weaken their grip on their identity, to severely restrict the kinds of identities that are open to members of the group, to undercut or render incoherent or splinter the identities of group members. To get a better sense of how these stunted or damaged identities are created, however, it will be necessary to examine not only oppression's several *manifestations* but also the various *forces* at work in abusive power systems. Some forces propel the members of different subgroups in different directions relative to the larger society, and others position the subgroups differently with respect to the dominant group. Since these forces serve as indicators of what kind of identity a given power arrangement might require of a subgroup, keeping track of which forces are present in the arrangement affords some idea of what kinds of work the dominant group's master narratives might need to do.

Master narratives associated with these forces could, for example, display the required behaviors for people who have been propelled in a given direction, or they could see to it that the forces that so propel them remain invisible.

Because the question of how various oppressive forces position people in a group with respect to the dominant group or the society as a whole is a tremendously complex one, any conceptual scheme purporting to represent these forces runs the risk of oversimplification. Still, it can be useful to identify at least some of the currents and crosscurrents at work in oppressive power relations. While the list I propose is not intended to be exhaustive, I believe it does capture four of the more important forces, some or all of which might be present in any given abusive group relation. The first force is *expulsive*: the subgroup is driven out of the larger society. The second is *dismissive*: the group is tolerated only on the fringes of the larger society. The third is *pressive*: the group is pressed into serving members of the dominant group. The fourth is *preservative*: the subgroup is the necessary Other that keeps the dominant ideology in place. While dismissive forces give rise to marginalization, pressive forces produce exploitation, and preservative forces are associated with cultural imperialism, the relationships between these forces and the faces of oppression that Young has identified are not tidy ones; dismissive and preservative forces, for example, might interact with the pressive forces at work in a particular system of exploitation.

Two of these forces are clearly visible in Laurence Mordekhai Thomas's distinction between "capricious" and "expectations-generating" power arrangements. In a capricious power arrangement, the fear of being harmed forces the subject to comply with the agent's demands, but the agent holds out no assurance that compliance will keep the subject safe from harm. The agent does not care whether the subject believes that the agent's power over the subject is legitimate, nor is the agent interested in establishing even a minimal trust relationship with the subject. Using the Holocaust as his example of a capricious power arrangement, Thomas writes, "There were no actions that Jews could perform whereby they could trust Nazis not to harm them, [which] is precisely what one would expect given the conception the Nazis had of the Jews, namely that they were irredeemably evil, for a relationship of trust is an inappropriate moral relationship to have with that which is irredeemably evil" (Thomas 1995, 164–65). Because there is no relationship of trust between agent and subject, Thomas declares that capricious power arrangements lack a normative component (154).

An expectations-generating power arrangement, on the other hand—
Thomas's example is slavery in the American South—is normative in
three respects. First, the agent believes that there are norms of behavior
for the subject. Second, the agent believes that she is morally justified
in forcing the subjects to comply with those norms. And third, although "the agent in an expectations-generating power arrangement
threatens to cause the subjects great harm if they fail to comply with
the agent's wishes, . . . the agent very much wants the subjects to believe that if they comply with the agent's wishes, then the agent will
voluntarily refrain from harming them" (Thomas 1995, 155). Subjects
are meant to reassure themselves on this point because they are supposed to believe that the agent is a *moral* agent, who acts out of a conception of the good rather than out of self-interest.

Thomas argues that in this third respect, an expectations-generating
power arrangement involves a trust relationship between agent and subject, even if it is only a "pocket of trust" (Thomas 1995, 157), and that
this kind of power arrangement therefore constitutes a moral relationship. There is an expectation that both parties will behave in certain
ways, and violation of this expectation is seen as a betrayal of the relationship. So, for example, Benjamin Schwarz writes of American slaves:

> The vast majority of runaways, after all, didn't seek to escape perma-
> nently. Rather, they absconded a short distance for a temporary period
> (usually days or weeks) and generally returned to bondage of their own
> accord. The trigger for slave flight . . . seems almost always to have
> been a breach by whites of what slaves regarded as standard expecta-
> tions, most commonly through excessive or unjustified punishment.
> (Schwarz 1999, 30)

Conversely, that American slaveholders regarded slaves as moral
agents, Thomas argues, is evident from the slaveholders' entrusting the
care of their children to slaves. They wanted the slaves to perform this
task well, and could not, he claims, have relied solely on coercive
threats to get them to do this (Thomas 1995, 162).

The forces that define capricious power arrangements are clearly *expulsive* ones. In the Holocaust, the aim was to expel certain ethnic
groups rather than enter into any kind of relationship with them.
Where the object is genocide, there is no need to establish trust, and as
Thomas tells us, from the dominant group's perspective, a relationship
of trust would be morally inappropriate. Indeed, *no* relationship is
deemed appropriate. Instead, the dominant group refuses to tolerate the

presence of the subgroup in the larger society and is interested in neither the subgroup members' own view of the matter or in any sort of mutual accommodation.

In Thomas's example of an expectations-generating power arrangement, by contrast, the predominant forces are *pressive* ones. American slave owners not only tolerated a relationship with their slaves—they insisted on it. Like the press gangs of the eighteenth-century British Navy, who rounded up able-bodied men to serve against their will as sailors on His Majesty's ships, the forces present in the institution of slavery pressed people into serving the members of the dominant group, appropriating their labor for the group's benefit. For slave societies to attain the stability that is necessary for a long-term relationship, there must be not only the threat of harm but also, as Thomas points out, a substantial degree of trust.

Consider another expectations-generating power arrangement in which pressive forces are at work—a patriarchal marriage in a society that does not permit women to own property and also forbids divorce. This power arrangement is expectations-generating in that there are well-defined norms for how the wife is expected to behave. She in turn may expect that if she complies with these norms, her husband will not harm her, though this expectation isn't always well founded. The pressive forces establish the norms with which she must comply: she is to meet her husband's sexual needs, care for his children, keep his house clean, defer to him, enter into no relationships with other men, and so on. The penalty for failure to comply can be quite severe. She might be raped by her husband if she is unwilling to have sex, have her children taken away by the state or other family members if she does not provide all their care, beaten if she does not defer to her husband, stoned for adultery if she takes a lover. If she refuses the relationship by running away she will become a social outcast and, having no money of her own, adds starvation to her other miseries. If, on the other hand, she is a compliant wife, then although her husband might still harm her, she has a reason to trust that he won't—particularly if she believes that her husband's authority over her is morally justified and that his exercise of this authority is governed by morality rather than self-interest. And just as she trusts that her husband is enough of a moral agent to refrain from harming her if she lives up to the norms, so he too trusts in her moral agency—he entrusts himself, his house, and his children into her care. When such trust is absent, the power arrangement cannot hold.

Not all expectations-generating power arrangements are ones in which pressive forces predominate, though. There are other ways of using people that don't involve requiring them to serve you. In social arrangements that enforce a strict gender binary, for example, women are expected to desire men and men to desire women; heterosexual desire is a part of what it means to be a woman or a man in these arrangements (Butler 1990). The *preservative* forces that flow through the arrangements police desire. These forces don't require a subgroup to perform services for heterosexuals; rather, they insist that all people *be* heterosexual. If some men and women refuse, the preservative forces push them into the role of Other, stigmatizing them so that they pose less of a threat to the gender ideology. The preservative forces assure that gender not only continues to be the identification with one sex, but that it also continues to entail the direction of sexual desire toward the other sex. Gays, lesbians, and bisexuals thus become the "not-us" that allows "us" to keep on defining itself in heteronormative terms.

And finally, there are *dismissive* forces. These circulate in many expectations-generating power arrangements, but they are also strong currents in arrangements that are neither expectations-generating nor capricious in Thomas's sense of these terms. While capricious power arrangements expel certain groups from the larger society altogether, the arrangements I have in mind are content to let the group exist on the fringes of society, as long as its members don't lay claim to the goods and opportunities that are enjoyed by those in the dominant group. So, for example, ageism pushes the elderly out on the margins of social life but doesn't, for the most part, insist on killing them. Native Americans are pushed onto reservations; the homeless are pushed to live under bridges; gays are pushed into their closets without actually being expelled outright. Because the forces at work here are dismissive rather than expulsive, the subgroup isn't apt to be characterized as "irredeemably evil." The terms employed are likely to be somewhat more restrained: the group is hopelessly dated, useless, unreliable, good for nothing, self-destructive, or perverted.[2] The point of abusive power arrangements characterized by dismissive forces is that the subgroup should have as little to do with the dominant group as possible. The dominant group doesn't want the subgroup to serve its members or preserve its ideology; it wants the subgroup to stay out of its way. And so it polices the subgroup, to make sure that it remains marginalized.

2. Some people apparently do think that gays and lesbians are irredeemably evil, but often the judgment is less harsh: a spokesman for the Boy Scouts of America recently insisted merely that homosexuals do not live up to the Scouting ideal of being clean in word and deed ("All Things Considered," National Public Radio, 4 August 1999).

This policing generates expectations of a kind, but the expectations don't bind the groups together, as they do in power arrangements characterized by pressive forces. As a consequence, the trust relationship isn't as strong, either. Because dismissive forces keep the subgroup at arm's length, the degree of trust required to sustain the power relation is minimal.

As the example of the oppressive treatment of gays and lesbians illustrates, dismissive forces and preservative forces can run alongside one another within a given power arrangement. Dismissive forces can also take on additional energy and become expulsive forces, or a power arrangement can contain both forces at once. Pressive forces can combine with any of these, lurk in the background, or dominate an arrangement for a while and then recede. Other forces might also run in tandem or at odds with these four. And what complicates the picture even further is that the impact of these forces on any one individual also depends on how she is situated *within* an oppressed subgroup, and on the number of other oppressed subgroups to which the individual might belong.

If you are poor, African American, and pregnant, for example, you are likely to be buffeted by the pressive forces running through racism and sexism; dismissive forces surrounding your poverty, race, and impending motherhood; preservative forces that keep ideologies of class, race, and gender in place; and possibly expulsive forces if you fail to comply with the norms of behavior to which pregnant women are held. You'll be confronted not only by the large signs in bars admonishing all pregnant or potentially pregnant women to refrain from alcohol, but also by medical professionals and professional social workers, who are ten times more likely to report you for a positive drug screen than they would a pregnant white woman who also tests positive (Nelson and Marshall 1998, 130). To one degree or another, the forces that run through this particular nexus of multiple oppressions bring it about that you are exploited, marginalized, powerless, and a victim of cultural imperialism. And violence, of course, is always a possibility.

I now want to take a close look at how three oppressive group identities are narratively constructed. I'll use the four forces I've identified as a conceptual grid that allows me to keep track of the different functions the master narratives might perform in creating the identity, since the forces are indicators of what kind of identity a given oppression could require of its victims. For instance, if the pressive forces that produce exploitation form a strong current in a particular power arrangement, one would expect to find identity-constituting master narratives that

set the norms for how the exploited group members are expected to behave. If the expulsive forces that manifest themselves in powerlessness
and violence are present in an arrangement, the odds are that the group
will be narratively identified in ways that either justify the expulsion or
hide the fact that any expulsion is occurring. The correlation between
the forces and the master narratives that do things with or because of
them is, for all I can tell, only a rough one; I'm claiming no more than
that the presence of a force is a tip-off to the possible presence of a story
that is in some way associated with that force.

The three groups whose identities I've chosen to examine are Gypsies, transsexuals, and mothers. Since they aren't the first groups that
spring to mind when one thinks about oppressive group relations, they
are worth exploring for potentially important aspects of oppressive
identities that might otherwise go unnoticed. The other reason for
choosing them is that they form instructive contrasts with one another,
particularly with respect to the forces that predominate in the power
arrangements that oppress them. As we'll see, dismissive forces play a
major role in the oppression of Gypsies, while many of the stories that
constitute transsexual identities are connected more directly with preservative forces; a strong current running through the power arrangement that damages the "mother" identity consists of pressive forces.
Instructive too are the differences among the three groups regarding
what is known in the wider society about the narratives that constitute
the groups' identities from the first-person perspective. Careful consideration of how these decidedly dissimilar groups are identified, then, reveals the range of possible tasks that the stories constituting group
identities might be required—or forbidden—to perform.

## Gypsies

The ancestors of the Gypsies are the Domba, who originated in
northern India and subsequently diverged into two linguistic branches.
One group migrated to Armenia, Egypt, and the Middle East, and the
other, the Romani-speaking people, went to Europe. The Gypsies who
went westward appear to have left India for Persia between A.D. 800 and
950, perhaps as artisans, musicians, or prisoners of war, and then, wandering through Byzantium, they settled in the Balkans at some time
after 1100. There they were soon enslaved. In the fourteenth century,
Moldavia and Wallachia also instituted Gypsy slavery, and at least half
the Gypsy population was forced into captivity. The other half escaped

only because they stayed perpetually on the move through northern, central, and southern Europe. In much of what is now Rumania, they were held as slaves and serfs for many centuries, to be emancipated only in the 1850s (Hancock 1987, 7–36).

Feared for their skin color and unfamiliar language and customs, the Gypsies were continually misidentified as marauding Tartars, Turks, or Muslims, and so encountered steady persecution wherever they tried to settle. A number of Italian and German duchies and principalities first tolerated and then repeatedly banished them in the fifteenth and six-teenth centuries, as did Spain, France, Scotland, and England: like bank-rupts, murderers, pickpockets, and other undesirables, they were shipped overseas to populate the European colonies of the New World, Africa, and India. Declared *Vogelfrei*—outside the protection of the law—in many parts of what is now Germany, in isolated instances Gypsies were still being hunted for sport as late as the 1830s (Trumpener 1995, 357). Where they could, they made their living by blacksmithing and mending pots and pans, horse trading, fortune telling, playing music, and working as itinerant agricultural laborers.

Beginning in the late eighteenth century, two contradictory sorts of master narratives were used to identify the group from the dominant European perspective. One set of narratives depicted the Gypsies as a romantic and free people, while the other set depicted them as savages who threatened the existing social order. Both ways of constructing the Gypsy identity are generated by the dismissive forces that pushed Gyp-sies to the edge of the European mainstream, but the sets of narratives differ in how they cooperate with those forces.

*The Gypsy of Romance.* The first set of master narratives built up the utopian picture of a carefree and genial Gypsy life seemingly outside of history, outside the Western nation-state and Western economic orders, and beyond the reach of the authorities. So, in *The Gypsy in Music*, Franz Liszt could write of the Romani people in 1859, "It is a people which exercises on civilised nations a fascination as hard to describe as to destroy; passing, as it does, like some mysterious legacy, from age to age; and one which, though of ill-repute, appeals to our greatest poets by the energy and charm of its types" (quoted in Trumpener 1995, 355). This is the Gypsy of Romance: the darkly beautiful and mysterious for-tuneteller, the laughing King of the Romany, the swarthy musician playing haunting music on a violin, all wandering the open road to-gether in the "gipsy caravan, shining with newness, painted a canary-

yellow picked out with green, and red wheels" so enchantingly described in *The Wind in the Willows* (Grahame 1908, 15). The master
narratives that construct the Gypsy of Romance implicitly appeal to
the wrongness of confining a wild, free spirit. They suggest that there is
something beautiful and adventurous in living outside civilized society,
and that it would be a pity to deprive these colorful travelers of the freedom to roam where they will. By implying that Gypsies choose to wander, not that they are forced to wander, the master narratives conceal
the dismissive forces that marginalize the group.

*The Gypsy of the Wild.* On the other hand, the Gypsies' very wildness
called into question Enlightenment definitions of civilization and nationalist definitions of culture. Katie Trumpener argues that the anxieties induced by this were projected onto the Gypsy identity via stories
of theft and displacement—the Gypsy baby as changeling in the Nor-
wegian, French, or German farm wife's cradle; the Gypsy beggar children who assail Harriet Smith and Miss Bickerton in the famous
episode of Jane Austen's *Emma*; the Gypsies in Sir Walter Scott's *Guy
Mannering*, who kidnap a young lord because his father has enclosed
the land on which they used to camp (Trumpener 1995, 361). In other
stories the Gypsies aren't merely thieves, they are animals: vermin,
beasts of the field, or even ogres.

This second set of master narratives purports to *justify* the forces
that dismiss the Gypsies by identifying the group as a dangerous threat
to the social order. Here there is nothing admirable that ought to be
protected by "allowing" Gypsies to run free, but rather an imputation
that their subhuman status renders them unfit for decent society. Indeed, as primitives, they came under the wildlife protection laws enacted in Germany in 1935: "mixed" Gypsies were incarcerated and
sterilized, but Himmler planned to preserve the Gypsy species by reset-
tling its "pure" specimens on special protected preserves (Trumpener
1995, 350).

Under the Nazis, the dismissive forces that had merely kept the Gypsies on the margins of European life snowballed into expulsive forces.
By 1945 at least 600,000 Gypsies—approximately a third of those living
in Europe—had been put to death, a percentage that is roughly the same
as for Jews who died under Hitler. After the war, when the genocide was
over, the expulsive forces subsided into dismissive forces once more,
but the Gypsy of the Wild narratives continue to be invoked to legitimate the dominant Europeans' treatment of the group. This narrative

construction may be seen lurking in the contrast between two job announcements posted side by side in England in 1985 by the City of Leeds Department of Environmental Health:

1. Assistant Gypsy Liaison Officer
    The postholder will assist in the enforcement of the Council's policy on Gypsies . . . serving eviction notices and physically evicting caravans from Council-owned land . . . assisting in the treatment of male clients for head, body or pubic lice, scabies and other conditions. . . .

2. Asian Liaison Officer
    To be responsible [for] housing welfare . . . involving the Asian ethnic minority in Leeds . . . to assist in bringing about a better understanding of the needs and requirements of ethnic minorities. To provide assistance by acting as interpreter to overcome the inevitable language problems which arise. (Quoted in Hancock 1987, 102)

The master narratives that were used to conceal and legitimate the dismissive forces exerted on Gypsies in Europe also served to conceal and legitimate their treatment in the United States, where approximately one million Gypsies now live (Sway 1988, 5). The literary figure with which the Gypsy is today most often associated in the United States is the Gypsy of Romance, who is, as Ian Hancock wryly puts it, "a composite Gypsy, wearing Spanish flamenco dancer's dress, traveling in an English Gypsy caravan, playing Hungarian Gypsy music." However, journalists also continue to perpetuate the Gypsy of the Wild identity that grossly misrepresents Gypsies via negative and defamatory stereotypes (Hancock 1987, 116, 119). These master narratives have undergirded anti-Gypsy laws that were designed, in the United States as in Europe, to keep the Romani people out of the way and on the move.

A Georgia law enacted in 1927 required bands of Gypsies who were not Georgia residents to pay $250 before they could conduct any business there. Indiana made it illegal for Gypsies to camp on any lands adjacent to public highways, and enforced the law so effectively that by the 1930s no Gypsies were to be found anywhere in the state. As late as 1969 any Gypsy caught in Pennsylvania without a license was subject to a fine of $100 and thirty days in jail, and another Pennsylvania law gave county departments of health the power to evict Gypsies from any municipality within their respective counties. In 1976 in Maryland, Gypsies were required to obtain a license costing $1,000 before settling or doing business, and sheriffs received a $10 bounty for any Gypsy they arrested who paid for the license after the arrest. In 1981 Texas law still referred to "prostitutes, Gypsies, and vagabonds" in the same breath, and charged Gypsies $500 to live there. These laws have since been repealed, but in *The Pariah Syndrome*, which was published in 1987, Hancock, himself a Romanichal Gypsy,[3] cites two state laws that were still in effect in that year: in Mississippi "gypsies . . . for each county . . . shall be jointly and severally liable with his or her associates [to a fine of] two thousand dollars," and in the state of New Jersey "the governing body may make, amend, repeal, and enforce ordinances to license and regulate . . . gypsies" (Hancock 1987, 105–6).

The Gypsies, then, have been what Europeans and Americans needed them to be—one of the many groups of "them" that allowed nation-states to make cultural and political sense of "us." In this respect the master narratives that constitute the Gypsy identity from the third-person perspective perform a third function. Not only do they justify or cover up the dismissive forces that keep Gypsies on the move, they also shore up the *preservative* forces at work in Gypsy oppression—the forces that preserve Western civilization from unruliness, lack of respect for authority, incomprehensibility, and the breakdown of the nation-state. The narratives fulfill this preservative function by drawing a very firm boundary between the law-abiding citizen and the lawless Gypsy. When Gypsies are figured as exotic or subhuman outsiders, they pose less of a threat to the values that are secured within the boundary.[4]

The third-person narratives that depict the Romani people as romantic or wild are scattered thickly on the ground, but most *gadže*[5]—non-Gypsies—don't know the first-person stories the Gypsies themselves tell. The narratives that constitute the Gypsy identity from the first-person perspective simply don't circulate in the wider community. There are a number of reasons for this. For one thing, the *gadže* haven't been very interested in finding out what these stories are—the linguists and linguistic anthropologists who have studied the Gypsies have tended to examine the Romani language much more closely than the Romani culture (Hancock 1987, 119). Secondly, since that culture is an oral one, the first-person narratives are not written down or published,

3. That is, a member of the Gypsy population from northern Europe, and especially the British Isles. Hancock's forebears were among the Hungarian Gypsies who came to England in the nineteenth century as circus and fairground entertainers.

4. The preservative function of Othering has been much discussed, particularly by French feminists. See, for example, Kristeva 1982.

5. The *dž* is pronounced like a hard *j* as in "judge."

so unless a *gadže* happened to know some Gypsies personally who were willing to tell her these stories, the *gadže* wouldn't have access to them. Indeed, even if the stories were written down, English-speakers couldn't understand them unless they were translated from the Romani.

The third and most important reason why the first-person stories don't circulate in the wider society, however, is that all but a very few Gypsies set themselves apart from the culture of the society they inhabit. Like the Amish and some groups of Jews, the Gypsies have a religious and cultural tradition bidding them not to mingle with those outside their group.

Marlene Sway argues that, in general, there are three "basic motivating factors" that lead Gypsies to preserve their cultural separation from the surrounding *gadže* society. The first is their religion, which is monotheistic and centers on the worship of a male god, *Del*. Although Gypsies not infrequently represent themselves to outsiders as Christians, in particular through veneration of certain Roman Catholic saints, this seems to be a form of protective coloration. When they are asked if Jesus is *Del*'s son, they say that he is not, and the representations of saints are found only in the Gypsies' places of business, never in their homes. Gypsies believe that they are *Del*'s chosen people, and that he has bidden them to remain a nation apart (Sway 1988, 28, 47).

The second factor that keeps the group from assimilating is its laws against fraternization with outsiders. Like Jewish *kosher* regulations, the Gypsy *marime* laws are purity laws and influence every aspect of life, from sexual relations between husband and wife to financial dealings with the *gadže*. Since all non-Gypsies and everything they touch are considered *marime*—unclean—the laws inhibit Gypsies from mingling with outsiders in any serious way. When *marime* laws are violated a trial is held, and if the Gypsy is found guilty he is banished from the tribe temporarily or permanently, depending on the severity of the violation. Sway reports that recent *marime* verdicts in California were handed down for sexual intercourse with a *gadže*, rape, incest, beating a member of one's family, joining the United States Army, and joining the Job Corps (Sway 1988, 53–56).

The third factor that sets Gypsies apart is their family and tribal structure, which regulates every phase of the group's life and keeps it self-sufficient, requiring contact with outsiders only for economic reasons—*gadže* are often considered fair game in economic transactions, since they are *marime* anyway. While Gypsies have repeatedly been forced out of various economic niches, they have tended to respond creatively by filling some other niche no one else wants. The *familia* works together to carve out that niche, relying on the labor of its children and its elders as well as that of the able-bodied adults. Although Gypsies permit their children to go to school to learn how to read, write, and master basic arithmetic, when the children reach the age of ten or eleven, they leave school and begin their apprenticeship with the adults of the *familia*. Girls assist their mothers, aunts, or grandmothers in their fortune-telling parlors, while boys help the men in the family, who earn their living by repairing or selling cars, blacktopping, carpentry, carnival work, and other jobs in which they can be self-employed (Sway 1988, 20, 28, 69, 72).

Gypsy religious beliefs, *marime* laws, and close-knit familial and tribal structures, combined with the high rates of illiteracy that accompany their way of life, have tended to insulate Gypsy Americans from *gadže* ideas and institutions. The Gypsies' fierce resistance to assimilation, however, is a two-edged sword. It is what has allowed them to preserve their culture despite many centuries of oppression in other people's lands, but it has also kept outsiders from learning about the first-person, self-constituting narratives that might serve to correct the morally degrading master narratives that constitute the Gypsy identity from the third-person perspective.

That said, it cannot be denied that the dismissive forces running through the power relation between the Romani people and their oppressors have played a major role in preventing the first-person accounts from circulating among outsiders as well. United States history books exclude any references to Gypsy American history, and Gypsies are the only ethnic minority that continue to be portrayed according to nineteenth-century stereotypes in the books children read in school. When taxed with this, governmental and educational sources have claimed that the Gypsies who populate children's literature "are not real people, and have nothing to do with the ethnic population of the same name" (Hancock 1987, 2), yet real Gypsies suffer because of these narrative representations. As we have seen, the narratives are functional. They serve the power system that oppresses Gypsies by papering over its dismissive forces or making them appear legitimate, and because they represent Gypsies as exotic Others, they align themselves with the preservative forces by which the dominant culture maintains its boundaries. The failure of the Gypsies' own stories to circulate within the wider U.S. and European society has made it terribly easy for the dominant group to use its master narratives of the group's identity as a justification for persecuting, suppressing, enslaving, or killing its members.

## Transsexuals

Unlike the members of most social groups, transsexuals have to find and even create their groups, or migrate to them and apply for acceptance. The term "transsexual" is currently in flux, but I'll use it to refer to someone whose gender identity is the opposite of the one normally associated with the person's bodily sex. Naomi Scheman has roughly this definition in mind when she writes that male-to-female (MTF) transsexuals see in the identity of girls and women "a variation of what they feel or want themselves to be" (Scheman 1997, 148); female-to-male transsexuals see the same in the identity of boys and men.[6] The subjective state that this dissonance induces in the person is gender dysphoria—the sense that one's body distressingly fails to conform to one's gender. Gender dysphoria is a medical diagnosis, for which the therapeutic interventions are extensive counseling, hormones, and surgery. It's impossible to know how many people bear a transsexual identity because most transsexuals aren't identifiable as such: they either perform the gender that is associated with their bodily sex, or they undergo hormonal therapy and sex-reassignment surgery, and then live according to the gender with which they identify. The figure that recurs in the literature, though, is 1 in 100,000.

I want to take a close look at a master narrative—I'll call it the Clinically Correct story—that constitutes the transsexual group identity from the third-person perspective but that also figures prominently in many transgendered people's own sense of who they are. According to this narrative, "passing" is a central feature of what it is to be a transgendered person. As the Clinically Correct story has it, a preoperative male-to-female transsexual living as a man isn't really a man in any ordinary sense of the term and certainly doesn't identify with that gender, but he passes for a man. If, postoperatively, she starts living as a woman, then in one sense she becomes a woman. But she can't tell the truth about herself because her story is not the story of a woman, so in another sense she can only pass for a woman. Either way, then, and no matter what she does, she is passing—or failing to pass. Like many an-

6. Until recently, it was thought that most transsexuals were MTF. Part of the reason is that gender clinics were set up originally to provide only MTFs with sex-reassignment surgery, since FTM genital surgery presented almost insurmountable technical difficulties. As a consequence, it was MTF transsexuals who were better known to the medical community. Now, however, more attention is being paid to FTM transsexuals, but as most transsexuals who have written about the identity are MTF, my discussion will inevitably be skewed in that direction.

other oppressive master narrative, the Clinically Correct story tries to have it both ways. It represents sex-reassignment surgery as the moment when the transgendered person passes from being a woman to being a man, or vice versa, but since it also insists that 'man' and 'woman' are natural kinds, it denies that transgendered people could actually be the men or women they appear to be.

People positioned as Other with respect to some dominant group are said to pass when they take up the group's norms for themselves, even though they don't "really" conform to those norms. Those who pass are stigmatized as duplicitous, lacking in integrity, trying to be something they're not. But this judgment, like the concept of passing itself, is premised on the unstated assumption that the norms of the dominant group are the proper ones for taking people's measure. Because the notion of passing valorizes the dominant norms, because it positions those who don't conform to the norms as not only different but deviant and defective, and because it stigmatizes those who do it, passing is arguably an oppressive concept. It would seem to follow that because the Clinically Correct story constitutes the transgendered group identity as one of continual passing, the story should be condemned as morally flawed. I'm going to criticize this master narrative on a number of grounds, but I want to problematize the notion of passing that inheres in it. I think a great many transgendered people *do* want to pass, though they'd rather employ a less negative term for it, and I'll argue that this desire ought to be respected.

*The Clinically Correct story.* The master narrative—itself a tissue of incompatible stories and fragments of stories—that represents transgendered people as passing no matter what they do has constituted the transgendered group identity from the medical point of view for the last thirty years and more. When the first academic gender dysphoria clinics were started in the 1960s, it was necessary to construct plausible criteria for candidacy for surgery, to justify what would otherwise be, from a professional point of view, medical mayhem. Researchers set out to find a test or differential diagnosis for transsexualism that didn't depend on anything as subjective as the feeling that one had been handed the wrong body at birth. But even after considerable research, no simple and unambiguous test could be developed, so criteria were defined recursively through a series of interactions with the candidates, using Harry Benjamin's definitive *The Transsexual Phenomenon*, published in 1966, as the researcher's standard reference (Stone 1991, 290). These criteria evolved into the Harry Benjamin standards, adopted in 1979 and repeatedly revised, the most recent version having been approved by the Harry Benjamin International Gender Dysphoria Association on 15 June 1998.

The problem, however, was that those seeking the correct diagnosis were reading Benjamin's book right along with the researchers, passing it from hand to hand in the transgendered community to find out what story they had to tell to be accepted for surgery (Stone 1991, 290–98). MTF transsexuals knew that if they said they enjoyed masturbating while in women's clothing they would be considered transvestites rather than "truly" gender dysphoric, and denied surgery. They knew that the question, "Suppose that you could be a woman in every way except for your genitals; would you be content?" must be answered in the negative. They knew they must say they had identified with the desired gender since childhood so as to establish a track record of gender dysphoria, and that suicidal ideation as a result of gender dysphoria would help rather than hurt their case. They knew that they must not say that they were erotically attracted to men, lest they be diagnosed gay rather than transsexual; on the other hand, if they said they were erotically attracted to women, that was proof that they weren't transsexuals either, since all MTF transsexuals, supposedly, want to be penetrated. They knew that they must display an eagerness to demonstrate the stability of their gender identity by living as a woman for a year or two before surgery.

The Clinically Correct story, then, represents transsexuals as people who have always felt themselves to be trapped in the wrong body—one with primary and secondary sex characteristics that do not conform to the gender with which they identify. It represents gender as based on biological sex, insisting that there are only two sexes—male and female—and only two corresponding genders, masculine and feminine. People whose subjective sense of their gender does not correspond to their bodily sex do not fit into either of the two allowable categories, so they suffer from a kind of birth defect, the diagnosis of which must be certified by professional experts and alleviated through medical and surgical interventions. Since these interventions can't convert or supply all sex-specific physical structures, and since they can't rewrite the person's history, they don't allow transgendered persons to become *real* men or women. But they have to pass as men or women, because those are the only two genders there are.

One important function of the Clinically Correct story is that it fuels the preservative forces that safeguard the ideology of a strict gender dualism. These forces draw a sharp boundary around the normally gendered dominant group, and impose on those who don't fit the norms the identity of "monster," "pervert," or, as activists in the transgendered community bitterly put it, "gender trash." Stigmatizing in this way the people who are marked as Other lessens the likelihood that their existence will destabilize the gender binary—if someone is a monster, s/he/it doesn't have to be taken seriously as a challenge to the system. But, since twenty-first-century Americans don't really believe in monsters, the people bearing the transgendered identity must be naturalized. The Clinically Correct story performs this function by pathologizing them. In treating transsexualism as a birth defect for which there are medical remedies, the Clinically Correct story denies that there is anything going on here that calls the sex-gender system into question. All that's going on is that there's something defective about transsexuals that needs to be fixed. In short, the Clinically Correct story is a narrative of passing because it first represents the person as pathologically abnormal and then offers to repair the pathology so that the person will appear normal, even though she isn't really.

The best-known book-length autobiographical narratives, all written by postoperative MTF transsexuals (Elbe 1933, Jorgensen 1967, Morris 1974, Conn 1977, Richards 1983), tend to converge on the Clinically Correct story. Because this story places a high premium on sex-reassignment surgery as the means for attaining the desired gender, Marjorie Garber claims that transsexuals "radically and dramatically *essentialize* their genitalia" (Garber 1992, 98). The suggestion is that if they would stop being dupes of the gender binary, they'd feel better. I believe that this way of understanding transsexualism gets the locus of the problem wrong. The profound and sometimes desperate need of very many transsexuals to have their bodies and their lives accord with the identity that's reserved for people of the opposite sex may be a sign that they inhabit an essentialist sex-gender ideology, but if there's gender essentialism going on here, it's arguably no more radical or dramatic than it is among people who do *not* bear a transgendered identity.

It is a common practice in our culture to determine a baby's gender identity on the basis of its sex. If a baby has a vulva, she is not only biologically female—she is a girl. This doesn't mean that she will automatically be wrapped in a pink blanket, but it does mean that she will be taught how to behave according to the norms for her gender. While she can, of course, call some of these norms into question, she does not thereby give up her gender identity—she merely expands the range of possible ways to be a woman. Although she might constitute her feminine identity via such character types as Lorelei Lee or June Cleaver, she is certainly free to identify herself with Gertrude Stein or Joan of Arc instead. Regardless of how she understands who she is as a woman, though, her conception of her gender identity will in all probability involve her sense of her body. For many of us, the features of our bodies that mark us male or female contribute importantly to our sense of ourselves as gendered beings.

Most people who are comfortable with their gender perform it in one of a wide range of ways that are perfectly intelligible to everyone else. What makes them intelligible are the norms for performing "woman" or "man" so that one may be identified as such. No one, perhaps, accepts all these norms without question, and many of us are happy to discard the grosser gender stereotypes. But it behooves us to bear firmly in mind that the gender norms to which many transsexuals wish to conform are the same norms that most nontranssexuals accept as well.

It's perfectly possible that the distress transgendered people feel is the result of a social construction which occasionally misfires very badly, but it is unfair of Garber to suggest that transsexuals' troubles would disappear if only they gave up *their* gender essentialism. Because a social construction is, precisely, social, these troubles will persist unless the larger society gives up *its* gender essentialism too. And that is easier said than done. What is socially constructed is often dreadfully hard to deconstruct. In the face of a gender ideology that is particularly intransigent, one might find it considerably easier to relieve one's gender dysphoria by reshaping one's body than by trying to reshape our culture's understanding of gender. In any case, that larger social understanding cannot be reshaped merely by a theoretical debunking of gender essentialism. What is required in addition are identity-constituting stories that offer alternative possibilities for being gendered—stories that transgendered people might then be able to incorporate into their own sense of who they are. As I'll argue in a moment, though, these new stories wouldn't necessarily preclude undergoing physical changes, including sex changes.

As transsexuals begin to live as the men or women they have needed to be, it's not at all uncommon for them to do it clumsily at first, drawing on sexist master narratives that neatly divide the world into tough, beer-drinking men and tender, domestic women. Noelle Howey, whose father told her when she was in the ninth grade that he had been "trapped in the wrong gender his whole life" and "couldn't live in a man's body anymore," recounts her first visit to her dad's apartment after her dad began living full-time as a woman:

> Three of the rooms were painted mauve, rose-shaped guest soaps lay in a cup in the bathroom, and everything was spic-and-span, as though she had just discovered housework. And in a way, she had, since the extent to which she had ever participated in housecleaning up until then was to lift up her legs while my mother vacuumed between the recliner and the ottoman.
>
> Beaming, she told me that she had taken up flower arranging in place of bowling—her guy obsession. Indeed, small vases of dried pink flowers sat on every tabletop on the first floor. One sat next to a plate of freshly baked chocolate chip cookies. The bile in my stomach grew as I walked from room to room. It seemed as though my father had liberated herself from her oppressive masculinity to become a Nick at Nite mom. (Howey 1999, 72)

The reruns of 1950s television sitcoms by which Noelle's dad was now constructing her "womanly" woman's identity were enough to make her feminist daughter want to throw up. These stories arise from within a power arrangement that is closely connected to the one in which transsexuals are not tolerated—namely, patriarchy. Under the guise of depiction, the master narratives that constitute women's identity within patriarchal power arrangements prescribe who women must be in relation to men. Women are fulfilled by marriage and motherhood; their natural place is in the home, which they keep clean, comfortable, and beautiful for their men; they defer to men and in general do not threaten men because they are gentle and noncompetitive— flower arrangers rather than bowlers.

It's not, of course, necessary for women to swallow these sexist stereotypes whole as they construct their self-conceptions, but it seems that Noelle's dad was doing just that. She was behaving as one might expect a man to behave if he were trying to pass as a woman. But that's because she didn't have her *own* identity as a woman down yet. She was caricaturing womanliness, in something like the way little girls do when they dress up in their mother's clothes and play house. But as Noelle conducted a lengthy series of debates with her father about whether transsexual desires are inherently sexist, she came to realize that she too had experimented with sexist narrative constructions of "woman" as she was growing up, trying on various feminine identities until she came to a self-conception that fitted her. Insightfully, I think, she recognized a similar process in her father, who was still growing into her own, particular womanhood.

Noelle's story of how she and her dad grew to be women shows us something quite interesting about the nature of master narratives. Because these narratives are used to constitute the identities of social groups, they generalize over many individuals. In this sense we may say that they are *generic*. The Nick at Nite mom isn't anyone's actual identity—it's a one-size-fits-all identity that has to be tailored to conform to the contours of an individual life. To insure a good fit, we have to mix the master narratives we use to constitute our own identities with all the other stories surrounding those of our acts, experiences, characteristics, roles, relationships, and commitments we care most about. Unless the mix is a judicious one, the identity won't be credible. Too much master narrative and your daughter will think you're only trying to pass as a woman, rather than being one.

None of this is to say that the Clinically Correct story doesn't need to be resisted. Indeed, a growing number of transsexuals have begun to challenge it explicitly, precisely because, as Garber charges, it reduces to biological sex what is better understood as a social construction. As Kate Bornstein puts it:

> I'm called "gender dysphoric." That means I have a sickness: a limited understanding of gender. I don't think it's that. I like to look at it that I *was* gender dysphoric for my whole life before, and for some time after my gender change—blindly buying into the gender system. As soon as I came to some understanding about the constructed nature of gender, and my relationship to that system, I ceased being gender dysphoric. (Bornstein 1994, 118–19)

Riki Anne Wilchins, cofounder of the activist group Transexual[7] Menace, agrees. She thinks that what is painful for many transsexuals is that their sense of self does not match closely with the socially dominant understanding of what their bodies are supposed to mean, and quips that transsexuality *is* a kind of birth defect—it's being born into the wrong culture (Wilchins 1997, 40, 30).

In a sendup of the intake interview at the gender dysphoria clinic, Wilchins offers this fragment of dialogue:

7. Her preferred spelling.

"How do you know you want rhinoplasty, a nose job?" he inquires, fixing me with a penetrating stare.

"Because," I reply, suddenly unable to raise my eyes above his brown wingtips, "I've always felt like a small-nosed woman trapped in a large-nosed body."

"And how long have you felt this way?" He leans forward, sounding as if he knows the answer and needs only to hear the words.

"Oh, since I was five or six, doctor, practically all my life."

"Then you have rhino-identity disorder," the shoetops state flatly. My body sags in relief. "But first," he goes on, "we want you to get letters from two psychiatrists and live as a small-nosed woman for three years . . . just to be sure." (Wilchins 1998, 63)

Wilchins's parody highlights one problem with the medical master narrative—namely, that the story devalues transgendered people's agency, depicting them as patients who are acted upon by medical professionals rather than agents in their own right. A second problem, as we've already seen, is that the story uncritically appropriates an essentialist view of gender that reduces it to genitalia, which fuels the preservative forces of the sex-gender ideology. A third problem, as we've also seen, is that the story uncritically embraces patriarchal gender stereotypes, inviting transsexuals, their physicians, and the psychiatrists who help them with their gender reassignment to reinforce rather than interrogate the reproduction of "manly" men and "womanly" women. A fourth problem with the Clinically Correct story is that it invites people to take its metaphors literally: "trapped in a man's body" makes it sound as if transsexuals were all Cartesian dualists living out a particularly Gothic version of the mind-body split. Fifth, in focusing on the "patient's" psychological "pathology," the story takes little account of the social pathologies that often cause untold misery in transsexuals' lives. Many transsexuals experience the crushing loneliness of feeling not only different, but grotesquely different, from everyone else. There is the continual sense of a lack of entitlement that comes of knowing that who you are isn't acceptable. There is the strong likelihood that you will be fired from your job or lose most of your clients if people find out that you are a transsexual.[8] And always, there is the threat of violence. Wilchins tells of an MTF prostitute who was ar-

8. The 27 September 1999 *New York Times* contains yet another story of a teacher with superb credentials and excellent teaching evaluations who was fired in California for being a transsexual. See "After Sex Change, Teacher Is Barred from School."

rested for soliciting and tossed overnight into the men's tank, where she was raped by forty-two men before she was let out in the morning (Wilchins 1998, 23). A horrifying number of other transgendered people are violently punished by family members for cross-dressing, beaten to death with baseball bats, drowned, strangled, shot, or stabbed.

The biggest problem with the Clinically Correct story, however, is that it makes it impossible for transsexuals to tell a credible story about their group identity. As Bornstein sees it, if you accept the medical story, with its insistence on a strict gender dualism, then the only way to be certified as a transsexual is to deny that you are one—the preservative forces of the sex-gender system require you to convince the doctors that you are really straightforwardly and simply a woman (or a man), despite what your body proclaims to the contrary (Bornstein 1994, 62). Moreover, the forces that simply will not tolerate the transsexual identity require that you falsify your identity so that you pass for someone who has never been anything but a normal woman or man. "The highest purpose of the transsexual is to erase him/herself, to fade into the 'normal' population as soon as possible," writes Sandy Stone. "Part of this process is known as *constructing a plausible history*— learning to lie effectively about one's past. What is gained is acceptability in society. What is lost is the ability to authentically represent the complexities and ambiguities of lived experience" (Stone 1991, 295). Naomi Scheman figures this loss as theft. "It is not only in our own memories but in the memories of others that our selves take shape, and the institutionalization of transsexuality functions as a theft of selfhood, in making a transsexual life not only closeted but literally untellable, incoherent" (Scheman 1997, 138).

The transsexual life is untellable and incoherent because it must draw on the master narrative of passing, a narrative so hegemonic that it undercuts the authority of any alternative story. Yet when transsexuals construct their own stories in accordance with that hegemonic script, the story explodes. To see this, we have only to consider the highly visible stories by transsexuals such as Renée Richards and Jan Morris that draw on that master narrative. The narrative requires that transgendered people pass as "natural" men or women. But when Richards and Morris incorporate the narrative into their own life stories, they are *not* passing. They are outing themselves as transsexuals in the most public manner possible. Thus in telling the story, they subvert it.

The existence of a master narrative so powerful that it delegitimates all other possible stories produces serious amounts of confusion and

bad faith for the members of the group. It also invites recurrent misun-
derstanding, stigmatization, and hostility from those outside the group,
who draw on either the Clinically Correct story or on the myths of
monsters and sexual perverts that are domesticated by the medical
story as they construct the transsexual identity—myths that are frequently internalized by transsexuals themselves, where they produce
shame and self-loathing.

What's needed are first- and third-person stories that aren't morally
degrading, that don't leave the entire burden of deconstructing the gender binary to transsexuals, and that allow the more interesting differences among transgendered people to emerge. If these alternative stories are to be both credible and morally acceptable, they clearly won't
*require* the person to pass as an ordinary man or woman. But might
such a story *allow* the person to pass? I think it might. While reading
Deirdre McClosky's memoirs I was struck by how much it mattered to
her that she pass as a woman, how worried she was that she might be
"read" (McCloskey 1999). Given the heavy punishment a transphobic
society imposes on people who are identified as transgendered, Mc-
Closky's desire to pass is surely defensible. Indeed, she herself repeatedly defends it on those grounds. Yet the wish to avoid the stigma that
accompanies being differently gendered was not McClosky's primary
reason for undergoing sex-change surgery and adopting a new gender
identity. Like many other transsexuals, she engineered these vast up-
heavals in her life because she profoundly longed to be Deirdre, not
Donald, and to receive the same sort of uptake from others that any ordinary woman would get. I think she would have wanted to avoid being
read even if there were no such thing as transphobia.

The wish to be ordinary should not be dismissed as false consciousness, nor yet as the sinister conspiracy that Janice Raymond conjures
up in *The Transsexual Empire* (Raymond 1979). A transgendered person
may feel she isn't ordinary, yet long to be accepted matter-of-factly as
just another woman. On her own terms, then, she needs to pass, although if we're going to use that word for what she's doing we'll have to
divest it of its morally negative connotations. For other transsexuals,
living as the man or woman they need to be *isn't* a matter of trying to
be something one is not. Instead, it's an attempt to shape the stories
that constitute one's identity from the third-person perspective so that
they will mesh harmoniously with the stories from the first-person perspective. Here, what is being revised isn't the concept of passing, but
the concepts of 'man' and 'woman' so that they include transgendered
people who identify with these genders. For yet a third group of trans-

sexuals—the group that includes Wilchins, Stone, and Bornstein—what is called into question is the idea that people have to be men or women at all. I note with interest that these three authors are also all perform-ance artists. As such, they are perhaps particularly skilled at imagining alternatives to the master narrative that more faithfully depict their own experience of gender difference.

Unless we insist that there is only one right way to understand who transgendered people are, it seems that at least three alternatives to the Clinically Correct story are needed. Some are stories that leave ordi-nary norms for 'man' and 'woman' in place but rehabilitate the concept of passing. Others are stories that expand the concepts of woman and man so that they include transgendered people who have adopted these identities. And still others are stories like Wilchins's and Stone's that allow people to *refuse* to be men or women. Until all these stories cir-culate much more freely in the wider community, transgendered people will continue to be relegated to the dark and unspoken corners of soci-ety, fearing for their jobs and sometimes their lives, and wondering how best to understand themselves.

## Mothers

Like other group identities, the "mother" identity is narratively con-stituted in a number of different ways, many of them highly contested. What the various conceptions of motherhood have in common, how-ever, is that they are dominated by stories clustering around the pres-sive forces that require the gestators and bearers of children—but not children's begetters—to keep children safe, tend to their physical needs, and teach them the morals and manners that allow them to take their place in society. The work of preserving children from harm, nurturing them, and socializing them continues to fall to women in grossly dis-proportionate amounts. In *The Second Shift: Working Parents and the Revolution at Home,* Arlie Hochschild presents evidence that even when women are full-time members of the labor force, they still almost invariably do the vast majority of unpaid family work, including child care (Hochschild 1989). Susan Lang reports that husbands on average perform only 20 percent of the domestic work (Lang 1991, 208–9), and much of this is yard work and home or auto maintenance rather than tending children.

The gender disparity is even more pronounced in the demographics of single-parent households: in a front-page story on 31 August 1993, the

*New York Times* reported that only 14 percent of all single-parent households in the United States are headed by men.[9] One study reports that when such households are formed in the aftermath of divorce, almost 70 percent of dependent children live with their mothers only, while 15 percent live in both their mother's and their father's households. Only 10 percent live solely with their fathers. Infants and toddlers, whose need for care is pronounced and prolonged, almost always lived with their mothers (Maccoby and Mnookin 1992).

Since the work of rearing children is labor-intensive, emotionally demanding, and time-consuming, and since corporations are organized "to suit a prototypical employee who is supposed to be exempt from caregiving obligations" (Meyers 2001, 98), mothers are often forced to take jobs that don't pay well but have flexible hours, or to occupy the "mommy track" in their chosen professions. They also have fewer opportunities and less leisure to pursue friendships or other interests; they are excluded from certain positions in the armed forces; they may be expected to take on additional care for elderly or ill adult family members or neighbors' children, on the grounds that they're good at it or at home so much anyway. But there is considerable disagreement about the extent to which the need to make these tradeoffs is oppressive. The "mommy track" seems to be just what many mothers want, although they don't want to use such a contemptuous term for it. Other mothers take great pride in doing their work on a full-time basis and count themselves fortunate that they are economically able to devote themselves wholeheartedly to maternal tasks they find deeply meaningful. Still others would be only too glad to sacrifice other goods and opportunities for the privilege of caring full-time for their children, but are kept by forces beyond their control from mothering in the way they would wish. And others again do not see the norms of full-time mothering as applicable to them, either because the members of their social class or ethnic group have never been governed by those norms or because individual women in a group so governed are actively contesting what *is* normative for their group.

Although the mother identity is differently constructed in different social contexts, what remains constant across all contexts is the nearly cosmic responsibility assigned to women, but not men, for their children's well-being. In the patriarchal, expectations-generating power

9. This figure is up from 10 percent in 1980. The *Times* seems to take the gender disparity for granted, focusing instead on the 4 percent increase. The headline reads, "More and More, the Single Parent Is Dad."

system that advantages men by pressing women into doing the work of child care while at the same time devaluing this work, two different sets of stories are used to constitute the mother identity from the dominant, third-person perspective. One set purports to legitimate the pressive forces requiring women to serve men's interests by explaining why women, and not men, must do the brunt of mothering labor. The other set establishes the norms for child care with which mothers are expected to comply. The first set of stories—the "who" stories—picks out the class of people who are supposed to do the job, while the second— the "how" stories—constitute the job description. Woven in among these are other stories, generated by the preservative forces protecting the patriarchal power arrangement, that draw a sharp line between good mothers and wicked women. The tendency of good mothers to stray over the line then serves as a justification for the massive amounts of social policing that is attendant on the mother identity.

*"Who" stories.* The master narratives that are used to justify requiring women, but not men, to be mothers in the relevant sense often appeal to putative facts about women's and men's natures. In *Emile*, perhaps the best-known "who" story of motherhood, Jean-Jacques Rousseau defends the idealized portrait of the submissive, gentle Sophie on the grounds that "the very law of nature" leaves men uncertain whether they actually sired the children they are expected to care for. From this it supposedly follows that women must be subordinated to men, and while that arrangement is admittedly unjust, the imperfections of men's nature require women to cultivate their natural propensity for enduring injustice (Rousseau 1979, 364, 370). In Allan Bloom's even cruder contemporary retelling of this narrative, men by nature neither need nor desire children. It's women who want them, so women must take care of them. To get their children's fathers to support them while they care for their children, women must first inveigle the fathers into marrying them and then keeping the fathers happy by catering to their needs and wants (Bloom 1987, 115, 128–31).

These stories are taken up primarily by the political right wing, but while other sectors of American society ridicule, dismiss, or ignore them, they continue to exert a certain amount of influence, particularly when coupled with their religious variants in a social climate that is overwhelmingly pronatalist. In many religious traditions there are stories of women—or fig trees—who are cursed because they do not bear fruit, and other stories depicting good women as good just in virtue of

the fact that they are mothers. The story of Mary, mother of Jesus, powerfully equates womanhood with motherhood, and in its representation
of Mary as patient, obedient, and unconditionally loving, also counts as
a "how" story that describes what mothers are supposed to do. And secular pronatalist stories abound, in novels, movies, and television programs that depict womanly fulfillment as maternal fulfillment.

In African-American communities, strong pronatalist forces may
arise in part from traditional understandings whereby becoming a biological mother was a mark of adult status. Patricia Hill Collins quotes
Joyce Ladner's description of how the link between adulthood and
motherhood operates in low-income, urban communities: "If there was
one common standard for becoming a woman that was accepted by the
majority of the people in the community, it was the time when girls
gave birth to their first child. This line of demarcation was extremely
clear and separated the *girls* from the *women*" (Collins 1991, 134).
Collins argues that motherhood remains a symbol of maturity in
African-American culture, but that among the poorest of black women,
having children is also a sign of hope. Deprived of material goods and
many opportunities for self-actualization, motherhood offers hope because children are often all that indigent women have (137).

If master narratives embodying pronatalist values offer positive depictions of women who are mothers, they also buttress these depictions
with their photographic negatives—women who have no children.
"Through the figure of the witch who consorts with the forces of evil,"
Diana Tietjens Meyers observes, "the childless woman is portrayed as
an outcast, and her freedom and vitality are branded wicked. . . . De-
fanged, the witch becomes the more ambiguous figure of the spinster.
As the spinster, the childless woman is portrayed as a failure, for she
has achieved neither of the defining feminine goals, namely, marriage
and motherhood. Yet, she seems more pathetic than odious—narrow,
rigid, and dry, to be sure, but effectively neutralized in her aseptic isola-
tion" (Meyers 2001, 122). These negative representations might be
thought of as anti-"who" stories. They feed the preservative forces that
keep the pronatalist ideology in place, by identifying women who do
not conform to the ideology as unnatural, pathetic, or evil. Not all
childless women are depicted as evil, of course. Many Catholics, for instance, honor women in religious orders who submit themselves to the
discipline of celibacy. What such women are doing, however, is typically understood by setting it within the larger narrative of their symbolic marriage to Christ, to whom they dedicate their sexuality. The

case could be made, however, that aside from the few purely contemplative orders, the work that nuns are expected to do in the world—tending and teaching children, caring for the sick—is largely the work of mothering. It may well be that nuns have escaped some of the opprobrium heaped on other childless women precisely because they have so often devoted themselves to maternal work.

The "who" stories that pick out women for the work of mothering also undergird the social policing that keeps mothers up to their jobs. One way they support this policing function is by dictating *when* women become mothers. Master narratives such as *The Silent Scream,* for example, which characterizes fetuses as unborn children, confer the "mother" identity on women from the earliest stages of pregnancy, as do the narratives of ensoulment that are currently told by the Roman Catholic church. If women are cosmically responsible for child care, and a conceptus is a child, then having an abortion automatically makes you a wicked mother, and wicked mothers must be policed. The best way to police them is by making abortion illegal, or, failing that, by intimidating their providers. But the policing function extends further still, thanks to other master narratives that identify women as mothers even before they have conceived. For instance, the March of Dimes "Think Ahead" campaign offers a story of maternal accountability whereby women, but not men, are to prevent birth defects by taking better care of themselves before sperm and egg ever join to form an embryo. Similarly, the stories of teratogenic hazards in the workplace that have been used to justify keeping women, but not men, from lucrative jobs identify *all* women of childbearing age as irresponsible mothers who must be forced to protect the health of their not-yet-conceived children.[10]

By assigning hypertrophied amounts of child-care responsibility to women, the "who" stories also undergird the social policing of women with actual, living children. The penalties for women who fail to perform the assigned tasks—especially the task of keeping children safe from harm—can be heavy indeed. Arguing that "courts are concerned only with a woman's compliance with an idealized standard of selfless, exclusive motherhood," Dorothy E. Roberts offers as an instance the

---

10. The Johnson Controls corporation, which manufactures automobile batteries, used stories of this kind to keep women from highly remunerative work from 1982 until 1991, when its policy was successfully challenged in court. That biohazards in the workplace can damage men's sperm went unnoticed or was accepted as a risk against which men could be trusted to protect themselves without company supervision. See *Automobile Workers v. Johnson Controls,* 499 U.S. 187, 111 S.Ct. 1196, 113 L.Ed.2d 158 (1991).

story of Denise Maupin, who was convicted by a Tennessee jury in 1991 of aiding and abetting the first-degree murder of her son Michael, who was then two years old. Maupin's crime was to go to her first day of work at a local fast-food restaurant, leaving Michael and his sibling in the care of her boyfriend, Thomas Hale. While she was at work, and apparently acting out of rage *because* she was at work rather than at home looking after the children, Hale beat Michael almost to the point of unconsciousness for wetting his pants. The boy died that night at the hospital. For her failure to protect him, Maupin was sentenced to life imprisonment (Roberts 1999, 39).

News reports of children killed by men in the home also tend to hold women responsible for men's violence. For example, in a *New York Times* article reporting the death of a five-month-old baby who was severely burned by the mother's boyfriend, the focus was solely on the failure of city social workers to supervise the mother adequately (Roberts 1999, 42). That men are violent is taken for granted. Indeed, according to the "who" stories, men's violence is one of the reasons why women must do the work of mothering. If they fail, as Denise Maupin did, the expulsive forces of the patriarchal power system can combine with the system's pressive forces to remove the women from society by incarcerating them for long periods of time.

*"How" stories.* In power arrangements characterized by pressive forces, then, identities are constituted in part by master narratives that pick out a subgroup of people who are to serve the interests of dominant others. At the same time, these "who" stories also assign a certain set of responsibilities to the subgroup: the "who" in question are responsible for their children's well-being. "How" stories, on the other hand, specify precisely how these responsibilities are to be carried out. Where Rousseau-type "who" stories identify *women* in a certain way, "how" stories identify *mothers* in a certain way. By depicting specifically what mothers are expected to do, they tell us how mothers are supposed to be. Master narratives specifying "how" must circulate widely in the larger society if the social group is to be kept in its proper place, and the power arrangement is most stable when group members also draw on these narratives as they construct their identities from the first-person perspective.

The master narratives that most powerfully establish the norms for white, middle-class mothering are the narratives that show such mothers in their proper setting: that of the "traditional" patriarchal family. As many historians of the family have pointed out, the traditional family isn't very old (Nicholson 1997, Mintz and Kellogg 1988). It has evolved from an earlier bourgeois family ideal which itself arose in Europe and the United States only in the 1830s. The earlier ideal, sometimes dubbed the "sentimental" family because it depicts the family as a haven of intimacy and emotional fulfillment, shares many of the features of what is now called the traditional family, differing from it in only two major respects—one having to do with the mother's employment, and the other with the permissibility of step-relationships. Embodied in stories as disparate as Louisa May Alcott's *Little Women*, Clarence Day's *Life with Father*, the "Dick and Jane" readers of the 1950s, and innumerable TV sitcoms from *Leave It to Beaver* to *The Simpsons*, the story of the sentimental family is one of a happy, nuclear household consisting of a committed father who is its head and who goes out to work; a loving, stay-at-home mother who runs the household and takes care of the children; and the children themselves, around whom the household revolves. It is private, sharply marked off from the public sphere (where it is represented by the father), and the labor of maintaining it is divided along strict gender lines (Mintz and Kellogg 1988). What mothers do in the sentimental family is to keep the home clean and attractive, making it a welcome haven for the children and for the fathers who return to it in the evening. Mothers cook and bake, especially for such family holidays as Thanksgiving and birthdays. Mothers nurse their children when they are ill or hurt and comfort them when they are upset, so naturally mothers are always there, whenever their children need them. Mothers provide moral and religious inspiration: they light the *shabbat* candles or are good Christian women. Mothers love their children unconditionally, no matter how their children treat them.

The "traditional" family began to supersede the sentimental ideal in the white middle class when women entered the labor force in large numbers during the Second World War. Except for a short time in the 1950s, when nostalgia for the sentimental ideal and the demands of returning GIs to receive preferential hiring sent women back into the home, the norm for middle-class married women has been to work for pay. As Linda Nicholson reports, "In 1890 in the United States, only 4.6 percent of married women were in the paid labor force. By 1950 the figure had climbed to 23.8 percent. By 1970 it was 40.8 percent. By 1985 it was 54.2 percent. Today, not only do a very high percentage of married women work in the paid labor force, but this is even true of married women with small children" (Nicholson 1997, 35). So, while families in which mothers work violate the norms of the sentimental ideal, they are now considered "traditional," as long as the mother is married to her children's father.

The second way in which the traditional patriarchal family deviates from the sentimental model is that it can contain stepchildren and stepparents, providing that the parents are a heterosexual couple and the household is nuclear. Nicholson argues that people have reconciled the older sentimental model with a divorce rate that now hovers at just above 50 percent of all marriages by "discounting the importance of prior marital history or means by which children have been acquired" (Nicholson 1997, 36). Modified in these two ways, then, the old senti-mental ideal has become the new traditional ideal. It is still patriarchal, although less so; it is still nuclear and private; it is still supposed to be a source of emotional security. And while its mothers may work and re-marry, they are still supposed to be at home when their children need them and to do for them the things that mothers on the sentimental model do.

The master narratives of the new traditional family set the norms not only for how mothers behave but for who counts as a mother. They stipulate, for example, that a child can have only one mother: the woman who gives birth to and rears the child with the material and emotional support of her husband, who is the child's father. In contract pregnancy arrangements, the woman who best conforms to this norm is the father's wife—particularly if she also supplied the egg, fertilized with her husband's sperm, that is carried to term by the hired gestator. In the states where pregnancy contracts are enforceable, it is she, not the gestator, who is almost always declared the legal mother in disputes where the gestator changes her mind and wishes to keep the baby (Oliver 1992, 328). Similarly, in a lesbian partnership, only the woman who actually gives birth to the child is counted as the child's mother, since she is the woman who most resembles the mother of the tradi-tional family. As Mary Lyndon Shanley's research confirms, when a les-bian partnership breaks up, the woman who is not genetically related to the child is routinely denied custody or even visitation rights. "It has proven very difficult," Shanley concludes, "for lesbian co-mothers to obtain legal recognition of their parental status" (Shanley 1999, 178).

Clearly, not all mothers stand in the same relation to these Anglo, middle-class "how" stories. Lesbian mothers, single mothers, women who became mothers postmenopausally via assisted reproductive technology, blue-collar mothers, impoverished mothers, and African-American mothers are not likely to see the norms embedded in these master narratives as pertaining to them. However, as is made clear by the lesbian child-custody struggles and by the case of Denise Maupin, who went to work instead of staying at home with her two-year-old, the courts and powerful others often hold mothers to these norms regardless of how well they fit their actual lives and circumstances. And sometimes the pressive, preservative, dismissive, or expulsive forces of power systems that interact with patriarchy produce additional identity-constituting master narratives that are imposed on mothers who are members of particular social groups.

In African-American communities, for example, the "how" stories of the Mammy, the Matriarch, and the Welfare Mother have been used to justify the forces that require African-American mothers to behave according to racist and sexist norms. The Mammy, once a slave and now a care giver for children of affluent white parents, is a persona created by whites to justify the economic exploitation of domestic servants. "By loving, nurturing, and caring for her white children and 'family' better than her own, the mammy symbolizes the dominant group's perceptions of the ideal Black female relationship to elite white male power" (Collins 1991, 71).

The Matriarch, the strong single mother who supports the household she heads by working outside the home, is a persona created by whites to deny the existence of racism. According to the narratives in which the Matriarch character appears, the reason that African Americans have not achieved racial equality is *not* that they are oppressed by institutions and economic arrangements that favor whites, but that black working mothers emasculate their husbands and fail to supervise their children adequately (Collins 1991, 74). It's these "bad" black mothers who cause, in Daniel Patrick Moynihan's infamous words, "the disintegration of the Negro family" (Moynihan 1965).

The persona of the Welfare Mother, which only became racialized in the 1930s (Gordon 1994, 48), has recently been held hostage to dismissive forces that want nothing to do with her. The Welfare Mother, Collins claims, is "an updated version of the breeder woman image created during slavery" and "provides an ideological justification for efforts to harness black women's fertility to the needs of a changing political economy" (Collins 1991, 76). While the Breeder Woman was valued for her ability to produce children who could then be sold or put

to work, the Welfare Mother produces children who "no longer represent cheap labor but instead signify a costly threat to political and economic stability" (76). The Welfare Mother, being unmarried, also fails
to conform to the master narratives of the new traditional family, and
therefore falls into the category of the "undeserving poor."

This was not always so. In the 1920s impoverished single mothers receiving public assistance were typically taken to be widows, and
throughout the social work literature of the time were identified as
"employees of the state, engaged in the care and training of the father-
less wards of the state" (Gordon 1994, 52). To be sure, these mothers
were policed. Social workers scrutinized their homes and refused aid to
mothers whose households did not conform to middle-class norms. "Illegitimate children or male friends, alcoholic beverages, boarders, or
alien methods of housekeeping and child care might disqualify a home.
In at least one jurisdiction, eligibility was dependent on the children
getting satisfactory school reports" (46). But their mothering work was
valued. Now it is not. From the perspective of the politically powerful,
whose class and racial biases incline them to take little responsibility
for the poor, welfare mothers are not rights-bearers who have already
paid into entitlement programs, as (supposedly) have recipients of Social Security—they are beneficiaries of undeserved governmental
largess, and should be coerced into paying back their benefits through
workfare programs (Fraser 1989, 152–53). The Welfare Mother, like the
Matriarch, is a bad mother. But where the Matriarch is too strong, the
Welfare Mother is too weak. She is depicted not only as the immoral
breeder of illegitimate children, but "as being content to sit around and
collect welfare, shunning work and passing on her bad values to her off-
spring" (Collins 1991, 77).

These three personae and the master narratives associated with them
have been vigorously contested within the African-American community. Collins, for one, has countered them with a "how" story that calls
into question their insistence that mothers have to take full and sole responsibility for the children they bear. In African-American communities, she explains, biological mothers are expected to care for their children, but this responsibility has traditionally been shared with other
women in the extended family or wider community—women she calls
"othermothers" (Collins 1991, 119). Citing a history of othermothering
in many West African, Caribbean, and other black societies that per-
sisted during the period of slavery and in the postbellum rural South,
Collins suggests that women who had no biological children of their

own served a crucial function in shielding vulnerable children from some of the worst damages of racial oppression, and have enjoyed significant social recognition within their communities because of this valued mothering labor (120–22).

On the other hand, some African Americans have demanded that black mothers reconfigure their families so that they conform *more* closely to the traditional, patriarchal norm. In concert appearances and recordings in the early 1990s, for instance, the rap artist Sister Souljah instructed African Americans that the means to achieving authentic blackness crucially involves strong heterosexual and patriarchal family bonds, with all that this implies for the "how" stories that are then supposed to constitute African-American mothers' identities. Louis Farrakhan's Nation of Islam and other black nationalist organizations have also called for "strengthening" black families along the lines prescribed by the new traditional patriarchal ideal. On these views, which Rhonda M. Williams asserts are widely prevalent in the black community, "families are *the* sanctioned site for the reproduction of authentic racial ethnic culture. Healthy families are monogamous, dedicated to masculine authority, and affirm traditional gender roles; unwell families include sexually promiscuous adults and foster female dominance" (Williams 1998, 144). However, when Farrakhan's Million-Man March proposed to fix the crisis of black masculinity by giving African-American men the opportunity to exert their authority over their families and so to rebuild the race, African-American and white feminists joined forces in condemning this "quasi-contractual view that promises men that they can be (seen as) providers, protectors, and unchallenged judges if only they will stay home or at least act fatherly from a distance" (Ruddick 1997, 214).

Whereas black nationalist ideology has been criticized for constructing the mother identity through a narrative that "insufficiently breaks with patriarchical modes of economic, political, cultural (especially familial) and social circulations of power that mimic Euro-American modes," as Wahneema Lubiano puts it (Lubiano 1998a, 234), black male scholars tend to construct the identity by glorifying black mothers—a move that some black women have viewed with almost equal suspicion. By fostering the persona of the "superstrong Black mother," Collins argues, African-American men inadvertently lose sight of the very real costs for African-American women of mothering under conditions of poverty, in the face of deteriorating social support and with no help from the children's fathers. Collins quotes Michele Wallace:

> I remember once I was watching a news show with a black male friend
> of mine who had a Ph.D. in psychology and was the director of an out-
> patient clinic. We were looking at some footage of a black woman. . . .
> She was in bed wrapped in blankets, her numerous small, poorly
> clothed children huddled around her. Her apartment looked rat-in-
> fested, cramped, and dirty. She had not, she said, had heat and hot
> water for days. My friend, a solid member of the middle class now but
> surely no stranger to poverty in his childhood, felt obliged to
> comment . . . "That's a *strong* sister," as he bowed his head in rever-
> ence. (Collins 1991, 117)

Collins believes that African-American women, concerned to present
a united front to dominant white Americans, have been reluctant to
criticize black men's well-intentioned efforts to replace negative white
male narrative constructions with positive black male ones. Nevertheless, she thinks that "how" stories about the "invincible strength and
genius" of the African-American mother can be just as damaging as the
stories about devoted Mammies and feckless Welfare Mothers.

The mother identity, then, has too often fallen afoul of the pressive,
dismissive, and preservative forces coursing through pronatalist, patriarchal, heterosexist, racist, classist, and ageist ideologies, each of which
has contributed stories that constitute the identity according to their
specifications. What is needed are "who" stories that don't insist that
all and only women must mother, and a wider variety of "how" stories
that take the enormous diversity of mothers' circumstances, abilities,
and resources into account. Until these stories are allowed to circulate
widely in the larger community, many mothers will continue to feel
conflicted or besieged, knowing, perhaps, who they would like to be,
but not always very sure of who they are.

## A Picture Holds Us Captive

The morally degrading master narratives that contribute in part to
oppressive group identities create a picture that holds us captive.
When—to return to our opening story—the physicians at Virginia Martin's hospital think about the nurses at all, the picture in their minds,
seemingly so normal and ordinary that it crowds out other possible representations, is that of the loving mother who tends to the bodily and
emotional needs of the sick. The image is latent rather than manifest,

not fully acknowledged even by the doctors themselves, but its latent quality is what gives it much of its power.

There are a number of interesting things to note about this latent picture. First, it is the picture of a character who crops up in a number of stories. She appears in master narratives about virtuous mothers living in traditional, patriarchal families (think of the maternally fulfilled Donna Reed character in *It's a Wonderful Life* who, but for Jimmy Stewart, would have ended up a childless, shriveled, bespectacled librarian). She also appears in master narratives about nursing, from stories of Florence Nightingale's selfless womanly devotion, to Cherry Ames's youthfully impulsive but well-meaning care, to Mother Teresa's saintly effacement of self in the service of others.

Second, because the picture of the nurse-mother is built up out of these various master narratives, it embodies two different sorts of moral norms: norms of *identity* and norms of *response*. Under the guise of nonmoral depiction it prescribes, without seeming to do so, how nurses ought to behave and hence who they ought to be: engrossed, other-directed, gentle, and steadfast nurturers who think with their hearts rather than their heads, who lovingly clean up people's bodily messes, and who make up for the father-doctor's intellectual detachment by providing comfort and emotional security. And again without seeming to do so, the picture directs its spectators (here, the physicians) to respond to what it depicts. What nurses do is women's work, the picture tells them—so while it's necessary and good and somebody's got to do it, it's not important or interesting, which means you don't have to take it or the people who do it seriously.

Third, the patent disparity between the picture's representation of nurses and the behavior of any of the actual nurses at Cranford Community Hospital doesn't count, for those held captive by it, as evidence that the picture is false. Neither Virginia Martin nor the other nurses at the hospital mother their patients; they certainly don't think of them as children, and the work they do is both skilled and important. But because of the power of the latent image, those facts don't stop the physicians from thinking of the picture as an accurate portrayal of nursing identity. Pictures derived from master narratives are "notoriously resistant to the impact of disconfirming instances. . . . [They] seem to circulate and become entrenched in the repertoires of many people and groups in the absence of many, or even, in the case of individuals' beliefs, in the absence of *any* observed instances that might provide a basis for forming beliefs about the behavior or characteristics of a stereotyped group" (Walker 1998, 193). That they're taken to be accurate despite any amount of evidence to the contrary is the reason why these pictures hold us *captive*. Evidence has little impact on them, so the belief that the people they represent are actually "like that" is hard to dislodge. Pictures created by master narratives are so strongly resistant to evidence because what they say about certain groups of people is only common sense, what everybody knows, what you don't have to think about, what's necessarily the case. Single instances to the contrary—even many of them—haven't much power to alter what everybody knows. Indeed, disconfirming instances tend to provoke a normative backlash: things are supposed to be the way the pictures show them to be, so if they aren't, it's they, not the pictures, that have gotten it wrong. Worse yet, even when we know that it's the picture and not the disconfirming instance that's false, the picture can still exert a good deal of power over us.

Fourth, because the physicians' picture of the nurses assigns to them an identity that is required by the pressive forces of an expectations-generating power system, there is a second sense in which it holds people captive: the nurses lose some of their freedom to act. The picture directs the physicians to see the nurses as less than fully formed moral agents, which causes the physicians to act on this perception, which constricts the nurses' moral agency. The picture thus captures the imagination and the captive imagination takes moral hostages. And should the nurses contest the required identity, there are plenty of ways in which the power systems within the hospital keep their complaints from being accorded full cognitive authority. Moreover, if the picture captures the nurses' imagination as well as the doctors', then the nurses will cooperate with the doctors in holding *themselves* morally hostage.

Not all the pictures that hold us captive are oppressive, of course. Some, such as the one Wittgenstein had in mind when he coined the phrase, might allow false beliefs about the world to dominate our imaginations without at the same time diminishing our moral regard for the members of some group. Others might not be false but still hold us captive (as benign jailers, so to speak) because we have never thought about whether we ought to let them inform our beliefs and guide our actions.[11] It might even be the case that we *ought* to be held captive by

---

11. Pictures of this kind, being accurate representations of some state of affairs, presumably encounter no serious evidentiary challenges.

certain pictures in the same way that we ought to consider ourselves bound by certain moral imperatives.

But the pictures that hold us captive are oppressive when they improperly identify certain social groups as useless, dangerous, or necessary means to a more powerful group's ends, since this produces or licenses diminished moral regard for members of the group. Members of the dominant group, guided by the norms in the master narratives that produce the picture, inflict on group members the harm I've been calling deprivation of opportunity. The oncologist brushes off Pilar Sanchez's request to reconsider the decision not to tell her patient Jake that he's dying of leukemia, because the doctor identifies her with the picture of the nurse-mother and knows—everybody knows—that nurse-mothers are to be taken seriously only within the limits of what's expected of them, and not when they act outside those expectations. People within the group, guided by the norms undergirding the picture, inflict on themselves the harm I've called infiltrated consciousness. Virginia Martin doesn't push it when the orthopedic surgeon brushes off her request for the medical consult for the patient with high blood pressure because, to some extent, she agrees with what everybody knows about not needing to take nurse-mothers seriously when they overstep the limits. She doesn't take them seriously then, herself. To the extent that her knowledge joins forces with that of the physicians in undermining her sense of her own worthiness to act, not only is her moral agency constricted, but she's treating herself with contempt.

The moral outlook for both nurses seems rather dire. How might the narratively constructed pictures of nursing that are holding these women captive be resisted? What can be done to repair the damage inflicted on their group identity? The proper tool for this sort of resistance and repair is the counterstory. So now we turn to an examination of the moral structure of the counterstory, paying particular attention to the question of how stories of this kind are to be assessed.

# 5 Counterstories

All things counter, original, spare, strange . . .
—Gerard Manley Hopkins, "Pied Beauty"

The connection between oppression and identity, I have claimed, lies in the master narratives that are generated by the forces circulating within particular systems of oppression, since these stories construct the identities that are required by those systems. The Gypsy of Romance or of the Wild, the Clinically Correct story, the "who" and "how" stories of mothering all identify specific groups of people in ways that mark them as morally undesirable or in need of policing. At the same time, these narratives elicit responses, whether on the part of those others or of the group members themselves, that unjustly constrict the group members' freedom of agency. Identities pick out certain people as candidates for certain treatments, and for the identities we have been considering, the treatments are morally indefensible. If you belong to a group that bears one of the required identities you may be hounded out of town, compelled to give up your job, or blamed for being too weak or too strong. You may think that you should always put others' interests ahead of your own, live in the conviction that there is something seriously wrong with you, or take pride in being the person others perceive you to be. In short, you are too much an object of others' actions, not fully enough a moral agent in your own right.

If agency that has been constricted in this manner is to be freed, the master narratives' morally degrading representations must be resisted. A means must be found for countering the faulty depictions of the members of the oppressed social group so that the members' status as competent moral agents can be affirmed. Counterstories, which root out the master narratives in the tissue of stories that constitute an oppressive identity and replace them with stories that depict the person as morally worthy, supply the necessary means of resistance. Here, resistance amounts to *repair:* the damaged identity is made whole. Through their function of narrative repair, counterstories thus open up the possibility that the person could attain, regain, or extend her freedom of moral agency.

The task of this chapter is to describe the features of a counterstory that allow it to perform its function. I'll proceed in three steps. In part one, I'll distinguish between counterstories and other stories that might serve as alternatives to master narratives, since not all such alternatives do what counterstories are designed to do. This initial pass lets us see what counterstories are by setting them against a background of what they are not. In part two, I'll look to the master narratives themselves to guide our understanding of the features that a counterstory must possess. Since counterstories set out to correct what the master narratives get wrong, an examination of the prevalence and vulnerabilities of master narratives points us to the elements that must be present in a counterstory if it is to repair the damage done to the identity. In part three, I'll offer means for distinguishing between a good counterstory and a bad one. I'll argue that a good counterstory meets the three credibility criteria of correlation to action, strong explanatory force, and heft; that it sets out to repair the group identity as well as the personal identity; and that its aim is to free agency.

Before I begin this discussion of what we might call the moral structure of the counterstory, however, I ought to point out that there is a difference between a counterstory that is well designed for the task of repair and a counterstory that actually succeeds of its aim. To be optimally successful, a counterstory must be culturally digestible and widely circulated, taken up not only by those who are on the receiving end of abusive power arrangements, but also by those who have benefited from those arrangements. People in the dominant group who have accepted the master narratives that identify subgroup members in morally degrading terms must be moved to endorse the counterstory even though they lose privileges, services, or cherished ways of thinking by doing so. In addition, members of the subgroup whose consciousnesses are infiltrated by the same master narratives must come to accept the counterstory as identity-constituting. I'll identify some of the material, political, social, and psychological conditions under which a good counterstory could actually be taken up in these ways, but I won't attempt a comprehensive discussion. Much of the question of what makes a counterstory politically successful is an empirical one, largely a matter for sociologists, psychologists, and other social scientists. As such, it falls outside the scope of my work.[1] For the most part, then, I'll confine myself to considering what makes counterstories

---

1. See Archer 1996, which is a careful and comprehensive examination of the conditions under which oppressive understandings can be shifted.

morally desirable, and I'll include among the desirable counterstories some that aren't politically successful at all. But I'll begin by discussing the difference between counterstories and other alternatives to master narratives.

## Counterstories and Other Alternatives

First, to recapitulate. Personal identities are constituted by the complex interaction of narratives from a first-, second-, and third-person perspective that create an understanding of who someone is. Many of the stories that constitute the identity from each of these perspectives are master narratives and fragments of master narratives—stories, drawn from the cultural store, that circulate widely within a society and embody its shared understandings. Some fragments of master narratives that constitute personal identities are stock *characters*. Others are the well-known *plot templates* that are associated with these characters. When we identify someone in terms of a familiar character, they become intelligible to us because we've seen that sort of character before; similarly, we infer from our knowledge of a stock plot how someone of that sort can be expected to (or is supposed to) behave. Because master narratives are generic, they identify groups of people; individuals derive some portion of their identities from their membership in the group. Many master narratives are benign and indeed socially indispensable, since they figure heavily in our ability to make sense of ourselves and one another. Others are morally compromised or flat-out evil, because they unfairly depict particular social groups as lacking in virtue or as existing merely to serve others' ends.

Not all the stories in the identity-constituting narrative tissue are master narratives, however. As we saw in the case of Noelle Howey's transgendered dad, whose initial attempts at living as a woman produced the effect of a Nick at Nite mom, even morally acceptable master narratives (and not all of hers were) must be mixed judiciously with other identity-constituting stories if the identity is to be credible. One way to mix them is to incorporate the scripts and personae of master narratives into the stories of the more significant acts, events, and experiences in a person's life. These mixtures, although they contain elements of master narratives, are not master narratives themselves. So, for example, when I make sense of my struggle to succeed in business by drawing on the master narrative of the career self, the resulting story will be *my* story, not another master narrative. Similarly, when a person draws on the personae of Martin Luther, Florence Nightingale, or Jesus—all figures from master narratives—in constructing the story of a commitment that partly constitutes the person as a moral agent, that story is not a master narrative. And in the same way, master narratives might be used as templates for the stories that allow a person to make sense of many of her personal characteristics, her social roles, or her relationships, but once the narratives have been tailored to fit the individual, they are no longer master narratives.

Self-constituting stories of this kind, which identify individuals rather than groups, are alternatives to master narratives on one understanding of "alternative"—they are something *other than* a master narrative. But they are clearly something other than a counterstory, too. They don't counter anything. They merely exploit the connective feature of stories, making sense of the particulars of a person's life and characteristics by tying them to the themes, personae, and plots of more general master narratives. These alternative stories personalize the identity that the master narrative leaves generic.

A slightly different alternative to a master narrative is one that need make no use of its connective capacities to link itself with any particular master narrative. Unlike the first alternative, where the story adapts the master narrative so that it conforms to the contours of a particular person's life, this one makes its contribution to the identity without necessarily referring to anything but itself. The story told repeatedly at the family reunion of how little Paul is just like his grandfather, illustrated with instances of little Paul's headstrong behavior, clearly contributes to Paul's identity from a third-person perspective, but it need draw on no master narratives to do so. The story of a personal achievement or a serious illness might likewise contribute to one's identity without connecting to a master narrative. This type of story doesn't constitute the identity by doing something to a master narrative; if it uses such a narrative at all, it does so only in passing. Like the first alternative, this sort of story is not a counterstory. Counterstories counter master narratives. These stories don't.

In both these instances, we've been using a broad understanding of "alternative," where the term is equivalent to "other than." On a narrower understanding, an alternative story isn't simply something other than a master narrative—it's something that *replaces* some portion of a particular master narrative. In this narrower sense, an alternative to a master narrative could be a story with only local circulation or it could be another master narrative. Counterstories are alternatives in this sense, but not all such alternatives are counterstories. Let's return to the example of the stranger in need who identifies you as a Good Samaritan because you have gone out of your way to help her. If, as it happens, you help her during the Christmas season, then, rather than invoking the master narrative of the Good Samaritan, she might instead draw on the story of Good King Wenceslas to make sense of who you are—she uses another master narrative. But this alternative to the story of the Good Samaritan is not a counterstory. Counterstories don't just offer a different but equally viable way of representing you. To one degree or another, they *resist* a representation.

A story that is an alternative to a master narrative in the narrow sense of the word and also resists its representation might still be something other than a counterstory, though. Suppose the adults in an Irish-American family teach the children in the family to take pride in their Irish heritage. The children are brought up on the master narratives of Irish culture—the legends of Finn McCool and other Irish folktales, the story of St. Patrick, Irish ballads, the poetry of William Butler Yeats, and so on. Now suppose that as she enters her teens, one of the children becomes ashamed of the family's immigrant status. She is embarrassed by her parents' pronunciation of English, their keen interest in Irish politics, the food that is served at home, and anything else that marks the family as different from the families of her friends. She repudiates her Irishness, constructing narrative self-understandings that focus on the American character of her experiences, roles, and relationships. The stories by which she constitutes her American identity are stories that resist the Irish master narratives, but they are not counterstories. Counterstories set out to *repair* damage to an identity, but the teenager's stories don't engage in the act of repair. She intends that they should, of course. Her stories are meant to repair perceived damage to her own identity and perhaps also to the identities of other Irish Americans. Since there is nothing shameful about her Irish ancestry, though, there is nothing here that needs to be repaired. The identity hasn't been damaged. If anything, she herself is damaging it by developing identity-constituting narratives that represent her Irishness as something to be ashamed of.

Note that in both these examples of alternatives to master narratives in the narrow sense, what disqualifies them from being counterstories is that they stand in for the wrong kind of master narrative. In the Wenceslas example, a benign and indeed admirable narrative persona replaces another that is equally benign and admirable. In the Irish-American example, the "I'm an American" stories replace a set of master narratives which, although they may be flawed, nevertheless credibly represent a group of people in terms that command respect. These aren't the sorts of master narratives that counterstories go after. The proper target of a counterstory is a master narrative that has been generated by an abusive power system to impose on a particular group an identity the system requires.

Again, though, not every story that goes after this sort of master narrative is a counterstory. Take, for example, the story that informs the romantic movement of the nineteenth century, perhaps most visibly in Schiller's "An die Freude" and Wordsworth's "Ode." According to this story, civilized man comes into the world trailing clouds of glory, but soon loses his innocence because he is alienated from nature. He longs to be reunited with God, his fellow man, and himself. In some variants on this story, the foil to civilized man is the Noble Savage, who is at one with nature, "naïve" rather than "sentimental," good because primitive and hence uncorrupted by civilization. This story is clearly an alternative, in the narrow sense, to the master narratives that characterize "savages" in less uplifting terms. The story surrounding the persona of the Noble Savage replaces the stories representing Native Americans as vicious, treacherous, and idle with a far loftier image, and thus sets out to repair rather than further damage the identity of an oppressed subgroup. But the story of the Noble Savage isn't a counterstory, because it doesn't aim to free the moral agency of the people it depicts. Instead, like the story of the Gypsy of Romance that is its cousin, it identifies Native Americans as Other, as outside the moral community, as primitive rather than fully human. It's not just that the story doesn't repair the identity as well as it should. What keeps it from being a counterstory is that it's no part of the story to allow members of the subgroup access to the opportunities that are available to the dominant group, and this constricts the subgroup members' freedom to act. By contrast, counterstories set out to free a person's moral agency rather than constrict it.

There is a final alternative to a master narrative that cannot be classified as a counterstory, even though it both resists and replaces a narrative that is oppressive, rehabilitates a damaged identity, and frees a person's agency. Here I am thinking, for instance, of the stories that have recently reidentified the computer hacker. Once widely depicted as brainy but socially inept—the pasty-faced, flabby or skinny adolescent who dreams of dating the prom queen but never does—the new hacker image is that of a sexy, well-dressed man of action, hip but dangerous and exciting to know. He is Keanu Reeves in *The Matrix* and Tom Cruise in *Mission: Impossible*, cool, confident, and clearly his own man. The upgraded image is arguably at least partly attributable to changing social attitudes toward computers, reflecting Americans' healthy respect for the vast fortunes that are made in the Silicon Valley, but reflecting too a greater familiarity with and reliance on a technology that many of us have come to take for granted. To the extent that the earlier, "nerd" identity was generated by preservative forces that fed people's anxieties about technology gone out of control, and by dismissive forces that ridiculed and marginalized people engaged in activities the dominant group didn't understand, that identity was an oppressive one. The new stories constitute the identity in a way that commands respect. But still they are not counterstories, because they aren't acts of purposeful self-definition. They simply reflect a shift in a cultural understanding. Counterstories, by contrast, don't merely *reflect* a shift in understanding. They set out to *cause* a shift.

A point made by Bernard Williams may be usefully applied here. In *Ethics and the Limits of Philosophy*, Williams argues that for a "thick" moral concept to be action guiding, there must be a socially shared evaluative perspective in which the concept can be put to active use (Williams 1985, 141). Because a concept such as, say, "honorable samurai" is world-guided, it can be correctly applied to certain activities, beliefs, and self-understandings only against a backdrop of specific religious values and metaphysical commitments shared by a society, since it's this backdrop that gives the concept its evaluative point. When the backdrop changes sufficiently, the concept loses that point. Cultural shifts that cause certain concepts to fall out of use can also cause identities associated with those concepts to fall out of use. In the United States at the start of the twenty-first century, the samurai identity is simply not a practical identity for anyone. For that reason, there is no socially shared perspective from which honor as the samurai understood it can function as a term of moral praise. What rendered the samurai identity obsolete and is now doing the same for the hacker-nerd identity are *not* new identity-constituting stories but rather shifts in the shared cultural background. Because the new hacker stories aren't purposive acts of moral self-definition, they aren't counterstories.

There are, no doubt, other alternatives to master narratives that can't be considered counterstories, but by clearing away the types of stories that I have identified here, we can get a better idea of what is left standing. We're now in a position to make some very general observations about counterstories. To begin with, they are identity-constituting stories that have a necessary relationship to certain types of master narratives. Second, the relationship is one of varying degrees of resistance.

Third, the master narratives resisted are those that are generated by oppressive forces within an abusive power system, and which impose on a subgroup an identity that marks its members as morally defective. Fourth, counterstories set out to repair the damage that has been inflicted on an identity by an oppressive master narrative. Fifth, through their function of repair, counterstories aim at freedom of moral agency. Sixth, counterstories are acts of purposive moral self-definition, even if at first they are not taken up self-consciously. And finally, it should be noted that a counterstory could itself be a master narrative, though it never oppresses the individual it identifies. Indeed, optimally successful counterstories *must* be master narratives, since success consists precisely in the counterstory's becoming widely circulated and socially shared.

## Master Narratives: The Lay of the Land

To understand more specifically what a counterstory must do to repair an identity damaged by an oppressive master narrative, it's necessary first to get a clear sense of the strengths and weaknesses of master narratives. The strengths tell us what a counterstory is up against, while the weaknesses show us the most promising avenues of resistance. In this section, then, we'll first examine the features of master narratives that account for their prevalence and durability, and then we'll see how some of these same features can leave a master narrative vulnerable to a counterstory. It will quickly become apparent that different kinds of oppressive master narratives have different strengths and weaknesses, depending on the nature of the forces that generated them and on whether the narrative purports to justify or to hide those forces. These differences explain why a one-size-fits-all counterstory is inadequate to the task of resistance. There can, then, be no cookbook description of how to create a counterstory. Each must be tailored to the particular master narrative it aims to resist.

### Strong Points: Bulwarks and Bridges

Master narratives retain their tenacious hold on a culture for a number of interconnected reasons: they are organic ensembles that grow and change, they constitute a world view, and they assimilate opposition. In addition, oppressive master narratives are often epistemically rigged. Taken in combination, these features produce a formidable resiliency and it's this, as well as their prevalence, that makes them so hard to uproot.

*Organic ensembles.* As is perhaps apparent by now, the term 'master narrative' is really only a *façon de parler*, since in many instances it doesn't designate any single narrative with a specific plot and a fixed cast of characters. Some master narratives actually *are* stories in the conventional sense of the word: the story of Adam and Eve, the Christmas story, "Sleeping Beauty," and *Hamlet* are all master narratives in English-speaking cultures. But most master narratives aren't so much stories as ensembles of repeated themes that take on a life of their own. Fragments of history, biography, film, fables, jokes, and similar narrative forms ring changes on the theme, as do proverbs, music, advertising slogans, and other cultural artifacts. Indeed, master narratives that are conventional stories often ring changes on the theme as well. "Sleeping Beauty," for instance, itself a master narrative, is nestled within the larger master narrative of "boy meets girl, boy overcomes obstacles, boy wins girl for his own." Master narratives are capacious, as cluttered and untidy as a Victorian attic, but unlike the attic they are dynamic, evolving in their own new directions.

The master narrative of the Gypsy of Romance, to take just one example, is a cultural accretion that is built up of all sorts of things—among them, Victor Hugo's portrayal of Esmeralda in *The Hunchback of Notre Dame*, the picture of the swarthy *Rom* on the lid of the tobacco can, the song of the Gypsy Rover, the child's Halloween costume, Liszt's *Zigeunerlieder*. The master narrative of the African-American Matriarch contains politician's speeches, *Amos 'n' Andy*'s Ruby Begonia character, "The St. Louis Blues," and other such items. These accretions allow the narrative to grow, but they also allow it to change its course. As the evolution of the master narrative of the Breeder Woman into the narrative of the Welfare Mother demonstrates, an altered political economy or other social contingency can push a master narrative in a new direction. What moves it along are additional images, stories, songs, and slogans.

Master narratives take on a fresh vigor with each new accretion, but they are also strengthened by their ties to other master narratives. We've already seen how the narratives that constitute the transsexual identity in medical terms are closely intertwined with the narratives that establish the norms for 'man' and 'woman' in patriarchal power systems. These same narratives, working in concert with the master narratives of the new traditional family, give aid and comfort to the narratives that constitute the oppressive "mother" identity—and these in turn contribute to the oppressive "nurse" identity. As we've also seen, the master narratives that allow the citizens of a nation-state to understand who they are by sharply dividing "us" from "not-us" have given crucial support to the narratives that damage the Gypsy identity.

By interlocking in these ways, master narratives reinforce one another, just as the items within a master narrative do. Because master narratives can incorporate an enormous diversity of even the humblest items in the cultural store, and because they can link themselves to any number of other master narratives that do the same thing, these stories infiltrate every corner of a society and lodge there tenaciously.

*World view.* Precisely because they are so ubiquitous, the master narratives of a society allow its members to understand who they are with respect to that society, as well as how the world works. As Alasdair MacIntyre puts it,

> It is through hearing stories about wicked stepmothers, lost children, good but misguided kings, wolves that suckle twin boys, youngest sons who receive no inheritance but must make their own way in the world and eldest sons who waste their inheritance on riotous living and go into exile to live with the swine, that children learn or mislearn both what a child and what a parent is, what the cast of characters may be in the drama into which they have been born and what the ways of the world are. Deprive children of stories and you leave them unscripted, anxious stutterers in their actions as in their words. Hence there is no way to give us an understanding of any society, including our own, except through the stock of stories which constitute its initial dramatic resources. (MacIntyre 1984, 216)

The stock of stories creates a picture of the world that is both comprehensive and reasonably unified because the narratives within that stock are not only wide-reaching but mutually reinforcing. A theme— say, that women are to be ruled by men—plays itself out not only in the master narratives of the patriarchal family but in the master narratives of modern science, which figure nature as feminine and reason as masculine, and represent man as dominating Mother Nature (Lloyd 1993, 10–17); in the narratives that feminize "lower" races (Rooney 1991, 89); in the narratives that prescribe what categories of men may have sexual access to what categories of women (MacKinnon 1987, 141–43); and in countless other master narratives as well. One master narrative thus confirms another, and the interlocking, intertwining web of these narratives creates a plausible world view.

Wielding the now famous metaphor of the "web of belief," W. V. O. Quine and J. S. Ullian remind us that "beliefs typically rest . . . on further beliefs" (Quine and Ullian 1978, 127). Their insight can usefully be extended to illuminate how narratives operate within world views. As with beliefs, some parts of a society's world view depend on other parts. The stories that lie farthest out on the periphery of this narrative web can be given up without much damage to the overall structure, but the closer the story is to the center, the more it supports. Tear out one strand there and a great deal of the web will have to be rebuilt. Since the beliefs at the center of the web are taken deeply for granted, they are hard to dislodge even in the face of evidence that calls them into question. As Quine and Ullian point out, though, this conservatism isn't always a bad thing. Indeed, they consider the reluctance to dismantle the framework of our most fundamental understandings to be one of the epistemic virtues (66).

Not all the master narratives we accept reach all the way into the center of our web of belief, but many do, and others are deeply entangled with these. That is why, as Diana Tietjens Meyers claims, oppressive master narratives are uprooted from people's belief systems only at great cost. "What is at stake in the perpetuation of culturally entrenched figurations of socially excluded groups is nothing less than a society's understanding of the human species and its place in the universe. . . . Even people who are victimized by these very figurations have reason to hesitate to overturn them. Insofar as members of socially excluded groups share the dominant culture's world view, their world view hangs in the balance, as well" (Meyers 1994, 54).

*Assimilation of opposition.* The intertangled web of master narratives possesses the ability to keep itself intact, not only because its roots reach down to our most fundamental beliefs, but because—like the pictures that hold us captive—it is capable of swallowing up disconfirming instances, complaints, and other forms of opposition. Master narratives' ability to respond to opposition is one of the ways in which they take on a life of their own. In this, they resemble the Borg—a relentless and enormously powerful character in the late TV series *Star Trek: The Next Generation*—which lives by attacking and then absorbing other creatures and even whole civilizations into its neural network, pro-

claiming as it does so, "Resistance is futile. You will be assimilated."
Master narratives assimilate resistance by enveloping it with plausible
stories. Some of these stories are benign responses to benign master
narratives: a finding that can't be accommodated by the theory is explained away by pointing out that the experiment lacked the proper
controls, or by attributing the aberration to a faulty memory or a trick
of perspective. Frequently, though, these stories deny the validity of the
thing the master narrative can't accommodate by undermining the cognitive authority of the person who is in a position to point out the incompatibility—a move that is often suspect.

One morally dubious way to undermine cognitive authority is to
blame the victim. A strategy for doing this is to deny the victim's complaints of being harmed and to accuse the victim of imagining things or
of being oversensitive (Harvey 1999, 81). Suppose that an airline passenger in a wheelchair challenges the master narrative that represents
physically disabled people as mentally disabled as well. The passenger
points out that, instead of speaking to her directly, the flight attendants
keep asking her traveling companion about the special accommoda-
tions she requires. The master narrative can assimilate this complaint
by wrapping it in a further story that characterizes the passenger as
pushy, or as the sort of person who imagines slights where none are intended. By sending out an offshoot that envelops the complaint in a
plausible subplot, the master narrative in effect dismisses the *reason*
for the complaint by assigning it a discreditable *cause*: namely, a defect
in the complainant's character.

A second form of victim-blaming is to grant that the victim has been
harmed, but to dismiss the harm as nonmoral and to claim that the victim has overreacted or is thin-skinned (Harvey 1999, 81). Since these
are moral failings, while the original harm is represented as nonmoral,
this response to opposition, like the previous one, puts the victim at a
disadvantage. Here, for example, the master narratives that are generated by the dismissive forces of racism might throw out a story that
weaves itself around the complaints of a black man who has on several
occasions been unable to hail a taxi in New York City. The spin the
story puts on his actions is that while he's understandably frustrated
and inconvenienced, he's also slightly paranoid—he's one of those people who thinks that *everything's* a racist conspiracy.

A third form of victim-blaming is to acknowledge that there was
moral harm but accuse the victim of having provoked the harm—the
classic example of this being the still too frequent response of police

and hospital staff to someone who has been raped. The master narratives that play out the theme of men's dominion over women can assimilate a complaint of rape by tying it up with an offshoot that makes the victim appear reckless or even psychologically disturbed. "The first staff member who saw me was a psychiatrist," recalls one rape victim. "His first words were, 'Haven't you really been rushing toward this very thing all your life?' He knew nothing about me, nothing! I had never been to a psychiatrist" (quoted in Harvey 1999, 82).

And a fourth form of victim-blaming is to acknowledge that there was moral harm and the agent was at fault, but to insist that the victim made things worse by how she acted or failed to act (Harvey 1999, 84). So, for example, the master narrative that assigns impossible amounts of responsibility for the care of children to their mothers could generate a further narrative that casts Denise Maupin's boyfriend in the role of the villain for having killed her two-year-old son while she was at work, but still portrays her as guilty of murder because she failed to protect the boy.

Victim-blaming is only one of master narratives' strategies for absorbing opposition. When it's someone other than the victim who complains, a master narrative can invoke the personae of the outside agitator, the rabble-rouser, the race-traitor, the prig. An even more effective means of assimilating resistance, perhaps, is for the master narrative to attach to itself the story that depicts complainers as socially inferior— they are "bounders," or "non-U," as the British say; they don't understand how "we" do things, and this is a sign that they aren't one of us.

*Epistemic rigging.* Any master narrative—even a benign one—possesses the Borg-like capacity to assimilate resistance by wrapping a narrative tendril around people or facts that call the master narrative into question. But oppressive master narratives in particular tend to meet the problem of opposition by stopping it before it starts. Rather than absorb resistance, they keep it from arising in the first place. As they construct the identities required by abusive power systems, these narratives hide the forces that subjugate or marginalize certain groups of people so that nothing morally objectionable appears to be going on. The resulting story is so smooth and slippery that the opposition can't grab hold of it.

Some master narratives hide the existence of coercion by *naturalizing* an oppressive identity. Naturalizing an identity is a matter of making it seem inevitable that certain groups of people must occupy certain places in society. Charles Mills has argued that this is how racial identities were constructed. The European expeditions of conquest in the Americas and then in Asia, Africa, and the Pacific were at first justified by the Catholic Church on religious grounds. If, by the natural light, a group of indigenous peoples didn't see the reasons for embracing Christianity, this proof of their "bestial irrationality" (Mills 1997, 22) licensed waging war against them, taking their lands away from them, and enslaving them. But Enlightenment morality and political thought couldn't officially countenance a religious justification for its New World conquests. Instead, it substituted "race" for "infidel" as a way of distinguishing the civilized from the subhuman, thereby setting up "a two-tiered moral code with one set of rules for whites and another for nonwhites" (23).

The substitution was advantageous in one important respect. While "infidels" who were enslaved might convert to Christianity and thereby undercut the religious justification for oppressing them, nonwhites could not undergo a similar conversion. Since, as Margaret Urban Walker remarks, "nothing denaturalizes situations quicker than evidence of coercion into them, the most effective implementation of naturalized identities is making them conditions of birth, ceasing at death. . . . Physical features or marks, body-types or conditions, are the very best bases for assignment at birth. It is then as if the individual's identity had come into the world with the individual, due to some straightforward fact about her or him" (Walker 1998, 171). The no-exit/no-entry identity of race simulated inevitability much better than did a religious identity, and the semblance of inevitability concealed the pressive, preservative, dismissive, and expulsive forces that allowed Europeans to vanquish the indigenous peoples of the New World.

Other master narratives *privatize* an identity (Walker 1998, 172). Confining groups of people to private spaces, in a way that makes it seem reasonable that they should be so confined, hides them from view and makes neglectful, unkind, or violent treatment of them disappear behind closed doors. Narratives of privatization, like those of naturalization, don't acknowledge the presence of the oppressive practice. Instead, they focus all the attention on the dominant players so that what's happening over there in private passes unnoticed. For example, narratives with courtship and marriage plots—"Cinderella," *Gone with the Wind*—attend so thoroughly to the norms of heterosexuality that same-sex relationships simply don't exist. We don't notice, speak of, or participate in such things. Conversely, when people who desire same-sex relationships try to circulate their own self-constituting stories in the public spaces of the dominant culture, master narratives generated by heterosexism portray them as exhibitionists or narcissists: they haven't the decency to keep their private lives private. It's by means of the epistemic mechanism of privatization that President Clinton's "don't ask, don't tell" policy for gays in the military achieved its seeming legitimacy.

Still other master narratives *normalize* an identity (Walker 1998, 172–73). Identities are normalized when the norms that purport to regulate certain kinds of behavior in fact create the identity. The identity is established narratively through stories focusing on the behavior that is expected under certain conditions, which deflects attention away from the conditions themselves. People become so intent on making sure that they or others are conforming to the norms for how to behave that they don't think to wonder if the conditions under which they are supposed to behave that way actually obtain, or whether they ought to obtain. The "how" stories constituting the "mother" identity concentrate on what mothers are supposed to do, matter-of-factly assuming, without dwelling on it, that mothering is women's work. Similarly, Booth Tarkington's *Penrod*, which is connected to master narratives of racism, matter-of-factly assumes that African Americans' raison d'être is to serve white folk and provide comic relief. In Penrod's world, *somebody's* got to be the yardman or the laundress, and they've got to do it with large helpings of charm and a bit of that old soft shoe. The focus on what black folk are supposed to do keeps us from asking why *they've* got to do it, or what might be wrong with imposing certain sanctions if they don't.

It seems, then, that counterstories are up against a formidable foe. The master narratives they set out to resist are capable of hiding what ought to be opposed, of absorbing such opposition as might be offered, of penetrating so deeply into a belief-system as to be uprooted only at great cost, of spreading their nets so widely across the culture that localized resistance can make no headway against them. Given their prevalence, toughness, and elasticity, it would seem that no counterstory could effectively engage these narratives. Yet we have seen that Gypsies, transsexuals, and mothers have vigorously contested the oppressive master narratives that partly constitute their identities. How is this contestation possible? This is a question about the respects in which master narratives are *vulnerable* to counterstories.

## WEAK POINTS: TENSIONS, FISSURES, AND GAPS

For all their many strengths, oppressive master narratives have at least three major defects, each of which may be conceptualized as a gap or an opening that lets a counterstory in. The first opening lies in the cracks among the many cultural accretions that, together, form the master narrative. The second opening lies in the poor fit between one master narrative and the others to which it is connected. And the third opening lies in the gap between what a master narrative demands of certain people and what those people actually do or are.

*Tensions within.* Most master narratives are not unified wholes. While the hodgepodge character of the maxims, sermons, stories, songs, commercials, and other elements that form the thematic ensemble contributes to the prevalence and tenacity of these narratives, the same quality of *bricolage* also opens avenues within the narrative that are vulnerable to a counterstory. The reason is that the elements of the ensemble don't all pull together. Tensions often exist among them, and it's the business of a counterstory to take advantage of that fact.

Consider just one of several master narratives used in Southern Baptist churches to exclude women from the pulpit. Mary Caldwell, herself an ordained Southern Baptist minister, argues that it's not the Bible per se but a particular interpretation of the Bible that can be thought of as the master narrative embodying the shared understanding in the life of the church. "Many Baptists believe Scripture is to be read, and followed, literally," says Caldwell, and on this literal interpretation, women are prohibited from church leadership (Caldwell 1999, 5). The primary text that is usually invoked is 1 Timothy 2:12, "I permit no women to teach or to have authority over men; she is to keep silent." But, as Caldwell points out, in Acts 18:26 a woman is portrayed as speaking publicly and is not condemned for doing so. Moreover, Paul forbids women to adorn themselves with "braided hair, or gold, or pearls, or costly array" (1 Timothy 2:9), but this prohibition is now not heeded literally. The tension that is created by a literal reading of verses of Scripture that pull in different directions, and the further tension caused by insisting on a literal reading of some verses of Scripture but not others, can be exploited by a counterstory. By engaging with the master narrative at these particular points, the counterstory can undermine the credibility of some of its parts. Note, by the way, that the literalist interpretation of the Bible constitutes a world view for Baptists, and as such it resides near the center of the narrative web. But even master narratives of this kind are susceptible to counterstories, because portions of the narrative are in tension with one another.

To take another example of internal inconsistency, consider the Clinically Correct story that constitutes an oppressive transgendered identity. One part of the story represents the sex-change operation as permitting a person with gender dysphoria to live more honestly, with greater accord between the person's subjective sense of gender and the person's bodily appearance. But another part of the story encourages the person to lie—to "construct a plausible history" that represents the person as having lived in the desired gender all along. The dissonance between these two parts of the story creates a soft spot that is vulnerable to a counterstory, but it isn't the only soft spot. Another portion of the story represents the moment of the sex-change surgery as the point at which the MTF transsexual becomes a woman and the FTM transsexual becomes a man, but this is contradicted by the portion of the story that insists that transsexuals aren't really men or women, no matter what they do. Counterstories can dig into either or both of these places where the parts don't agree, and so call the master narrative into question.

*Tensions among.* Just as there are gaps and inconsistencies *within* a given master narrative, so are there inconsistencies *among* interconnected master narratives. When several master narratives work together to constitute a world view, a counterstory can be lodged in the fissures and cracks that are formed at the interstices, since the narratives are almost sure not to fit together smoothly. Let's return to the master narratives that are used to keep Southern Baptist women out of the pulpit. Caldwell observes that, in addition to the literal interpretation of Scripture, one of the narratives that constitutes the Southern Baptist group identity is the Protestant story about the "priesthood of all believers"—a narrative that represents every Christian as a priest in his or her own right. According to this story, "each person is competent to read, understand, and interpret Scripture, to communicate personally and directly with God, and be guided individually and directly by the Holy Spirit. These notions are sometimes referred to as 'soul liberty,' and the logical expression of such views would hold that if a woman believes she is called by God to ordination, no other believer has the right to question her call." As Caldwell points out, "this situation creates a contradiction that few Baptists are willing to acknowledge" (Caldwell 1999, 5). There is surely a tension between the master narrative that depicts all Baptists, including Baptist women, as authorized by God to decide for themselves whether they have received the call to ordination, and the master narrative of Holy Writ, which in First Timothy, at any rate, prohibits women from speaking in church. If a counterstory is inserted between these two contradictory narratives, it might be able to loosen their grip on Baptist women's identity. Even when a master narrative is entrenched at the center of one's web of belief, as this one is, some portion of it can be dislodged by setting a counterstory between it and another master narrative that is at odds with it.

*Prescription and description.* The final weakness of an oppressive master narrative lies in the gap between the norms of conduct that it prescribes for a particular class of people and how such people actually behave. Oppressive master narratives depict groups of people as engaged in certain activities, but because these depictions are really prescriptions in disguise, there is a difference between the narrative's representation of the group and what members of the group actually do. So, for instance, the patriarchal master narratives that constitute gender identity contain such maxims as "a lady never contradicts" and "real men don't ask for directions," which duplicitously purport to represent an actual state of affairs. In point of fact, however, ladies sometimes do contradict and even he-men have been known to ask for directions, so there is a lack of fit between prescription and practice. The lack of fit creates an opening into which a counterstory can be inserted.

Here it might be objected that master narratives' ability to absorb disconfirming evidence was just described as one of their greatest strengths. As we've seen repeatedly, oppressive master narratives are notoriously evidence-resistant. They run roughshod over what actually happens in the world, papering over or distorting the inconvenient facts that might call the narrative's credibility into question, and undermining the cognitive authority of people who are in a position to point out those inconvenient facts. How, then, is the lack of fit between what they prescribe and how things actually are a weakness? It is a weakness because no oppressive master narrative can absorb *all* disconfirming evidence—there is simply too much of it. No matter what the narrative distorts or papers over, there are always more inconvenient facts that it hasn't yet caught up with, and these are visible from some perspective or other.

We can see how the incongruity between prescription and practice is generated by the "who" stories that assign responsibilities to certain groups of people on the basis of "facts" about their natures that aren't facts at all. Allan Bloom's "who" story of why women, but not men, must mother, depicts men as by nature neither needing nor wanting children, while women do. On those grounds, Bloom absolves men of responsibility for the care of children and imposes it all on women. The gap between Bloom's portrayal of men and women and the far more complicated picture of what individual men and women actually think and feel lets a counterstory get a purchase here. Any master narrative that falsely naturalizes an identity is vulnerable to a counterstory, because the master narrative's representation of the group will fail to capture morally salient details of how group members in fact behave. When a narrative is epistemically rigged in this way, a counterstory can work its way inside the rigging.

If the difference between what master narratives assert and how people actually behave leaves an opening that can be filled by a counterstory, so does master narratives' silence about the conditions under which people actually live their lives. The master narrative about the African-American Matriarch who undermines her husband's masculinity, for example, carefully diverts attention away from the patterns of child-rearing in a patriarchal system that make it easy for fathers to absent themselves. When fathers are present neither as distant providers nor as hands-on care givers, mothers and othermothers must assume both roles. The absence of fathers necessitates strong mothers. But by making it appear as if single black mothers deliberately choose to take on all the responsibility for familial breadwinning and child tending so that they can emasculate their husbands and cause "the disintegration of the Negro family," the Matriarch narrative omits something important about the conditions under which many African-American women have to mother.

Similarly, by representing it as a shame that Gypsies should be cooped up in a town rather than roving where their fancy dictates, the master narrative of the Gypsy of Romance conceals the dismissive forces of an oppressive power system that compel Gypsies to stay on the move. The story depicts the subgroup as exercising choices, just as the Matriarch story does, but this is a way of maintaining silence about the coercive conditions that actually govern many Gypsies' lives. Like

Bloom's narrative of mothering, the Matriarch and Gypsy narratives are epistemically rigged. When that is the case, there is something morally discreditable that the narrative is trying to conceal. The narrative's strength lies in doing so successfully, but the very fact that something is hidden is a weakness that a counterstory can exploit.

## How Counterstories Resist

The cracks and fissures within and among master narratives, and the gap between the oppressive narratives' description of certain people and what those people actually do and are, allow a counterstory to get an initial purchase on an identity-constituting story that needs to be resisted. But the counterstory then has to do something to interfere with some portion of the master narrative. What it does can vary greatly, depending on which sort of opening gives the counterstory its purchase, what the master narrative is doing to falsify the identity, and which part of the master narrative the counterstory is taking on.

Just as it's a mistake to conceptualize master narratives as single, unified stories, so is it mistaken to think of counterstories as full-blown stories that preexist their encounter with any given master narrative. Counterstories come into being through a process of ongoing engagement with the narratives they resist. Many of them start small, like a seed in the crack of a sidewalk, but they are capable of displacing surprising chunks of concrete as they grow.

How much of the sidewalk a counterstory displaces is a function of the degree to which it resists the master narrative. Because the purpose of a counterstory is to repair an identity, the resistance it offers must, at a minimum, aim to dislodge some portion of a master narrative from a person's understanding of who she herself is, even if there is no attempt to push the counterstory into the broader community. Maximal resistance consists in aiming to uproot a master narrative altogether, so that even the members of the dominant group stop using it to identify a subgroup. Roughly, then, we can distinguish three levels of resistance: refusal, repudiation, and contestation. To *refuse* a master narrative is to deny that it applies to oneself and to tend one's own counterstory, perhaps without serious effort or any hope that others will take it up. To *repudiate* a master narrative is to use the self-understanding arising from a counterstory to oppose others' applying the narrative to oneself, but the opposition is piecemeal. To *contest* a master narrative is to oppose it with a counterstory both publicly and systematically.

*Refusal.* Within a subgroup that recognizes its subjugation or exclusion, there can be counterstories circulating for the group members, but not outside the group. These counterstories run parallel with the master narratives that configure the group identity according to the requirements of the dominant group. Subgroup members are conscious of the need to cope with the expectations set by the master narratives, but they refuse to see themselves as the master narratives depict them. The point of counterstories that *refuse* master narratives is not to change the dominant perception of the group—it's to shift how individuals within the group themselves understand who they are. These stories are not for general consumption. They are developed to uproot some portion of a master narrative from the group members' self-conception, and so to repair the damage of an infiltrated consciousness. The audience for this sort of counterstory is the members of the subgroup.

Consider, for example, how women in a sexist workplace are likely to be identified by their male coworkers. The master narratives generated by the pressive, dismissive, and preservative forces of patriarchy require women to dress in ways that men find sexually attractive, to defer to men, to make the coffee and do the photocopying. Women therefore have to choose whether to go along with these sexist expectations. Should they use nail polish? Wear something feminine? Laugh at the joke about the dumb blonde? Spend their lunch hour doing personal errands for their boss? From their own point of view, women so positioned could develop a counterstory that allows them to understand themselves differently from the way the patriarchal master narratives depict them. Using the self-understanding that is partly constituted by the counterstory, a female employee might think to herself, "We have to work with these guys who don't get it, but that doesn't mean we don't know what's going on. Sure, we give them what they want and make them feel important. It's the game we play so we can get around them. Let them think we're sex kittens if it makes them happy—that's not who I am to me."

Counterstories that refuse an oppressive identity offer only minimal amounts of resistance to the master narratives they counter. Questions therefore arise about them. Is the person who creates this sort of counterstory kidding herself? Is it possible to adopt a strategy of accommodation without seriously compromising one's sense of who one is? In some circumstances this sort of counterstory may well be an improvement over other possible alternatives, but they cannot free the person's moral agency altogether, because they don't repair the identity from the

third-person perspective. The person will therefore continue to suffer
the harm of deprivation of opportunity.

*Repudiation.* Members of a subgroup who wish to repudiate a master
narrative don't merely deny that the master narrative is identity-constituting from their own point of view—they use the self-conception that
is shaped by a counterstory to try, in limited ways, to shift dominant
understandings of who they are. Counterstories that repudiate master
narratives offer a patchwork form of resistance, bucking the narratives
in certain situations but not in others. The point of the counterstory is
to limit the amount of damage inflicted on the identity from a third-
person as well as a first-person point of view. The counterstory thus attempts to repair the damage of deprivation of opportunity as well as infiltrated consciousness, but it's a spot-repair job. The audience for
counterstories that *repudiate* master narratives is not only the members of the subgroup who bear the oppressive identity, but also some
members of the dominant group.

   To return to the example of the sexist workplace, let's suppose our female employee draws certain lines, pointedly withholding the girlish
responses that are expected of her. In doing so, she is sending her
coworkers a message: What does my sweater have to do with this project? How does knowing with whom I spent the evening help us to meet
our production quotas? The counterstory guides the woman's attempts
to reidentify herself in her coworkers' eyes, but she repudiates their
story of who she is only when their treatment of her oversteps a boundary she has set for herself.

*Contestation.* Members of a subgroup who contest a master narrative
use the self-understanding generated by their counterstory for the political purpose of challenging, in the public domain, the dominant perception of the subgroup. Counterstories that contest a master narrative
offer wholesale resistance, saying, in effect, "We don't buy that story. It
oppresses us. Now you're going to hear what *we* have to say about who
we are." The point of the counterstory is to repair systematically the
damage done to the identity from both the first-person and the dominant perspective. The audience for counterstories that contest master
narratives is thus the members of the subgroup and the members of the
dominant group. The counterstories of the black power movement and
those of gay and lesbian activists are examples of this level of resistance.

There are, then, not only a number of ways for a counterstory to get a foothold on a master narrative, but also a number of ways for it to proceed when it gets there. We've seen that two of the strengths of master narratives—their consisting of a hodgepodge of repeated themes and their connections to other master narratives—are also weaknesses, because counterstories can be inserted into the cracks among the various elements of a narrative, or among several narratives, even when the narratives are central to one's world view. We've also seen that an additional strength of oppressive master narratives—their epistemic rigging—permits a gap between the narratives' representation of certain people and what those people are and do, and this too provides a counterstory with an avenue of entry. Once it's gone in via any of these three openings, the counterstory can refuse the narrative, repudiate the narrative, or contest the narrative, depending on the audience at which it aims and how much of the dominant perception it sets out to shift. The degree of resistance that makes the most sense in a given case depends on what is personally at stake for those who develop the counterstory and how likely it is that the story will be taken up by the designated audience.

There remains, however, a strength of master narratives that we haven't yet addressed. Recall that master narratives have the Borg-like capability of assimilating resistance, and that one of the most effective ways they do this is by generating further stories that undermine the cognitive authority of the person who is in a position to complain. So far, nothing we've said about counterstories tells us how they might overcome this problem.

## LEGITIMATION

As a number of feminist epistemologists have argued, cognitive authority is dependent on social position—it requires a certain standing within one's community (Addelson 1994; Nelson 1990; Potter 1993). What a scientist can know, for example, and with whom she can work to advance knowledge, depends crucially on how she is situated vis-à-vis those who know authoritatively (Harding 1986). Nor is social situation relevant only to the production of formally bounded, public bodies of knowledge. A sense of competence regarding what we know about ourselves and our relationships to others, about the world and our personal possibilities for living well in it, also requires social standing within the community of those who know (Code 1991; Scheman 1993).

People who have been morally degraded by being identified according to the requirements of an oppressive group relation lack the social standing to be taken seriously when what they claim to know falls outside the limits of what is expected of them. So, for instance, the physicians in Virginia Martin's hospital, who carry considerable clout within the community, freely grant that nurses have authoritative knowledge regarding unimportant matters such as prepping a patient for surgery, but they do not recognize Pilar Sanchez's authority to know whether her fifteen-year-old patient should be told that he is dying, or Virginia Martin's authority to know when a medical consultation is necessary for an orthopedic patient. The physicians view the nurses with what Marilyn Frye has called "the arrogant eye" (Frye 1983, 66)—a gaze that takes the physicians' own standpoint as central, their needs, opinions, desires, and projects as the salient ones, their experience and understanding as what is the case. Arrogant perception permits physicians to absorb nurses' identities into their own. From the point of view of the arrogant eye, insofar as the nurses exist, they exist for physicians.

Oppressive master narratives commonly construct the identities of certain classes of people from the perspective of an arrogant eye, dismissing and degrading anything about the members of the class that does not bear directly on their value to the dominant group. Because these narratives are arrogant, the norms embodied within them for evaluating the subgroup must inevitably produce the judgment that the subgroup members are cognitively below par. As viewed by the arrogant eye, subgroup members can't possibly know what they are talking about, can't be concerned with anything significant, must be stupid or unreliable or devious or crazy. The narratives that depict them in these ways typically represent the group members as morally impaired as well as cognitively defective.[2] The trouble here is not just that the group members *don't* conform to the evaluative standards adopted by those in the mainstream, as Paul Benson claims (Benson 1990, 58)—it's that the stories depict them as being *incapable* of conforming to those standards.

When entire groups of people fail to measure up to the evaluative norms of the mainstream, something is wrong with the norms of the mainstream. If the cognitive authority of the group members is to be recognized, then, they must either find or create a community with better norms. Such communities constitute what Cheshire Calhoun calls

2. The picture is more complicated for women, who in many American subcultures are expected to be the standard-bearers of morality. The moral code they are expected to uphold, however, is one that is biased in favor of men's interests, not their own, since that is how they conform to patriarchal norms for good women.

"abnormal moral contexts." In a normal moral context, the participants "share a common moral language, agree for the most part on
moral rules, and use similar methods of moral reasoning" (Calhoun
1989, 394–95). The moral context is normal when the participants' actions say something about who they are as moral agents, because the
standards by which their actions are evaluated are shared by virtually
all the morally developed members of the community. By contrast,

> abnormal moral contexts occur when some segment of a society pro-
> duces advances in moral knowledge that outrun the social mecha-
> nisms for disseminating and normalizing that knowledge in the soci-
> ety as a whole. In that case, a gap opens between what "everyone
> knows" is the right thing to do and what from a (presumably) advan-
> taged epistemic position is viewed as the right thing to do. The gap, of
> course, will be obvious only to those who take themselves to be rea-
> soning from a more advanced, socially critical point of view—as femi-
> nists, for example, generally take themselves to be doing. (Calhoun
> 1999, 89)

In an abnormal moral context, the standards for evaluating what people do are not keyed to the requirements of those who perceive certain
others with an arrogant eye. People who by the standards of the mainstream are seen as morally subnormal and lacking in cognitive authority can in the abnormal context be viewed lovingly rather than arro-
gantly. "The loving eye," Frye asserts, "knows the independence of the
other. . . . It is the eye of one who knows that to know the seen, one
must consult something other than one's own will and interests and
fears and imagination" (Frye 1983, 75). Under the loving eye, people
who lay claim to certain kinds of knowledge aren't unauthorized or
delegitimated solely in virtue of their belonging to the class of people
who are not, in the eyes of the dominant group, in a position to know.
The loving eye confers social standing on those who have been dismissed and degraded by the arrogant eye. Abnormal moral contexts permit loving perception because they allow people to evaluate one another according to moral and cognitive norms that are better than the
ones shared by the dominant group.
    The nurses who make up the Nurse Recognition Day committee in-
habit an abnormal moral context. By according each other the social
standing that the physicians at Cranford Community Hospital with-
hold from them, they confer on one another the cognitive authority
that is withheld by the arrogant eye. Viewing one another with a loving

eye, the committee members judge their actions according to the evaluative standards of their chosen community—standards less morally defective than those used by the moral mainstream. The committee members' authority to develop their counterstory thus derives from their own standing within that little community.

Those who create counterstories, then, acquire their cognitive authority from communities that constitute abnormal moral contexts. Within such communities, however, the stories must be generated self-consciously, since, as I have argued, a story that counters an oppressive master narrative must be purposive for it to qualify as a counterstory. It's not enough that there are alternative evaluative standards available in the community—the members of that community must intentionally avail themselves of these standards to bring about change. From its inception, the Nurse Recognition Day committee possessed the moral resources to evaluate nurses' actions according to feminist standards rather than the sexist standards of the moral mainstream. But as long as these feminist resources lay dormant, the most the committee members could do about the conditions in the hospital was grouse. It wasn't until Patricia Kent deliberately marshaled the alternative evaluative standards available to the committee that the group could begin to develop its counterstory.

This is not to say that only a group can develop a counterstory. The story the female employee uses to refuse the identity imposed on her by the sexist master narratives circulating in her workplace is one she creates for herself, by herself. But by herself, the employee can't *legitimate* what she knows. She needs a community for that, and social standing within the community. Her found community, evaluating her according to the standards of the normal moral context, denies her social standing. So she must seek out a community whose evaluative standards are morally abnormal, in Calhoun's sense of the term. Because the members of that chosen community would possess the ability to see the office worker with a loving eye, they could accord her the social standing that her coworkers deny her, and so confer on her the authority to tend her story. If a counterstory is to resist absorption by the master narratives it opposes, then, those who develop it—even if they do it only for themselves—must be must be authorized by a chosen community that avails itself of moral resources that are underutilized in the normal moral context.

While a community that constitutes an abnormal moral context can *legitimate* those who create a counterstory by recognizing that they are in a position to know, it can't *justify* the story. What justifies any identity-constituting story is how well it correlates to action, how much it explains, and whether it possesses enough heft—the three credibility criteria I proposed in Chapter 3. In addition, counterstories are justified to the extent that they meet the functional criteria for identity-constituting stories of this kind: Does the story reveal the person to be a developed moral agent? Does the story reidentify the group as well as the individual? Does the story loosen the constraints on moral agency? The community cannot, by majority vote or in any other way, bring it about that the counterstory is true, properly connected to reality, accurate, or worthy of being believed. What it can do is keep a counterstory from being absorbed, Borg-like, by the master narrative it attempts to resist. The community does this by endorsing the credibility of the person who develops the counterstory. Because there is a difference between legitimation (which attaches to the person) and justification (which attaches to the story), a community of choice might very well authorize a bad counterstory.[3]

## The Assessment of the Counterstory

Now that we have a clearer sense of what counts as a counterstory, what counterstories are up against, the different stances they can take toward the particular master narratives they set out to undermine, and how those who develop them acquire cognitive authority, one question still remains—namely, how to tell a good counterstory from a bad one. Which ones are morally desirable, and which are less so? Which ought to be taken up and which repudiated? On the assumption that we'll be in a better position to see what makes good ones good if we can establish the negative conditions that make bad ones bad, I want now to describe four of the many ways in which a counterstory can misfire.

### WHEN COUNTERSTORIES GO BAD

I call the four types of bad stories that I have chosen the boomerang story, the hostage story, the "we are who I am" story, and the bathwater story. These categories don't exhaust the list of possibilities, but they do, I think, represent some of the more common kinds of failure.

---

3. I am indebted to Jonathan Dancy for helping me to clarify my thinking on this point in a conversation on 18 March 2000.

*The boomerang story.* This type of counterstory is politically meaning-less, because it doesn't do anything to repair the damage done to the group identity. It merely reidentifies an individual who belongs to the group, representing the person as an exception, a stand-out, different from the rest. By attempting to repair one person's identity but leaving the other members of the group untouched, the story boomerangs. It ends up reinforcing the master narrative it's trying to undermine.

The first variant of the boomerang story is a counterstory that identi-fies an individual as a credit to her group. This sort of counterstory measures the individual according to the norms established by the dominant group for the subgroup members' behavior, and judges that the individual measures up to the norms exceptionally well. The indi-vidual is then exceptional *according to those norms*—she is a credit to her sex, for example, because she behaves the way good women are sup-posed to behave in a patriarchal power arrangement. He is a credit to his race (never the white race) because he does what whites expect of him cheerfully, industriously, and with a certain amount of initiative. This sort of counterstory misfires because it not only leaves the oppres-sive group identity intact, it also leaves the individual identity intact. She just "does" her race, gender, or ethnicity better than the other group members do. Although these stories keep in place all the oppres-sive master narratives that identify the individual as well as the group, they aren't total failures. Often, members of the subgroup are galva-nized by them, finding that they kindle hope and self-respect. More-over, insofar as the story invites the dominant group to treat the indi-vidual with greater respect than it accords the other members of her group, it may enable her to exercise her agency a bit more freely.

In Gareth Williams's description of one woman's interaction with the British National Health Service we have a fine example of this vari-ant of the boomerang story. As Williams tells it, the Thatcher adminis-tration, whose reigning tactic was to blame the poor for their poverty and the ill for their illness, invoked the master narratives of Protes-tantism in support of the view that health is a matter of right conduct, while illness is "a sign of sinfulness and a warning to the individual to alter his or her behaviour" (G. Williams 1993, 92). According to these narratives, people who are poor and chronically ill have brought their troubles on themselves through shiftlessness, indolence, and dirty habits.

But Williams reports that Mrs. Fields, an impoverished sixty-two-year-old widow with acute rheumatoid arthritis, self-consciously repudiates this characterization. Keenly aware of the narrative construction the government imposes on her, she develops a counterstory whose aim is to shift how the representatives of the National Health Service see her. Guided by her counterstory, she remains physically independent, stays out of debt, and keeps her house clean. She buys her own bath seat, though the government would have supplied her with one, explaining that now nobody will come "knocking at the door saying 'Have you finished with that?' It's mine, I can go up and use it when I want" (101). And she proudly tells Williams,

> The other week, the district nurse came running in saying, "Do you mind if I use your toilet?" Now the first thought in my mind was "She's a nurse, they're particular, she wouldn't ask to go to my toilet if I was dirty." You know, you think you've achieved something. I know it may sound simple to you, but it's not. That was something important. She can't think I'm careless, and she's not frightened of touching anything in the house. (98)

Mrs. Fields's counterstory of independence, cleanliness, and financial responsibility allows her to resist being seen as just another drain on the National Health. But she only constitutes her *own* identity with this counterstory. The story leaves untouched the Protestant and Thatcherite master narratives that constitute the identity of the other chronically ill people in her socioeconomic class. So while it allows the district nurse to see her as a competent moral agent, it does nothing to free the moral agency of the others who share her plight. If the counterstory concedes too much because it seems to accept the master narratives' representation of these others, however, it might nevertheless be better than no counterstory at all. Sometimes a local repair job is the best that a person can do.

A second variant of the boomerang story allows a member of an oppressed group to pass as a member of a dominant group. While, as I've already argued, not all instances of passing are morally undesirable, they do all fail to overturn the master narratives that contribute to the identity of the subgroup, so they have no direct political force. Developing a counterstory that attempts to repair your identity by denying your group membership does nothing to shift the terms in which the group is identified—it just sets you outside the group. Whether a counterstory of this kind is a bad one, though, depends largely on what is at stake for the person who enacts it and for the others she can hurt by it.

The American writer and critic Anatole Broyard, for example, resisted the master narratives that portray African Americans as incapable of intellectual activity by refusing to be identified as African-American, passing for white until his death in 1990. He told his sister he "had resolved to pass so that he could be a writer, rather than a Negro writer" (quoted in Gates 1996, 68), and it seems clear that passing in this way advanced his career. Henry Louis Gates suggests, however, that once Broyard became established as one of the more important voices in U.S. literary criticism, he would have suffered relatively few adverse consequences from acknowledging his African-American identity, and he might have played a constructive role in defusing the dominant expectation that African Americans must write about the black experience. Instead, he not only failed to help other African-American writers but also harmed his relationships with his family, distancing himself from his darker-skinned sister and hiding his racial identity even from his own children, which caused anguish to his wife. If indeed it was unnecessary for Broyard to tell this particular counterstory, then given the amounts of damage it inflicted on his family, and given too that he commanded enough social prestige to influence white opinion concerning black writers, the story is morally more objectionable than others he might have developed.

*The hostage story.* Whereas the boomerang story ends up reinforcing the master narrative it aims to unseat, the hostage story unseats the master narrative at which it aims by reinforcing *other* oppressive master narratives. The groups who are identified by these other master narratives may be thought of as innocent bystanders, held hostage by the counterstory. While this sort of story is capable of repairing the original group's identity, it does so at the expense of the other groups.

Consider a master narrative that constitutes, in part, the identity of the elderly. The "decline narrative," as Margaret Morganroth Gullette (1997) calls it, generally harkens back to a golden age in which those now grown old possessed desirable qualities—beauty, independence, a capacity for many friendships, physical strength, a sense of the *Zeitgeist*—and then moves to the present, in which sadly, or in the nature of things, these individuals have lost these qualities. Now suppose that an elderly woman repudiates the decline narrative with a counterstory that emphasizes the many ways in which she and other elderly people continue to grow and flourish. According to her counterstory, the fact that she has broken her hip is not a sign of "decline" but rather an unfortunate result of osteoporosis—a consequence of aging, to be sure, but not an indication that she is on a downhill slide. She's much more patient about her disability than she would have been twenty years ago, having learned in the interim how to accept what can't be changed and to make the most of what she has. Acting on the self-understanding made possible by her counterstory and with her daughter nearby to help, she dresses better than she ever did, is more assiduous in maintaining her friendships, continues to live independently, and has recently learned how to use a computer.

It's worth pointing out that by declining to decline, the elderly woman in effect confirms that decline in old age is a fearsome phenomenon. While this leaves much of the master narrative in place, it does disrupt the connection between decline and aging, and this might involve revaluing what counts as decline. But the counterstory would still be problematic, because it leaves out how heavily the elderly woman depends on—and how heavily she discounts—her daughter's financial, logistical, and emotional support. It's her daughter who buys the gifts with which she remembers her friends' birthdays and anniversaries, her daughter who takes her nice clothes to the cleaner's, her daughter who taught her to use her computer. Because the elderly woman's counterstory makes use of patriarchal master narratives that require adult daughters, but not sons, to care for their elderly parents while at the same time devaluing this caring work and rendering it invisible, it repairs the elderly woman's identity by holding her daughter hostage.

A similar misfiring occurs when proponents of "black authenticity," resisting racist master narratives by encouraging African Americans to take pride in their race, set out to repair the damage done to the African-American group identity with counterstories that oppress gays and lesbians. Kendall Thomas has written of "the heteronormative logic that conditions the ascription of 'authentic' black identity on the repudiation of gay and lesbian sexualities," citing as an example the words of gangsta-rapper Ice Cube, who declares that "true niggers ain't gay" (Thomas 1998, 120). Advocates of black authenticity, Thomas claims, appeal to "the African tradition" as the source of their authority, but in their insistence that gay and lesbian sexuality is alien to that tradition and was unknown before Africans encountered whites, they falsify the historical narratives that constitute the African-American group identity. By constructing true "blackness" with the help of master narratives that depict gay men as effeminate objects of contempt and lesbians as unnatural—and barren—perverts, these counterstories offer a picture of African Americans that allows many of them to feel pride in themselves, but they do so by dishonoring both those within their group and those outside it whose behavior does not conform to heterosexual norms. And since these stories are developed within what Thomas calls "a culture of violence," their endorsement of homophobic master narratives puts actual gays and lesbians at risk. Consider these lyrics, from reggae rapper Buju Banton's "Boom Bye Bye" (quoted in Thomas 1998, 128):

> Homeboys don't condone nasty men
> They must die
> Two men necking
> Lying in a bed
> Hugging each other
> And caressing one another's legs
> Get an automatic or an Uzi instead
> Shoot them now, let us shoot them

Now, *that's* a bad counterstory.

*The "we are who I am" story.* A third way in which a counterstory can misfire is by overgeneralizing from an individual case, as if all the members of the group whose identity has been damaged by a particular set of master narratives were similarly situated. The mistake here is to suppose that because one member of the group is capable of reidentifying herself in a certain way, all of the group members could do it that way too. Think, for example, of Betty Friedan, who identified the "problem that has no name," that "lay buried, unspoken, for many years in the minds of American women" (Friedan 1963, 15). The problem, which she dubbed "the feminine mystique," was not really a problem for "American women" as such; rather, it was a problem for middle-class, heterosexual, college-educated, married housewives with children—American women like Friedan herself. The feminine mystique, which traps such women and makes them seriously unhappy, is a patriarchal master narrative that prescribes, under the guise of depiction, domestic and maternal behavior that is supposed to be deeply satisfying and fulfilling for any "true" woman, and it depicts women who are bored and unfulfilled in the identity of the suburban housewife as psychologically maladjusted and insufficiently feminine. Friedan contests this master narrative, developing a counterstory that allows stay-at-home mothers to reinvent themselves as career selves. The counterstory offers us a picture of women who attend college for the purpose of preparing themselves for professions rather than simply to find husbands, and who solve the problem of child care and housework by hiring domestic help.

In describing the "rationalizations" the feminine mystique can generate to keep a woman from reidentifying herself, Friedan reports:

> Another woman, a psychiatric social worker, said that she could not take a regular agency job, only volunteer jobs without deadlines that she could put down when she felt like it, because she could not count on a cleaning woman. Actually, if she had hired a cleaning woman, which many of her neighbors were doing for much less reason, she would have had to commit herself to the kind of assignments that would have been a real test of her ability. Obviously she was afraid of such a test. (Friedan 1963, 349)

More obviously still, this passage makes it clear that women who avail themselves of Friedan's counterstory mustn't come up with insubstantial excuses for remaining in the home—they must confidently hire the help they need so that they can construct their new identities. The trouble, though, is that not all American women *can* avail themselves of Friedan's counterstory. Some of them will be too busy looking after the kitchens and children of the women who *do* get to reidentify themselves in accordance with the story. Because she overgeneralizes her own situation, Friedan fails to acknowledge her counterstory's inapplicability to the other "American women" who must be pressed into service if women like her are to be freed. Friedan's story is a variant on the hostage story, but where it goes wrong in the first place is in its assumption that the only women who count are women like her.

*The bathwater story.* The fourth kind of counterstory misfires because, in dislodging the oppressive master narrative at which it aims, it also dislodges too many other understandings, some of which are fundamental. I am thinking here, for example, of the master narratives that identify disabled people in terms of their disability, depicting the disabling trait as if it stood for the whole. Then, since the trait is devalued, the disabled person is devalued: the narratives depict the person as helpless, disgusting, or greatly to be pitied. Some disability-rights activists have countered these narratives with an identity-constituting story that represents disability as simply one more form of "neutral" human variation, like eye color. According to this story, "having a characteristic like cystic fibrosis or spina bifida is of no more consequence than being left-handed or being a man who is five feet, three inches tall" (Parens and Asch, 1999, S11). This counterstory throws out the narrative bathwater that degrades people with disabilities, all right, but it also throws out the baby—the fundamental understandings of what we owe one another. If spina bifida were merely a neutral human variation, there would be no need for publicly funded health care systems to expend resources on correcting the condition surgically or through other therapeutic means, and parents who withheld such therapies from their children could not be guilty of neglect. Eating spinach or taking folic acid supplements during pregnancy to prevent the condition wouldn't make much sense either, unless one happened to prefer intact neural tubes for one's children.

In its attempt to affirm the moral status of people with disabilities, this story sends too much down the drain. As Parens and Asch put it, "The majority community sometimes uses the trait to deny the moral significance of the person; the disability community sometimes [as with this counterstory] uses the moral significance of the person to deny the significance of the trait" (S15). The trouble lies in not remaining clear about a value as one tries to protect people who have been degraded in terms of that value.

If the "neutral trait" counterstory misfires when understood assertorically, however, it might still possess considerable rhetorical force. By calling radically into question the common wisdom regarding the desirability of disabling traits, the story forces us "to grapple with what many think is disvaluable or undesirable about these traits" (Parens and Asch 1999, S16). For that reason, even though the counterstory is a bathwater story, it might nevertheless perform a useful political function.

GOOD COUNTERSTORIES

When counterstories go bad, then, they do it either by toppling too many morally valuable beliefs or by freeing too few people—some faulty counterstories go much too far and others don't go far enough. Good counterstories aim to free not only individuals but the entire group whose identity is damaged by an oppressive master narrative. They don't try to free one group by oppressing another, nor do they throw out moral understandings that ought to be left in place. They are credible because they offer the best available explanation of who the

group members are, they correlate strongly with the group members'
actions, and they weight the various characteristics of the group accurately, so that the representation of the group members is a faithful one.

To describe how a counterstory might be evaluated with the help of
these criteria, a demonstration is in order. Let's consider a master narrative that contributed to the identity of gay men in the middle of the
twentieth century. George Chauncey, Jr., argues that sexual categories
for men underwent a significant shift just prior to the Second World
War. The gender-based contrast between "men" (who might be homosexual, heterosexual, or heterosexual men who accepted advances from
homosexual men) and "fairies" (who were effeminate) gave way to the
current, desire-based binarism between homosexual and heterosexual.
Real manhood ceased to be a matter of avoiding feminine behavior and
instead became a matter of exclusive heterosexuality (Chauncey 1994).
The depiction of gay men as violent child molesters in the sex panics of
1937–40 and 1949–55 further cemented the boundary between "real"
men and homosexuals, as did the McCarthy-era purging of "sex perverts" from government jobs on the grounds that they threatened not
only children but the national security and the heterosexuality of adult
men and women as well (Calhoun 1997, 141–42).

The master narrative of the dangerously sexual homosexual who
could not be trusted to observe the prohibition against molesting children clearly damaged gay men's identities. It deprived them of opportunities to take certain jobs, to create legally recognized families, to be
safe from the threat of harm at school, at work, or on the streets. It also
infiltrated many gay men's consciousnesses, causing them to feel socially isolated or undermining their self-respect. It was a narrative that
needed to be uprooted.

The gay liberation movement of the 1970s began to develop a counterstory that would attempt to do just that. The story contested the
"Dangerously Sexual" master narrative purposefully and publicly, replacing it with personal stories of gay men's struggles in the face of homophobia and a collective narrative of gay pride. Some of the counterstory was developed in consciousness-raising sessions, not unlike
Virginia Martin's Nurse Recognition Day committee meetings. Other
parts were developed at Wigstock and in gay pride marches. As the
story grew, it tapped into changing heterosexual mores, such as the acceptability of nonprocreative sex, and it depicted gay men as engaged in
all sorts of activities that had nothing to do with their erotic inclina-
tions. Although it has not yet succeeded in displacing the master narra-

tive it set out to resist, the "We're here, we're queer, get used to it!" story is nevertheless morally desirable.

The counterstory gets its purchase in the gap between the master narrative's depiction of homosexuals and gay men's actual behavior. Because it takes better account of how gay men actually behave than the master narrative does, it meets the credibility criterion of action, and because it depicts gay men as engaging in activities other than sexual ones, it also meets the criterion of heft. Moreover, the story begins to develop a hypothesis about who the group members are—a diverse group of men seemingly no better or worse than are heterosexual men—that has strong explanatory force. When compared to the Dangerously Sexual master narrative, then, this counterstory is much better, not only because it is more credible, but because it also depicts gay men as worthy of respect and so aims to free their moral agency. It undertakes its task of repairing the gay identity without oppressing other groups or implausibly undermining important moral values. And because it was developed within the gay community, whose members self-consciously made use of the abnormal evaluative standards available there, those who put the story forward acquired a certain degree of cognitive authority, even though the story is not fully accepted in the wider community.

Like bad counterstories, good ones are apt to have tradeoffs, since as a general rule they can create some openings but not others for freeing agency. The "We're here, we're queer" story has allowed more gay men to live uncloseted, but it might be argued that it has also accepted the terms, laid down by the master narrative, that construe homosexuality as an identity at all. Because, as the argument has it, the counterstory must work within the constraints of the preservative forces of an abusive, heterosexist power arrangement that marks a firm boundary between a heterosexual "us" and a homosexual "them," the story doesn't ask why a particular erotic desire should generate an identity in the first place when other desires don't.

While many good counterstories do have to make this sort of tradeoff, I don't think this one does. In my view, the counterstory being developed in the gay community positions itself orthogonally with respect to the Dangerously Sexual story, issuing a note of defiance in its insistence that we're here *as* queer, in perhaps more ways than one, and contesting the idea that we must be recognized as morally upstanding folk to get our basic rights. Seen in that light, the counterstory *doesn't* fully accept the terms the dominant culture has set for discussion and simply deny what the terms assert, but rather, it displaces that discussion. In any case, a story needn't uproot the entire master narrative to be a good counterstory. If it manages to dilute the moral poison of the narrative and so free the group members' moral agency, then despite any constraints under which it operates, the story is good enough.

## DAMAGED IDENTITIES, NARRATIVE REPAIR

The dynamic of oppression produces both the need for counterstories and the conditions for their proper functioning. By pulling apart the master narratives that construct a damaged identity and replacing them with a more credible, less morally degrading narrative, counterstories serve as *practical* tools for reidentifying persons. They serve to repair the damaged identity.

As an *analytical* tool for moral theorizing, the concept of the counterstory can also be profitably put to work on the four problems posed for narrative ethics by the approaches of Nussbaum, Rorty, MacIntyre, and Taylor. Nussbaum's work, recall, raises questions about the spirit in which one approaches a story. What, it seems to ask, are you trying to *do* with the story? An answer suggested by the concept of the counterstory is that you aim to identify people as fully developed moral agents. Rorty's work raises the problem of the limits to narrative self-creation. Who gets to *tell* the story? One answer is that many people do. An account of self-creation that leaves out the ways in which identities get imposed on us is disastrously incomplete, and as I hope I have shown, full repair of an identity damaged by oppression requires the co-operation of quite a number of people. Taylor's and MacIntyre's narrative understanding of the self raises questions about the plot of a life-story. What, it seems to ask, should be the *form* of the story that identifies you? In light of what counterstories reveal about the inter-penetration of personal identities, it is easier to see that there is no particular "should" about this—the tissue of an individual's (auto)biographical narratives can take many forms and still qualify as the stories that constitute the person's identity. As for the questions of exclusion and inclusion raised by MacIntyre's use of historical narrative, we are now in a position to reply: the way you keep stories from *edging you out or forcing you in* is by countering them with identity-constituting stories that loosen the constraints on a person's moral agency.

The communities in which we find ourselves do more than provide us with a language, a social niche, a culture, and a particular form of life—they also constitute us. Living by our communal allegiances, as Michael Sandel observes, "is inseparable from understanding ourselves as the particular persons we are—as members of this family or community or nation or people, as bearers of this history, as sons and daughters of that revolution, as citizens of this republic" (Sandel 1982, 179). These understandings are narrative understandings, made up of the stories and fragments of stories that circulate widely in the community and that allow us to make sense not only of ourselves but also of those around us.

When the master narratives of the found community are used to constitute an identity according to the requirements of an oppressive group relation, however, the identity takes on what is sometimes an unbearable weight. Group members are not only deprived of opportunities to enjoy valuable roles, relationships, and other goods on offer in the society, but often also come to operate, from their own point of view, as the identity requires. These twin injuries to the identity, which I have been calling deprivation of opportunity and infiltrated consciousness, can be repaired if the master narratives that have inflicted the damage can be sufficiently dislodged so that alternative identity-constituting stories can replace them. By resisting in just this way the defective master narratives that weigh so heavily on some of its members, good counterstories challenge the moral understandings of the found community.

But it's important to notice the precise nature of the challenge. In our found communities there exists not only what besieges, deprives, and violates us but also our moral good: a considerable portion of the richness and variety of life lies in the given. The goods of familial relationships, interesting work, education, personal safety, opportunities for travel and recreation, health care, pleasant surroundings, freedom from want, political and cultural influence, social standing, a sense of belonging—all are on offer in the found community, and all are worth having. The trouble has been that the goods of found communities have been preferentially available to their dominant members. By giving people whose identities have been damaged greater confidence in their worthiness to be the authors of their own action, and by allowing these actions to be taken up by the members of dominant groups as the expressions of morally developed persons, counterstories function as avenues of access to the goods of the found communities. Moreover, if the counterstory is widely accepted, it also reshapes the group relations within those communities.

The story that I have developed in these pages about how damaged identities can be narratively repaired is intended to contribute to our understanding of the role of stories in our moral lives. Some of the stories bear down heavily on certain people. My hope, in developing the concept of the counterstory, has been not only to explain why some identities weigh so much more than others, but also to remove some of that weight.

# Bibliography

Adams, Hazard, and Leroy Searle. 1986. *Critical Theory Since 1965.* Talla-hassee: Florida State University Press.

Addelson, Kathryn Pyne. 1994. *Moral Passages: Toward a Collectivist Moral Theory.* New York: Routledge.

Alcoff, Linda Martín. 1995. "The Problem of Speaking for Others." In Bell and Blumenfield, *Overcoming Racism and Sexism.*

Alcoff, Linda Martín, and Elizabeth Potter, eds. 1993. *Feminist Epistemologies.* New York: Routledge.

Antony, Louise, and Charlotte Witt, eds. 1992. *A Mind of One's Own: Feminist Essays on Reason and Objectivity.* Boulder: Westview.

Appiah, Kwame Anthony, and Henry Louis Gates, Jr. 1995. *Identities.* Chicago: University of Chicago Press.

Archer, Margaret Scotford. 1996. *Culture and Agency: The Place of Culture in Social Theory.* Rev. ed. New York: Cambridge University Press.

Arras, John. 1997. "Nice Story, but So What? Narrative and Justification in Ethics." In Nelson, *Stories and Their Limits.*

Babbit, Susan E. 1996. *Impossible Dreams: Rationality, Integrity, and Moral Imagination.* Boulder: Westview.

Baier, Annette C. 1986. "Trust and Antitrust." *Ethics* 96, no. 1:231–60.

——. 1995. *Moral Prejudices: Essays on Ethics.* Cambridge: Harvard University Press.

——. 1997. *The Commons of the Mind.* Paul Carus Lecture. Chicago: Open Court Press.

Bakhtin, Mikhail M. 1981. "Discourse in the Novel." In *The Dialogic Imagination,* ed. Michael Holquist, trans. Caryl Emerson and Michael Holquist. Austin: University of Texas Press.

Bal, Mieke. 1985. *Narratology: Introduction to the Theory of Narrative.* Trans. Christine van Boheemen. Toronto: University of Toronto Press.

Bartky, Sandra Lee. 1990. *Femininity and Domination: Studies in the Phenomenology of Oppression*. New York: Routledge.

Bell, Linda A., and David Blumenfield, eds. 1995. *Overcoming Racism and Sexism*. Lanham, Md.: Rowman & Littlefield.

Belsey, Catherine. 1980. *Critical Practice*. New York: Routledge.

Benson, Paul. 1990. "Feminist Second Thoughts about Free Agency." *Hypatia* 5, no. 3:47–64.

——. 1994. "Free Agency and Self-Worth." *Journal of Philosophy* 91, no. 12:650–68.

Bloom, Allan. 1987. *The Closing of the American Mind: How Higher Education Has Failed Democracy and Impoverished the Souls of Today's Students*. New York: Simon and Schuster.

Bornstein, Kate. 1994. *Gender Outlaw: On Men, Women, and the Rest of Us*. New York: Routledge.

Brison, Susan J. 1997. "Outliving Oneself: Trauma, Memory, and Personal Identity." In Meyers, *Feminists Rethink the Self*.

Butler, Judith. 1990. *Gender Trouble: Feminism and the Subversion of Identity*. New York: Routledge.

Caldwell, Mary. 1999. "Not in My Pulpit: Counterstories of Women in Baptist Ministry." Unpublished paper, Department of Philosophy, University of Tennessee.

Calhoun, Cheshire. 1989. "Responsibility and Reproach." *Ethics* 99, no. 2:389–406.

——. 1992. "Emotional Work." In Cole and Coultrap-McQuin, *Explorations in Feminist Ethics*.

——. 1995. "Standing for Something." *Journal of Philosophy* 92, no. 5:235–60.

——. 1997. "Family's Outlaws: Rethinking the Connection between Feminism, Lesbianism, and the Family." In Nelson, *Feminism and Families*.

——. 1999. "Moral Failure." In Claudia Card, ed., *On Feminist Ethics and Politics*. Lawrence: University Press of Kansas.

Card, Claudia. 1996. *The Unnatural Lottery: Character and Moral Luck*. Philadelphia: Temple University Press.

——, ed. 1991. *Feminist Ethics*. Lawrence: University Press of Kansas.

Carroll, Lewis. 1978. *Alice's Adventures in Wonderland* and *Through the Looking Glass*. London: Methuen.

Cavell, Stanley. 1979. "Knowledge and the Basis of Morality." In *The Claim of Reason: Wittgenstein, Skepticism, Morality, and Tragedy*. New York: Oxford University Press.

Charon, Rita. 1997. "The Ethical Dimensions of Literature: Henry James's *The Wings of the Dove*." In Nelson, *Stories and Their Limits*.

Chauncey, George, Jr. 1994. *Gay New York: Gender, Urban Culture, and the Making of the Gay Male World, 1890–1940*. New York: Basic Books.

Christman, John. 1991. "Autonomy and Personal History." *Canadian Journal of Philosophy* 21, no. 1:1–24.

Code, Lorraine. 1991. *What Can She Know? Feminist Theory and the Construction of Knowledge*. Ithaca: Cornell University Press.

Cole, Eve Browning, and Susan Coultrap-McQuin, eds. 1992. *Explorations in Feminist Ethics: Theory and Practice.* Bloomington: University of Indiana Press.

Collins, Patricia Hill. 1991. *Black Feminist Thought: Knowledge, Consciousness, and the Politics of Empowerment.* New York: Routledge.

Conn, Canary. 1977. *Canary: The Story of a Transsexual.* New York: Bantam.

Davidson, Donald. 1980. *Essays on Actions and Events.* New York: Oxford University Press.

Delgado, Richard, ed. 1995. *Critical Race Theory: The Cutting Edge.* Philadelphia: Temple University Press.

Dennett, Daniel. 1984. *Elbow Room.* Cambridge: MIT Press.

——. 1988. "Why Everyone Is a Novelist." *Times Literary Supplement* 4, no. 59.

DePaul, Michael. 1993. *Balance and Refinement: Beyond Coherence Methods of Moral Inquiry.* London: Routledge.

Dillon, Robin. 1992. "Care and Respect." In Cole and Coultrap-McQuin, *Explorations in Feminist Ethics.*

Dunn, Allen. 1999. "The Limits of Particularism in the Ethical Criticism of the Novel." *Proceedings of the American Society for Aesthetics.* Pacific Division Annual Meeting.

Dworkin, Gerald. 1970. "Acting Freely." *Nous* 4, no. 4:367–83.

——. 1988. *The Theory and Practice of Autonomy.* New York: Cambridge University Press.

Dworkin, Ronald. 1986. *Law's Empire.* Cambridge: The Belknap Press of Harvard University Press.

Elbe, Lili. 1933. *Man into Woman: An Authentic Record of a Change of Sex. The True Story of the Miraculous Transformation of the Danish Painter, Einar Wegener.* Ed. Niels Hoyer. Trans. H. J. Stenning. New York: E. P. Dutton.

Epstein, Julia. 1995. *Altered Conditions: Disease, Medicine, and Storytelling.* New York: Routledge.

Epstein, Julia, and Kristina Straub, eds. 1991. *Body Guards: The Cultural Politics of Gender Ambiguity.* New York: Routledge.

Flanagan, Owen. 1990. "Identity and Strong and Weak Evaluation." In Flanagan and Rorty, *Identity, Character, and Morality.*

Flanagan, Owen, and Amélie O. Rorty, eds. 1990. *Identity, Character, and Morality: Essays in Moral Psychology.* Cambridge: MIT Press.

Foucault, Michel. 1995. *Discipline and Punish: The Birth of the Prison.* Trans. Alan Sheridan. New York: Vintage.

Frank, Arthur. 1995. *The Wounded Storyteller: Body, Illness, and Ethics.* Chicago: University of Chicago Press.

——. 1997. "Enacting Illness Stories: When, What, and Why." In Nelson, *Stories and Their Limits.*

Frankfurt, Harry G. 1971. "Freedom of the Will and the Concept of a Person." *Journal of Philosophy* 68, no. 1:5–20.

——. 1988. *The Importance of What We Care About: Philosophical Essays.* Cambridge: Cambridge University Press.

Fraser, Nancy. 1989. *Unruly Practices: Power, Discourse, and Gender in*

*Contemporary Social Theory*. Minneapolis: University of Minnesota Press.

Friedan, Betty. 1963. *The Feminine Mystique*. New York: W. W. Norton.

Friedman, Marilyn. 1992. "Feminism and Modern Friendship: Dislocating the Community." In Cole and Coultrap-McQuin, *Explorations in Feminist Ethics*.

Frye, Marilyn. 1983. *The Politics of Reality: Essays in Feminist Theory*. Freedom, Calif.: Crossing.

———. 1995. "White Woman Feminist." In Bell and Blumenfield, *Overcoming Racism and Sexism*.

Garber, Marjorie. 1992. *Vested Interests: Cross-Dressing and Cultural Anxiety*. New York: Routledge.

Gardiner, Judith Kegan, ed. 1995. *Provoking Agents: Gender and Agency in Theory and Practice*. Carbondale: University of Illinois Press.

Gates, Henry Louis, Jr. 1996. "White Like Me." *New Yorker*, 17 June, 66–81.

Gordon, Linda. 1994. *Pitied but Not Entitled: Single Mothers and the History of Welfare, 1890–1935*. New York: Free Press.

Grahame, Kenneth. 1908. *The Wind in the Willows*. 1986. Reprint, London: Orbis/Beehive.

Gullette, Margaret Morganroth. 1997. *Declining to Decline: Cultural Combat and the Politics of the Midlife*. Charlottesville: University Press of Virginia.

Hacking, Ian. 1986. "Making Up People." In *Reconstructing Individualism: Autonomy, Individuality, and the Self in Western Thought*, ed. Thomas C. Heller, Morton Sosna, and David E. Welbery. Stanford: Stanford University Press.

Hampton, Jean. 1998. *The Authority of Reason*. New York: Cambridge University Press.

Hancock, Ian. 1987. *The Pariah Syndrome: An Account of Gypsy Slavery and Persecution*. Ann Arbor: University of Michigan Press.

Hanen, Marsha, and Kai Nielsen, eds. 1987. *Science, Morality, and Feminist Theory*. Supplementary volume 13. *Canadian Journal of Philosophy*. Alberta: University of Calgary Press.

Hanigsberg, Julia E., and Sara Ruddick, eds. 1999. *Mother Troubles: Rethinking Contemporary Maternal Dilemmas*. Boston: Beacon.

Harding, Sandra. 1986. *The Science Question in Feminism*. Ithaca: Cornell University Press.

Hardwig, John. 1997. "Autobiography, Biography, and Narrative Ethics." In Nelson, *Stories and Their Limits*.

Harper, Phillip Brian. 1995. "Nationalism and Social Division in Black Arts Poetry of the 1960s." In Appiah and Gates, *Identities*.

Harry Benjamin International Gender Dysphoria Association. 1998. *Standards of Care: The Hormonal and Surgical Sex Reassignment of Gender Dysphoric Persons*. Palo Alto: Harry Benjamin International Gender Dysphoria Association.

Harvey, Jean. 1999. *Civilized Oppression*. Landham, Md.: Rowman and Littlefield.

Hawkins, Anne Hunsaker. 1993. *Reconstructing Illness: Studies in Pathography*. West Lafayette, Ind.: Purdue University Press.

Hill, Thomas E., Jr. 1991. *Autonomy and Self-Respect*. Cambridge: Cambridge University Press.

Hochschild, Arlie. 1989. *The Second Shift: Working Parents and the Revolution at Home*. New York: Viking Penguin.

hooks, bell. 1989. *Talking Back: Thinking Feminist, Thinking Black*. Boston: South End Press.

Howey, Noelle. 1999. "Studying Womanhood." *Ms.*, October/November, 69–73.

Hunter, Kathryn Montgomery. 1991. *Doctors' Stories: The Narrative Structure of Medical Knowledge*. Princeton: Princeton University Press.

Jaggar, Alison M. 1983. *Feminist Politics and Human Nature*. Totowa, N.J.: Rowman and Allenheld.

Jaggar, Alison M., and Iris Marion Young, eds. 1997. *A Companion to Feminist Philosophy*. Malden, Mass.: Blackwell.

Jorgensen, Christine. 1967. *Christine Jorgensen: A Personal Autobiography*. New York: Paul S. Eriksson.

Kalin, Jesse. 1992. "Knowing Novels: Nussbaum on Fiction and Moral Theory." *Ethics* 103, no. 1:135–51.

Korsgaard, Christine M. 1989. "Morality as Freedom." In *Kant's Practical Philosophy Reconsidered*, ed. Yirmiahu Yovel. Dordrecht, The Netherlands: Kluwer.

———. 1996. *The Sources of Normativity*. Cambridge: Cambridge University Press.

Kristeva, Julia. 1982. *Powers of Horror: An Essay in Abjection*. New York: Columbia University Press.

Lang, Susan S. 1991. *Women without Children: The Reasons, the Rewards, the Regrets*. New York: Pharos Books.

Levine, Peter. 1998. *Living without Philosophy: On Narrative, Rhetoric, and Morality*. Albany: SUNY Press.

Lewis, David. 1983. *Philosophical Papers*. Vol. 1. Oxford: Oxford University Press.

Lieberman, Marcel S. 1998. *Commitment, Value, and Moral Realism*. Cambridge Studies in Philosophy. Cambridge: Cambridge University Press.

Little, Margaret Olivia. Forthcoming. "Moral Generalities Revisited." In *Moral Particularism*, ed. Brad Hooker and Margaret Olivia Little. Oxford: Clarendon.

Lloyd, Genevieve. 1993. *The Man of Reason*, 2d ed. Minneapolis: University of Minnesota Press.

Longino, Helen. 1993. "Subjects, Power, and Knowledge." In Alcoff and Potter, *Feminist Epistemologies*.

Lubiano, Wahneema. 1998a. "Black Nationalism and Black Common Sense: Policing Ourselves and Others." In Lubiano, *The House That Race Built*.

———, ed. 1998b. *The House That Race Built*. New York: Vintage.

Lugones, María C. 1987. "Playfulness, 'World'-Travelling, and Loving Perception." *Hypatia* 2, no. 2:3–19.

———. 1990. "Hispaneando y Lesbiando: On Sarah Hoagland's *Lesbian Ethics*," *Hypatia* 5:138–46.

———. 1991. "On the Logic of Pluralist Feminism." In Card, *Feminist Ethics*.

Lugones, María C., and Elizabeth V. Spelman. 1983. "Have We Got a Theory for You! Feminist Theory, Cultural Imperialism, and the Demand for 'The Woman's Voice.'" *Women's Studies International Forum* 6, no. 6:573–81. Reprinted in Tuana and Tong, *Feminism and Philosophy.*

McCloskey, Deirdre. 1999. *Crossing: A Memoir.* Chicago: University of Chicago Press.

Maccoby, Eleanor E., and Robert H. Mnookin. 1992. *Dividing the Child: Social and Legal Dilemmas of Custody.* Cambridge: Harvard University Press.

MacIntyre, Alasdair. 1984. *After Virtue: A Study in Moral Theory.* 2d ed. New York: Oxford University Press.

———. 1988. *Whose Justice? Which Rationality?* Notre Dame, Ind.: Notre Dame University Press.

MacKinnon, Catharine. 1987. *Feminism Unmodified.* Cambridge: Harvard University Press.

Macklin, Ruth. 1996. "Cultural Difference and Long-Acting Contraception." In Moskowitz and Jennings, *Coerced Contraception?*

Mahowald, Mary, and Cathleen Harris. 1997. "Women and Alcohol Abuse." In *Advances in Bioethics: Values, Ethics, and Alcoholism,* ed. Wayne Shelton and Rem Edwards. Greenwhich, Conn.: JAI Press.

Mann, Patricia S. 1994. *Micro-Politics: Agency in a Postfeminist Era.* Minneapolis: University of Minnesota Press.

Meyers, Diana Tietjens. 1994. *Subjection and Subjectivity: Psychoanalytic Feminism and Moral Philosophy.* New York: Routledge.

———. 1997. "The Family Romance: A *Fin de Siècle* Tragedy." In Nelson, *Feminism and Families.*

———. 2001. "The Rush to Motherhood: Pronatalist Discourse and Women's Autonomy." *Signs* 26, no. 3:97–135.

———, ed. 1997. *Feminists Rethink the Self.* Boulder: Westview.

Michaels, Walter Benn. 1995. "Race into Culture: A Critical Genealogy of Cultural Identity." In Appiah and Gates, *Identities.*

Mills, Charles. 1997. *The Racial Contract.* Ithaca: Cornell University Press.

Minow, Martha. 1990a. *Making All the Difference: Inclusion, Exclusion, and American Law.* Ithaca: Cornell University Press.

———. 1990b. "Words and the Door to the Land of Change." *Vanderbilt Law Review* 43:1665, 1687–95.

Mintz, Steven, and Susan Kellogg. 1988. *Domestic Revolutions: A Social History of American Family Life.* New York: Free Press.

Minuchin, Salvador. 1974. *Families and Family Therapy.* Cambridge: Harvard University Press.

Moynihan, Daniel Patrick. 1965. *The Negro Family in America: The Case for National Action.* Washington: Government Printing Office.

Morreall, John. 1983. *Taking Laughter Seriously.* Albany: SUNY Press.

Morris, Jan. 1974. *Conundrum.* New York: Harcourt Brace Jovanovich.

Moskowitz, Ellen, and Bruce Jennings, eds. 1996. *Coerced Contraception? Moral and Policy Challenges of Long-Acting Birth Control.* Washington, D.C.: Georgetown University Press.

Murray, Thomas H. 1997. "What Do We Mean by Narrative Ethics?" In Nelson, *Stories and Their Limits*.

Narayan, Uma. 1997. *Dislocating Cultures: Identities, Traditions, and Third World Feminism*. New York: Routledge.

Narayan, Uma, and Julia J. Bartkowiak. 1999. *Having and Raising Children: Unconventional Families, Hard Choices, and the Social Good*. University Park: Pennsylvania State University Press.

Neely, Wright. 1974. "Freedom and Desire." *Philosophical Review* 83, no. 1:32–54.

Nelson, Hilde Lindemann. 1995. "Resistance and Insubordination." *Hypatia* 10, no. 2:23–40.

———. 1996. "Sophie Doesn't: Families and Counterstories of Self-Trust." *Hypatia* 11, no. 1:91–104.

———. 1999. "Stories of My Old Age." In Walker, *Mother Time*.

———, ed. 1997. *Feminism and Families*. New York: Routledge.

———. 1997. *Stories and Their Limits: Narrative Approaches to Bioethics*. New York: Routledge.

Nelson, Hilde Lindemann, and James Lindemann Nelson. 1992. "Frail Parents, Robust Duties." *Utah Law Review* 1992, no. 3:747–63.

Nelson, James Lindemann. 1998. "The Silence of the Bioethicists." *GLQ* 4, no. 2:213–30.

———. 1999. "Agency by Proxy." In *Proceedings of the 21st International Wittgenstein Symposium*, ed. Peter Kampits et al. Vienna: Holder-Pichler-Tempsky.

Nelson, Lawrence J., and Mary Faith Marshall. 1998. "Ethical and Legal Analyses of Three Coercive Policies Aimed at Substance Abuse by Pregnant Women." A report to the Robert Wood Johnson Foundation.

Nelson, Lynn Hankinson. 1990. *Who Knows? From Quine to a Feminist Empiricism*. Philadelphia: Temple University Press.

Nicholson, Linda. 1997. "The Myth of the Traditional Family." In Nelson, *Feminism and Families*.

Nisbett, Richard, and Lee Ross. 1980. "Judgmental Heuristics and Knowledge Structures." In *Human Inference: Strategies and Shortcomings of Social Judgment*. Englewood Cliffs, N.J.: Prentice-Hall. Reprinted in *Naturalizing Epistemology*, ed. Hilary Kornblith. 2d ed. Cambridge: MIT Press, 1994.

Noggle, Robert. 1998. "The Web of Self: Reflections on the Structure of Personhood." Paper presented at the Pacific Division Meetings of the American Philosophical Association, Berkeley, Calif.

Nussbaum, Martha C. 1986. *The Fragility of Goodness*. New York: Cambridge University Press.

———. 1990. *Love's Knowledge: Essays on Philosophy and Literature*. New York: Oxford University Press.

———. 1993. "Equity and Mercy." *Philosophy and Public Affairs* 22, no. 2:83–125.

———. 1995. *Poetic Justice: The Literary Imagination and Public Life*. Boston: Beacon.

———. 1998. "Exactly and Responsibly: A Defense of Ethical Criticism." *Philosophy and Literature* 22, no. 2:343–65.

Oliver, Kelly. 1992. "The Matter of Baby M: Surrogacy and the Courts." In *Issues in Reproductive Technology 1: An Anthology*, ed. Helen Bequaert Holmes. New York: Garland.

Paltrow, Lynn M. 1999. "Punishment and Prejudice: Judging Drug-Using Pregnant Women." In Hanigsberg and Ruddick, *Mother Troubles*.

Parens, Erik, and Adrienne Asch. 1999. "The Disability Rights Critique of Prenatal Genetic Testing." Special Supplement. *Hastings Center Report* 29, no. 5:S1–S22.

Parfit, Derek. 1984. *Reasons and Persons*. Oxford: Clarendon.

Perry, John. 1976. "The Importance of Being Identical." In A. Rorty, *The Identities of Persons*.

Potter, Elizabeth. 1993. "Gender and Epistemic Negotiation." In Alcoff and Potter, *Feminist Epistemologies*.

Quine, W. V. O., and J. S. Ullian. 1978. *The Web of Belief*. 2d ed. New York: Random House.

Quinn, Warren. 1993. *Morality and Action*. Cambridge: Cambridge University Press.

Rawls, John. 1971. *A Theory of Justice*. Cambridge: Harvard University Press.

Raymond, Janice. 1979. *The Transsexual Empire: The Making of the She-Male*. Boston: Beacon.

Reagon, Bernice Johnson. 1983. "Coalition Politics: Turning the Century." In *Home Girls: A Black Feminist Anthology*. Ed. Barbara Smith. New York: Kitchen Table/Women of Color Press.

Richards, Renée. 1983. *Second Serve*. New York: Stein and Day.

Roberts, Dorothy E. 1999. "Mothers Who Fail to Protect Their Children." In Hanigsberg and Ruddick, *Mother Troubles*.

Rooney, Phyllis. 1991. "Gendered Reason: Sex Metaphor and Conceptions of Reason." *Hypatia* 6, no. 2:77–103.

Rorty, Amélie, ed. 1976. *The Identities of Persons*. Berkeley and Los Angeles: University of California Press.

Rorty, Richard. 1989. *Contingency, Irony, and Solidarity*. Cambridge: Cambridge University Press.

Rousseau, Jean-Jacques. 1979. *Emile; or, On Education*. Trans. Allan Bloom. New York: Basic Books.

Rovane, Carol A. 1998. *The Bounds of Agency: An Essay in Revisionary Metaphysics*. Princeton: Princeton University Press.

Ruddick, Sara. 1997. "The Idea of Fatherhood." In Nelson, *Feminism and Families*.

Sandel, Michael J. 1982. *Liberalism and the Limits of Justice*. Cambridge: Cambridge University Press.

Scanlon, T. M. 1972. "A Theory of Freedom of Expression." *Philosophy and Public Affairs* 1:204–26.

Schechtman, Marya. 1996. *The Constitution of Selves*. Ithaca: Cornell University Press.

Scheman, Naomi. 1993. *Engenderings*. New York: Routledge.

———. 1997. "Queering the Center by Centering the Queer: Reflections on Transsexuals and Secular Jews." In Meyers, *Feminists Rethink the Self*.

Schiller, Friedrich von. 1966. "Naïve and Sentimental Poetry." In *Naïve and Sentimental Poetry, and On the Sublime; Two Essays*. Trans. Julius A. Elias. New York: Frederick Ungar.

Schwarz, Benjamin. 1999. Review of *Runaway Slaves: Rebels on the Plantation*, by John Hope Franklin and Loren Schweninger. *New York Times*, Book Review section, 15 August, 30.

Shanley, Mary Lyndon. 1999. "Lesbian Families: Dilemmas in Grounding Legal Recognition of Parenthood." In Hanigsberg and Ruddick, *Mother Troubles*.

Shrage, Laurie. 1994. *Moral Dilemmas of Feminism: Prostitution, Adultery, and Abortion*. New York: Routledge.

Smith, David Lionel. 1998. "What Is Black Culture?" In Lubiano, *The House That Race Built*.

Spelman, Elizabeth V. 1997. *Fruits of Sorrow*. Boston: Beacon.

Statman, Daniel, ed. 1993. *Moral Luck*. Albany: SUNY Press.

Steinberg, Stephen. 1998. "The Liberal Retreat from Race during the Post-Civil Rights Era." In Lubiano, *The House That Race Built*.

Stocker, Michael. 1976. "The Schizophrenia of Modern Ethical Theories." *Journal of Philosophy* 73, no. 14:453–66. Reprinted in *The Virtues: Contemporary Essays on Moral Character*, ed. Robert B. Kruschwitz and Robert C. Roberts. Belmont, Calif.: Wadsworth, 1987.

Stone, Sandy. 1991. "The Empire Strikes Back: A Posttranssexual Manifesto." In Epstein and Straub, *Body Guards*.

Strawson, Peter. 1962. "Freedom and Resentment." *Proceedings of the British Academy* 48:1–25. Reprinted in *Free Will*, ed. Gary Watson. New York: Oxford University Press, 1982.

Sway, Marlene. 1988. *Familiar Strangers: Gypsy Life in America*. Chicago: University of Illinois Press.

Taylor, Charles. 1989. *Sources of the Self*. Cambridge: Harvard University Press.

———. 1992. *Multiculturalism and the "Politics of Recognition."* Princeton: Princeton University Press.

Thomas, Kendall. 1998. "Ain't Nothin' Like the Real Thing." In Lubiano, *The House That Race Built*.

Thomas, Laurence Mordekhai. 1995. "Power, Trust, and Evil." In Bell and Blumenfield, *Overcoming Racism and Sexism*.

Trumpener, Katie. 1995. "The Time of the Gypsies: A 'People without History' in the Narratives of the West." In Appiah and Gates, *Identities*.

Tuana, Nancy, and Rosemarie Tong, eds. 1995. *Feminism and Philosophy: Essential Readings in Theory, Reinterpretation, and Application*. Boulder: Westview.

Walker, Margaret Urban. 1987. "Moral Particularity." *Metaphilosophy* 18, no. 3/4:171–85.

———. 1993. "Keeping Moral Space Open: New Images of Ethics Consulting." *Hastings Center Report* 22, no. 4:33–40.

——. 1997a. "Moral Epistemology." In Jaggar and Young, *A Companion to Feminist Philosophy*.

——. 1997b. "Picking Up Pieces." In Meyers, *Feminists Rethink the Self*.

——. 1998. *Moral Understandings: A Feminist Study in Ethics*. New York: Routledge.

——, ed. 1999. *Mother Time: Women, Aging, and Ethics*. Lanham, Md.: Rowman & Littlefield.

Watson, Gary. 1975. "Free Agency." *Journal of Philosophy* 72:205–20.

White, Hayden. 1973. *Metahistory: The Historical Imagination in Nineteenth-Century Europe*. Baltimore: Johns Hopkins University Press.

Wilchins, Riki Anne. 1997. *Read My Lips: Sexual Subversion and the End of Gender*. Ithaca: Firebrand Books.

Williams, Bernard. 1981a. "Moral Luck." In *Moral Luck*. New York: Cambridge University Press.

——. 1981b. "Persons, Character, and Morality." In *Moral Luck*.

——. 1985. *Ethics and the Limits of Philosophy*. Cambridge: Harvard University Press.

——. 1993. *Shame and Necessity*. Berkeley and Los Angeles: University of California Press.

——. 1995. "How Free Does the Will Need to Be?" *Making Sense of Humanity and Other Philosophical Papers*. Cambridge: Cambridge University Press.

Williams, Gareth. 1993. "Chronic Illness and the Pursuit of Virtue in Everyday Life." In *Worlds of Illness: Biographical and Cultural Perspectives on Health and Disease*, ed. Alan Radley. London: Routledge.

Williams, Rhonda. 1998. "Living at the Crossroads: Explorations in Race, Nationality, Sexuality, and Gender." In Lubiano, *The House That Race Built*.

Wittgenstein, Ludwig. 1958. *Philosophical Investigations*. 3d ed. Trans. G. E. M. Anscombe. New York: Macmillan.

——. 1972. *On Certainty*. Ed. G. E. M. Anscombe and G. H. von Wright. Trans. Denis Paul and G. E. M. Anscombe. New York: Harper & Row.

Wolf, Susan. 1990. *Freedom within Reason*. New York: Oxford University Press.

Woolf, Virginia. 1929. *A Room of One's Own*. New York: Harcourt Brace Jovanovich.

Young, Iris Marion. 1989. "Policy and Group Difference: A Critique of the Ideal of Universal Citizenship." *Ethics* 99, no. 2:250–74.

——. 1990. *Justice and the Politics of Difference*. Princeton: Princeton University Press.

# Index